WEIRD FISHES

Written and Drawn by
Jamaica Dyer

Story Assistance
Caleb Finch

Published by SLG Publishing

P.O. Box 26427
San Jose, CA 95159
www.slg-comic.com

President and Publisher: Dan Vado
Editor-in-Chief: Jennifer de Guzman

First Printing: October 2009
ISBN-13: 978-1-59362-177-3

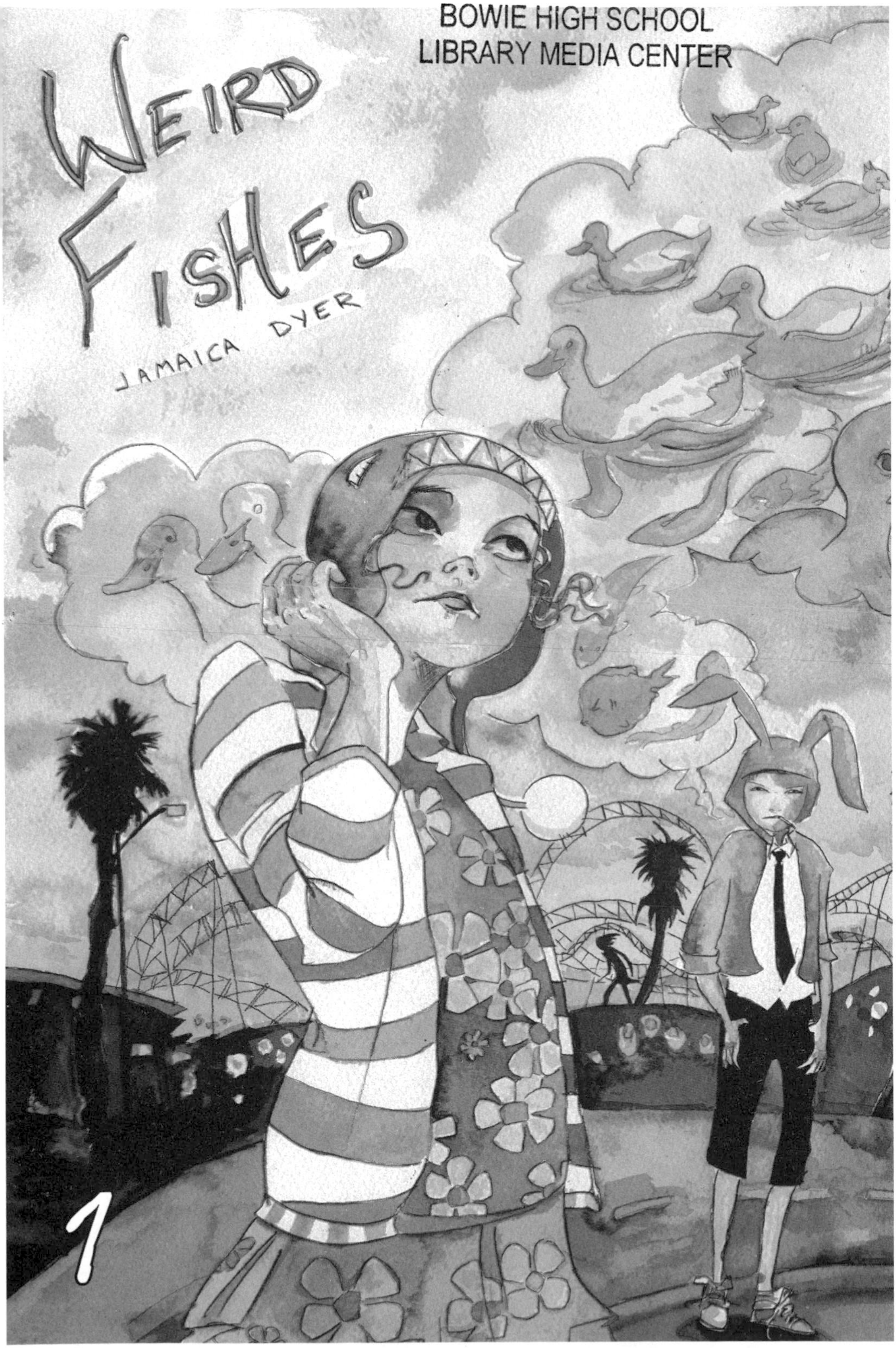
WEIRD FISHES
JAMAICA DYER
1

Special Thanks to...

Suzie for always understanding what I'm trying to say and do, my teachers who pushed me, my favorite comic book rockstars who encouraged me when I was young, SLG for being awesome, the cool kids at Ghostbot, Joe Ferrara and the Atlantis family, the Allen Spiegel team, my friends who'll stay up late and talk art, everyone who's been reading my comics online, and Batman. Always thank Batman.

How Dee Met that Bunny Boy...

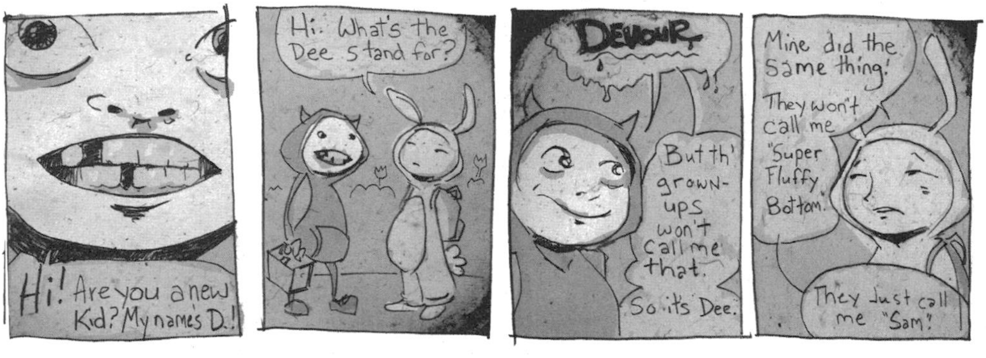
Hi! Are you a new Kid? My name's D.!
Hi. What's the Dee stand for?
DEVOUR!
But th' grown-ups won't call me that.
So it's Dee.
Mine did the same thing!
They won't call me "Super Fluffy Bottom."
They just call me "Sam."

Social Links

Chapter One

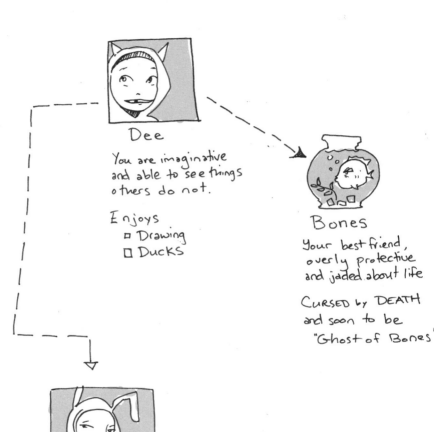

Dee

You are imaginative
and able to see things
others do not.

Enjoys
☐ Drawing
☐ Ducks

Bones

Your best friend,
overly protective
and jaded about life

CURSED by DEATH
and soon to be
"Ghost of Bones"

Bunny Boy

You have made
a new friend!
The new kid in town
with an interest in
the easter bunny.

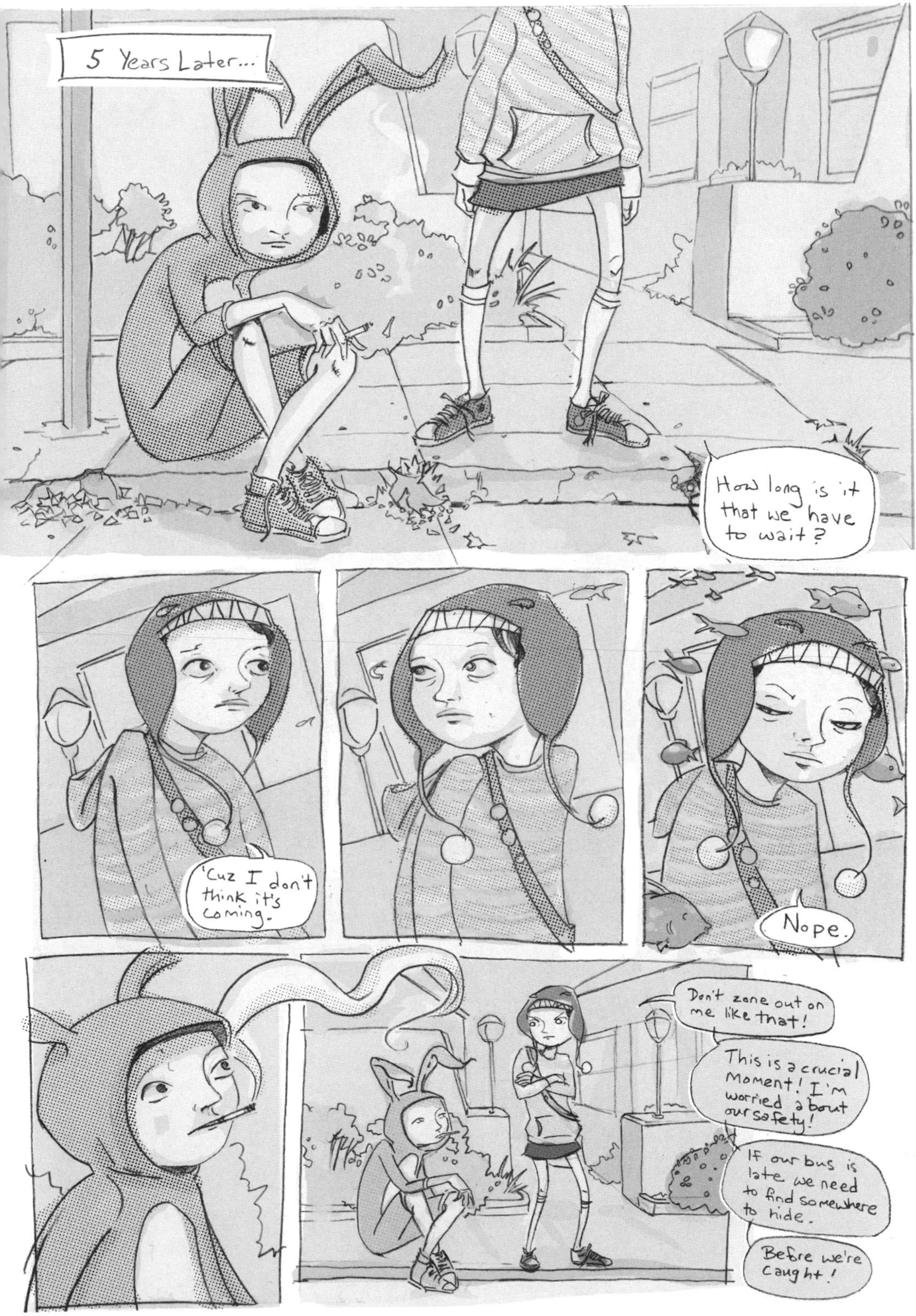
5 Years Later...
How long is it that we have to wait?
'Cuz I don't think it's coming.
Nope.
Don't zone out on me like that!
This is a crucial Moment! I'm worried about our safety!
If our bus is late we need to find somewhere to hide.
Before we're caught!

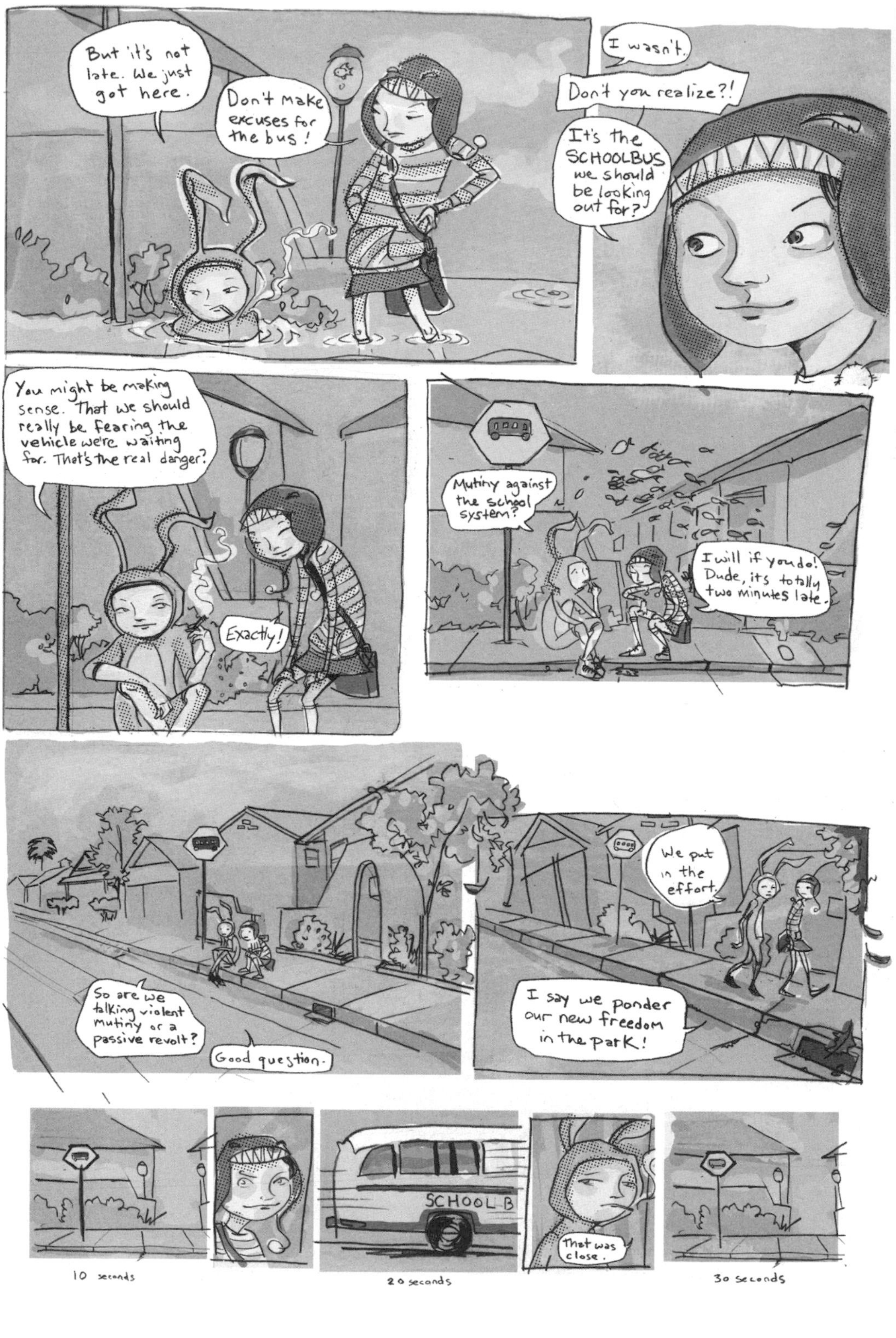
But it's not late. We just got here.
Don't make excuses for the bus!
I wasn't.
Don't you realize?!
It's the SCHOOLBUS we should be looking out for?
You might be making sense. That we should really be fearing the vehicle we're waiting for. That's the real danger?
Exactly!
Mutiny against the school system?
I will if you do! Dude, its totally two minutes late.
So are we talking violent mutiny or a passive revolt?
Good question.
We put in the effort.
I say we ponder our new freedom in the park!
SCHOOL B
That was close.
10 seconds
20 seconds
30 seconds

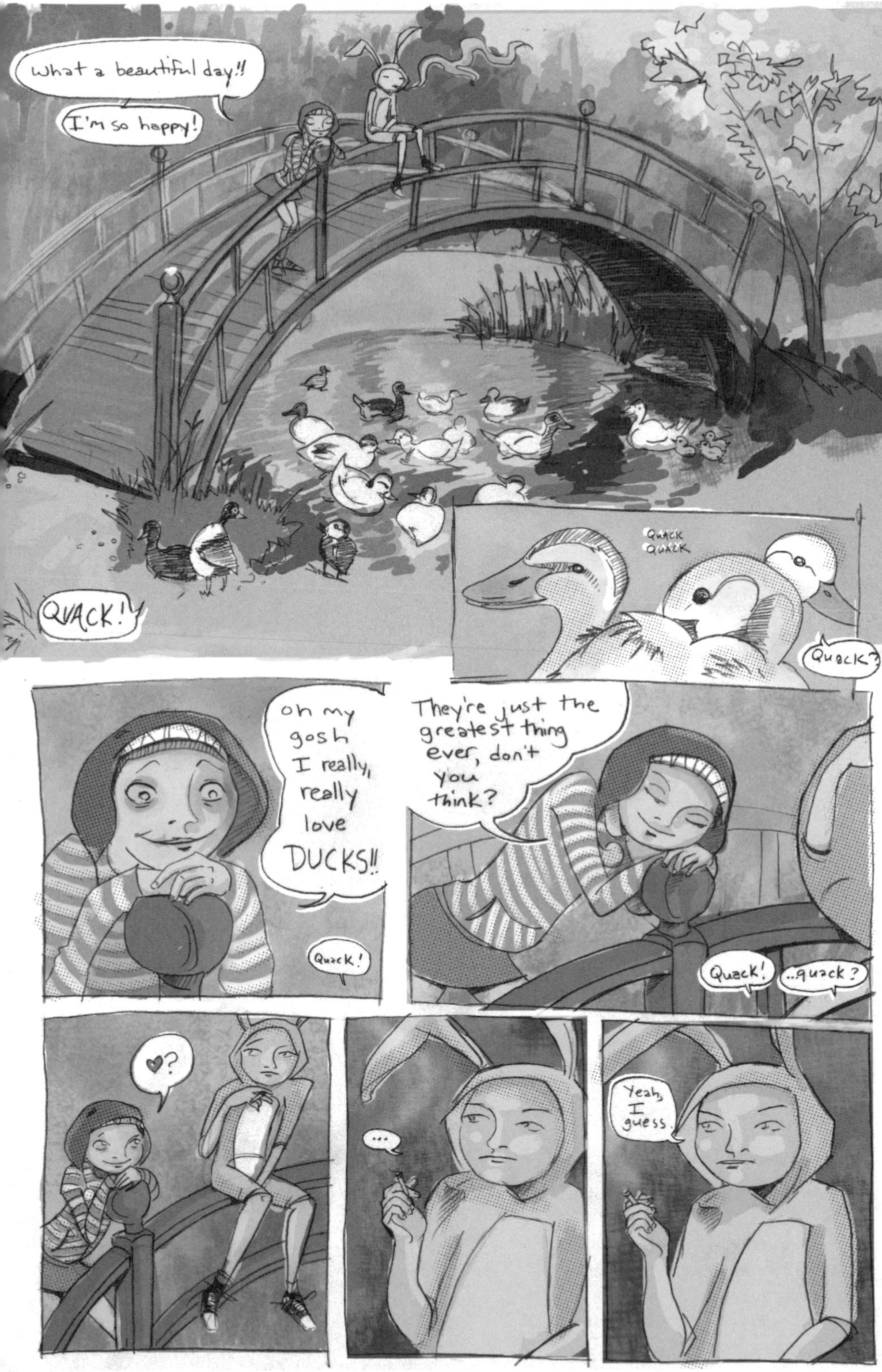
what a beautiful day!!
I'm so happy!
QUACK!
QUACK
QUACK
Quack??
oh my gosh I really, really love DUCKS!!
Quack!
They're just the greatest thing ever, don't you think?
Quack!
..quack?
♥?
...
Yeah, I guess.

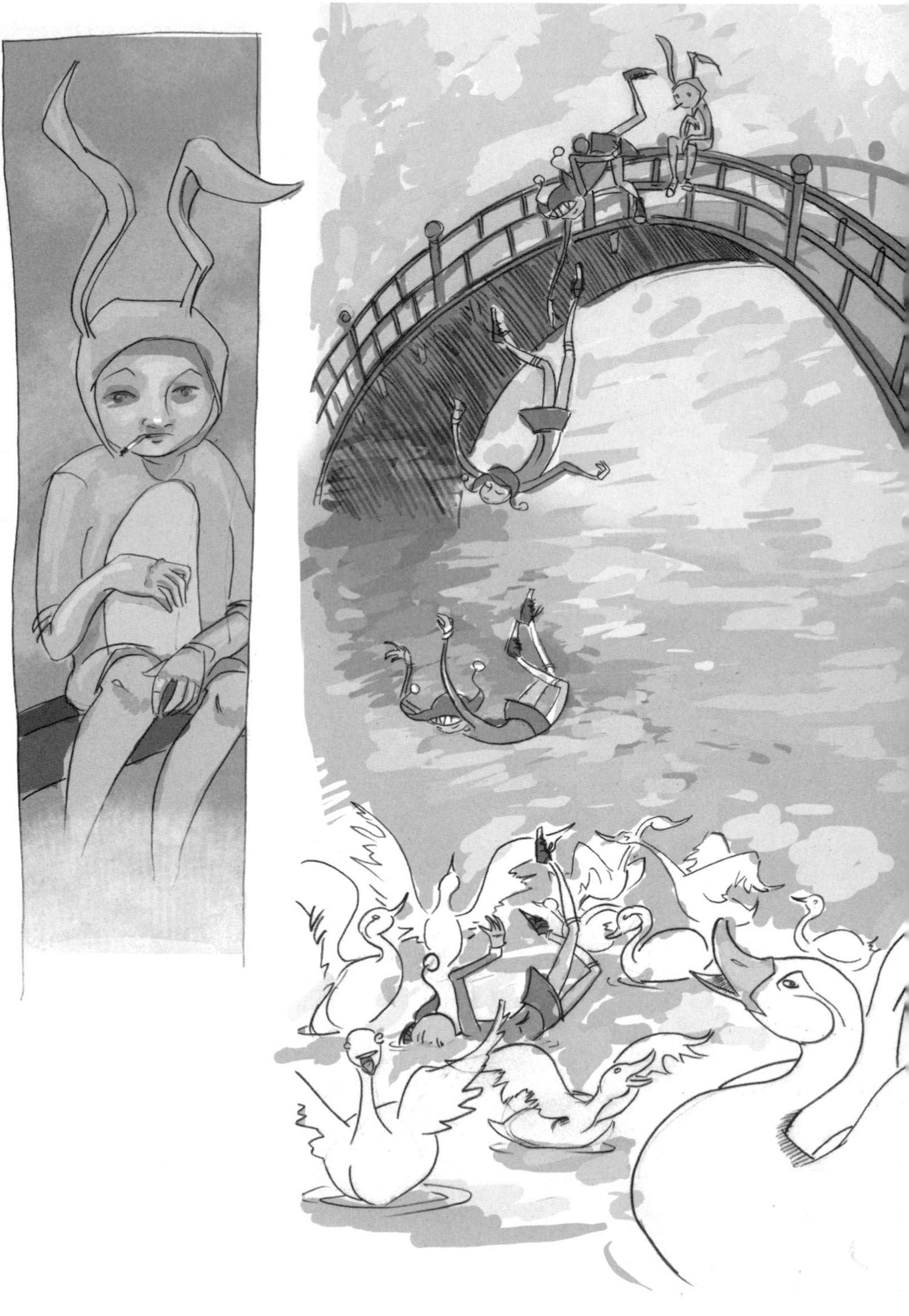

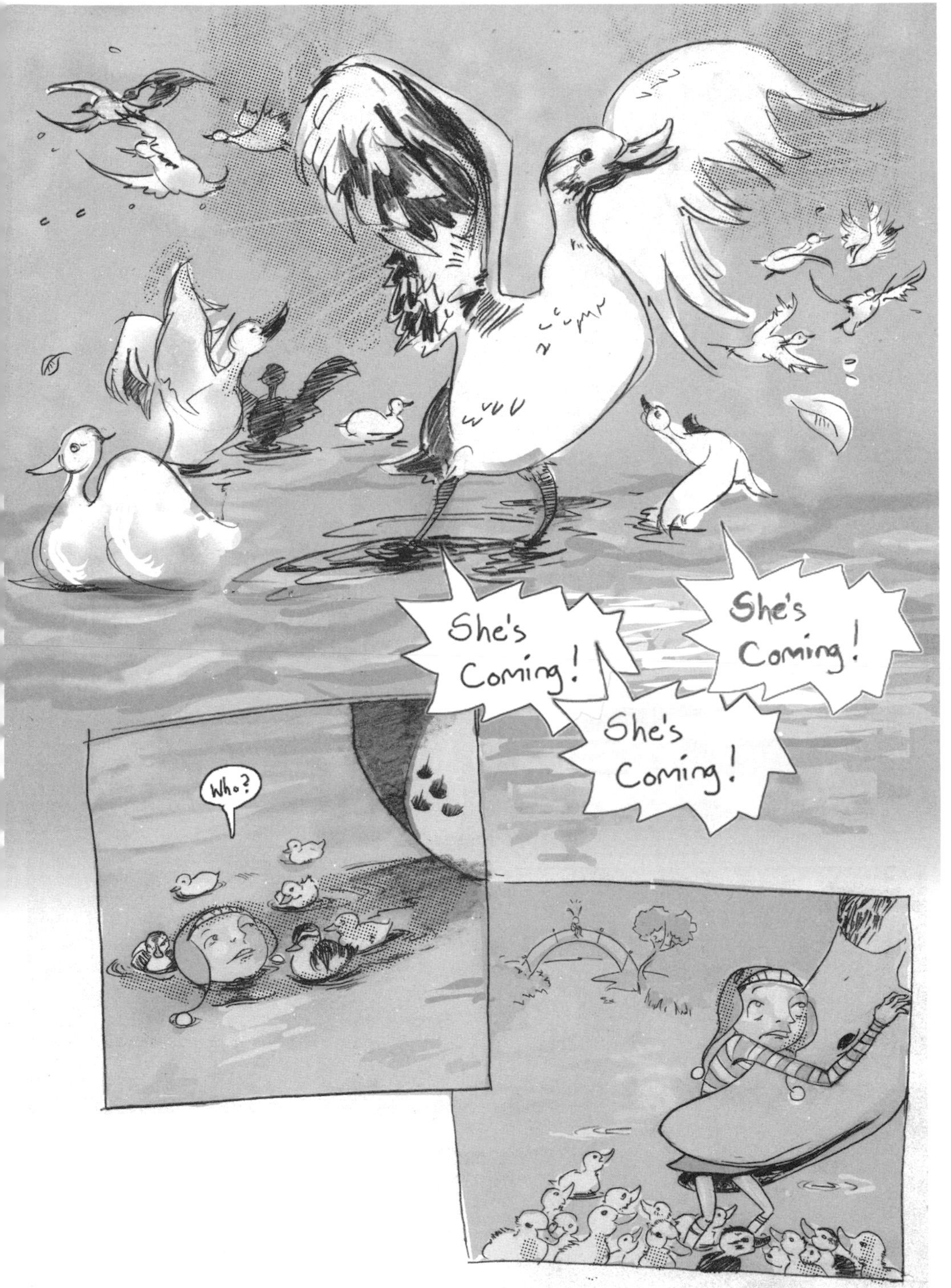
She's Coming!
She's Coming!
She's Coming!
Who?

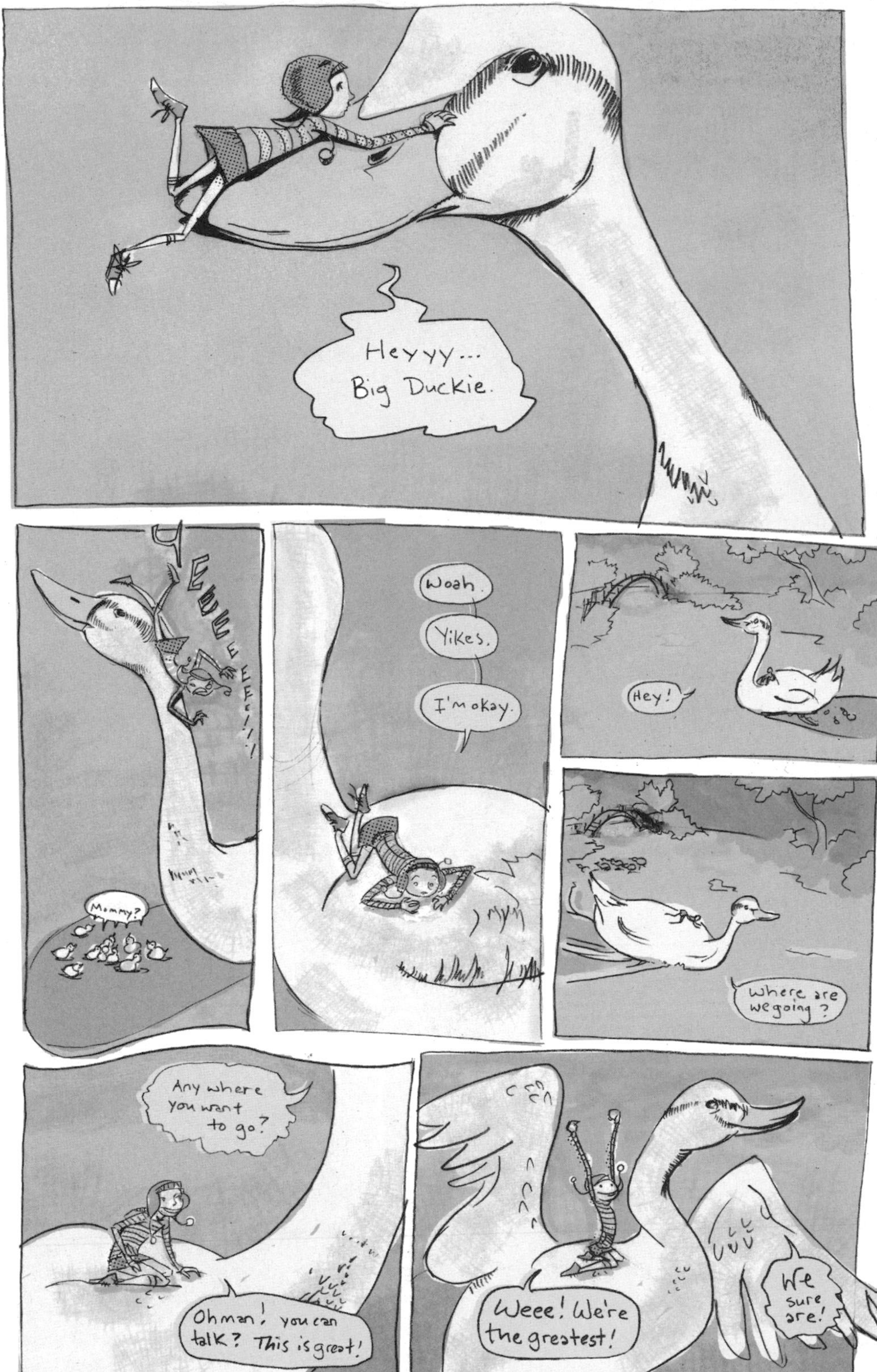
Heyyy...
Big Duckie.
EEEEEEE!!!
Mommy?
Woah.
Yikes.
I'm okay.
Hey!
Where are we going?
Any where you want to go?
Ohman! you can talk? This is great!
Weee! We're the greatest!
We sure are!
JAMAICA D

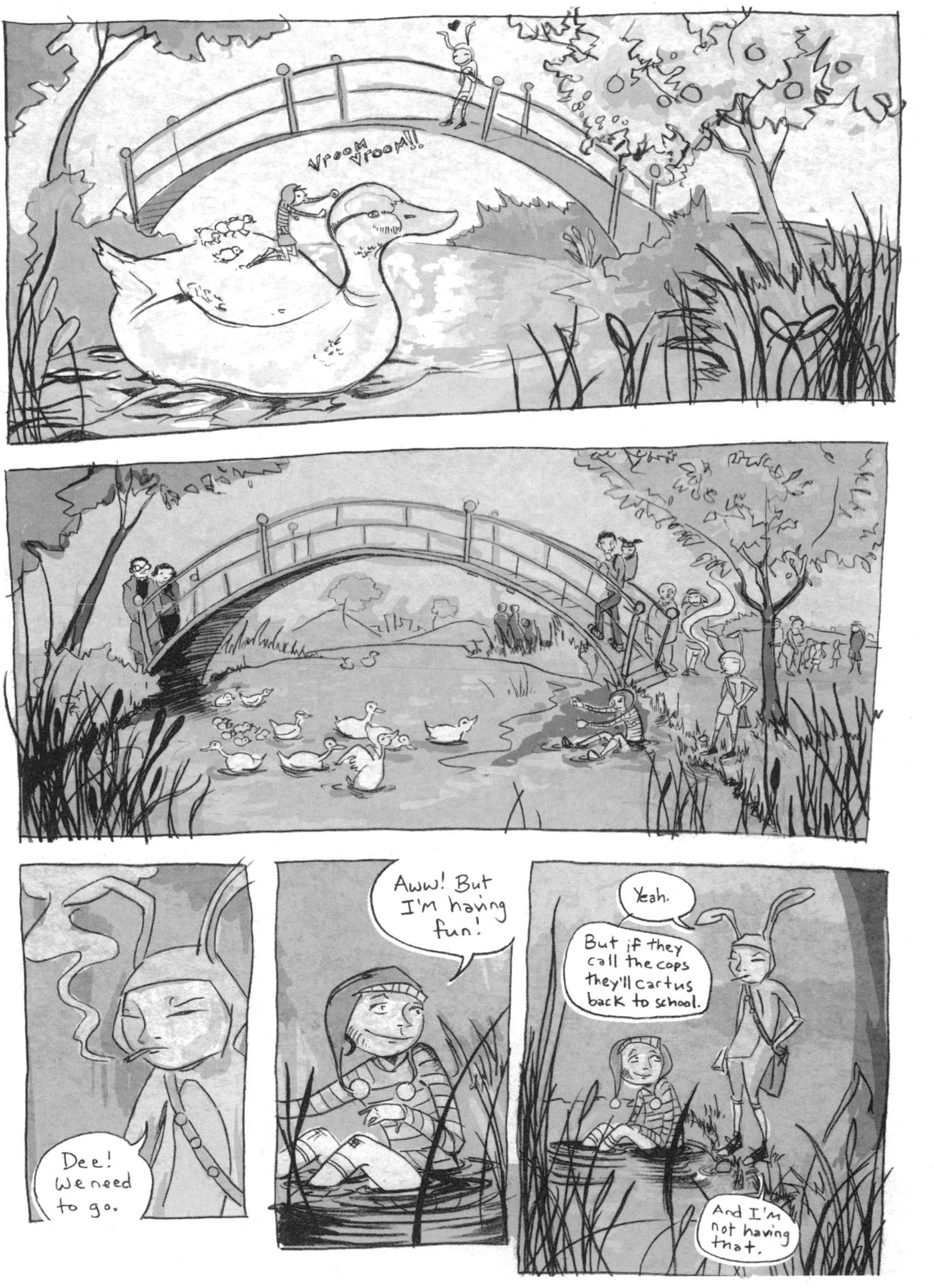
Vroom Vroom!!
Dee! We need to go.
Aww! But I'm having fun!
Yeah.
But if they call the cops they'll cart us back to school.
And I'm not having that.

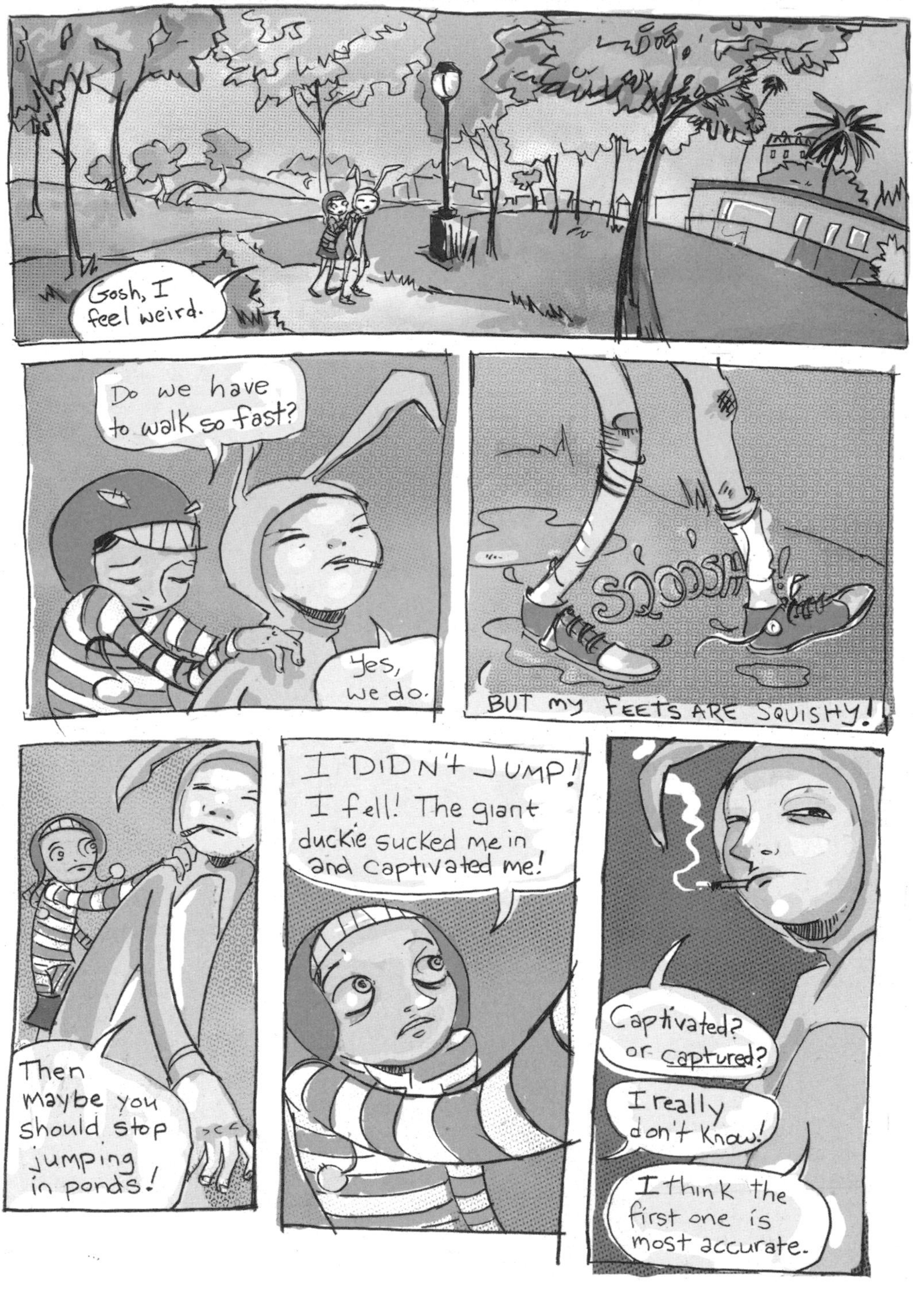
Gosh, I feel weird.
Do we have to walk so fast?
Yes, we do.
SQOOSH!
BUT MY FEETS ARE SQUISHY!
Then maybe you should stop jumping in ponds!
I DIDN'T JUMP! I fell! The giant duckie sucked me in and captivated me!
Captivated? or captured?
I really don't know!
I think the first one is most accurate.

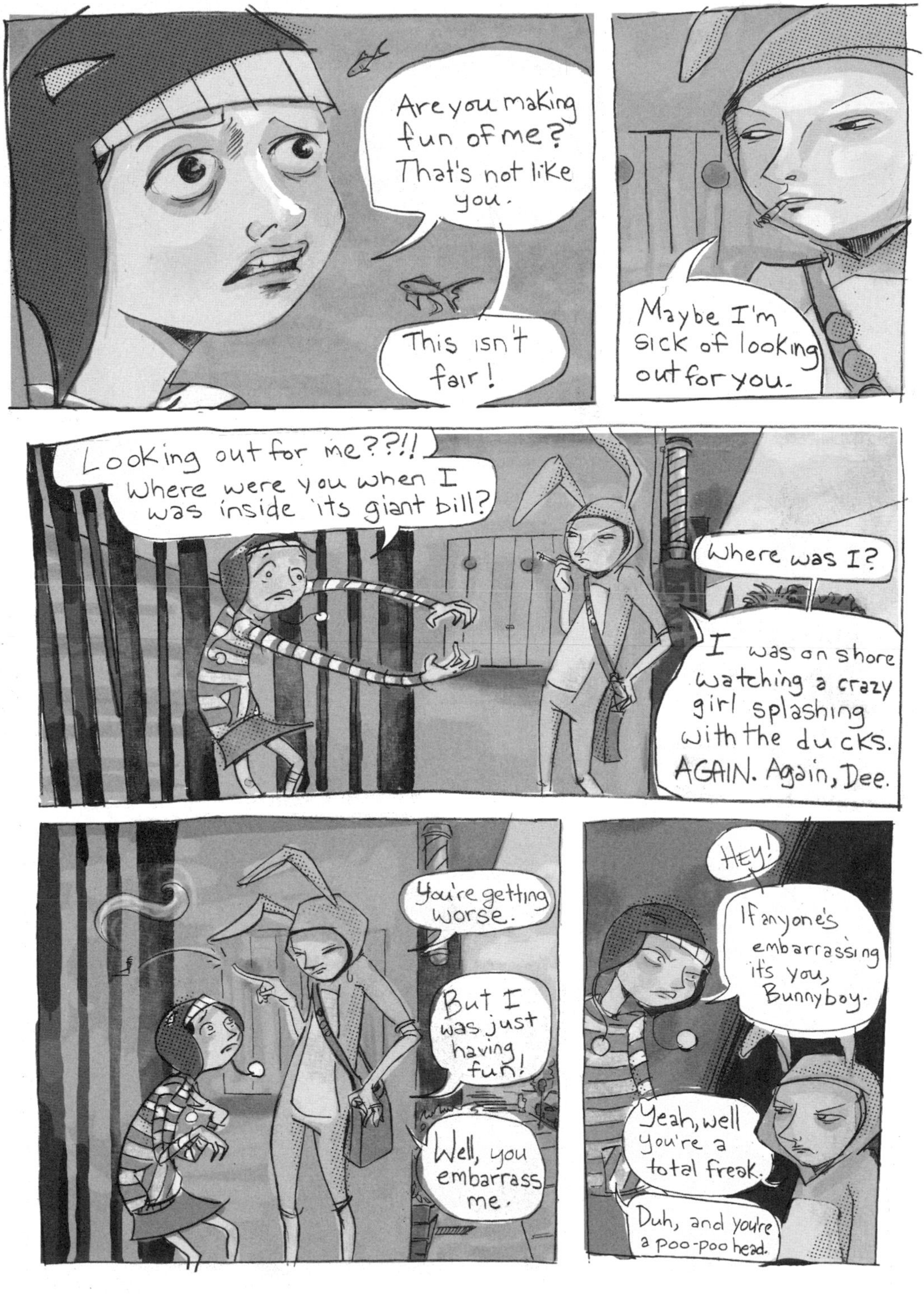
Are you making fun of me? That's not like you.
This isn't fair!
Maybe I'm sick of looking out for you.
Looking out for me??!! Where were you when I was inside its giant bill?
Where was I?
I was on shore watching a crazy girl splashing with the ducks. AGAIN. Again, Dee.
You're getting worse.
But I was just having fun!
Well, you embarrass me.
HEY!
If anyone's embarrassing it's you, Bunnyboy.
Yeah, well you're a total freak.
Duh, and you're a poo-poo head.

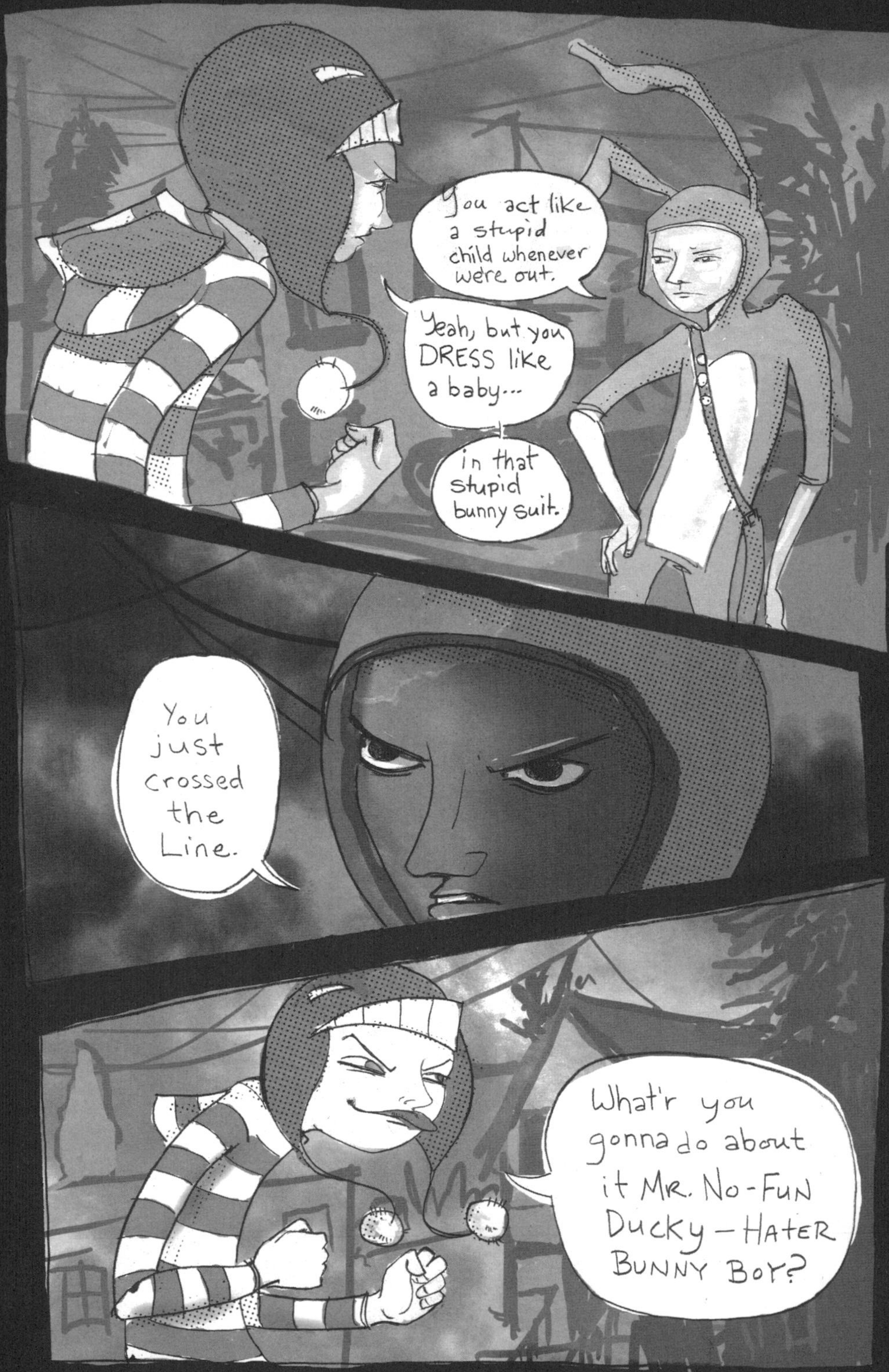
You act like a stupid child whenever were out.
Yeah, but you DRESS like a baby...
in that stupid bunny suit.
You just crossed the Line.
What'r you gonna do about it MR. NO-FUN DUCKY-HATER BUNNY BOY?

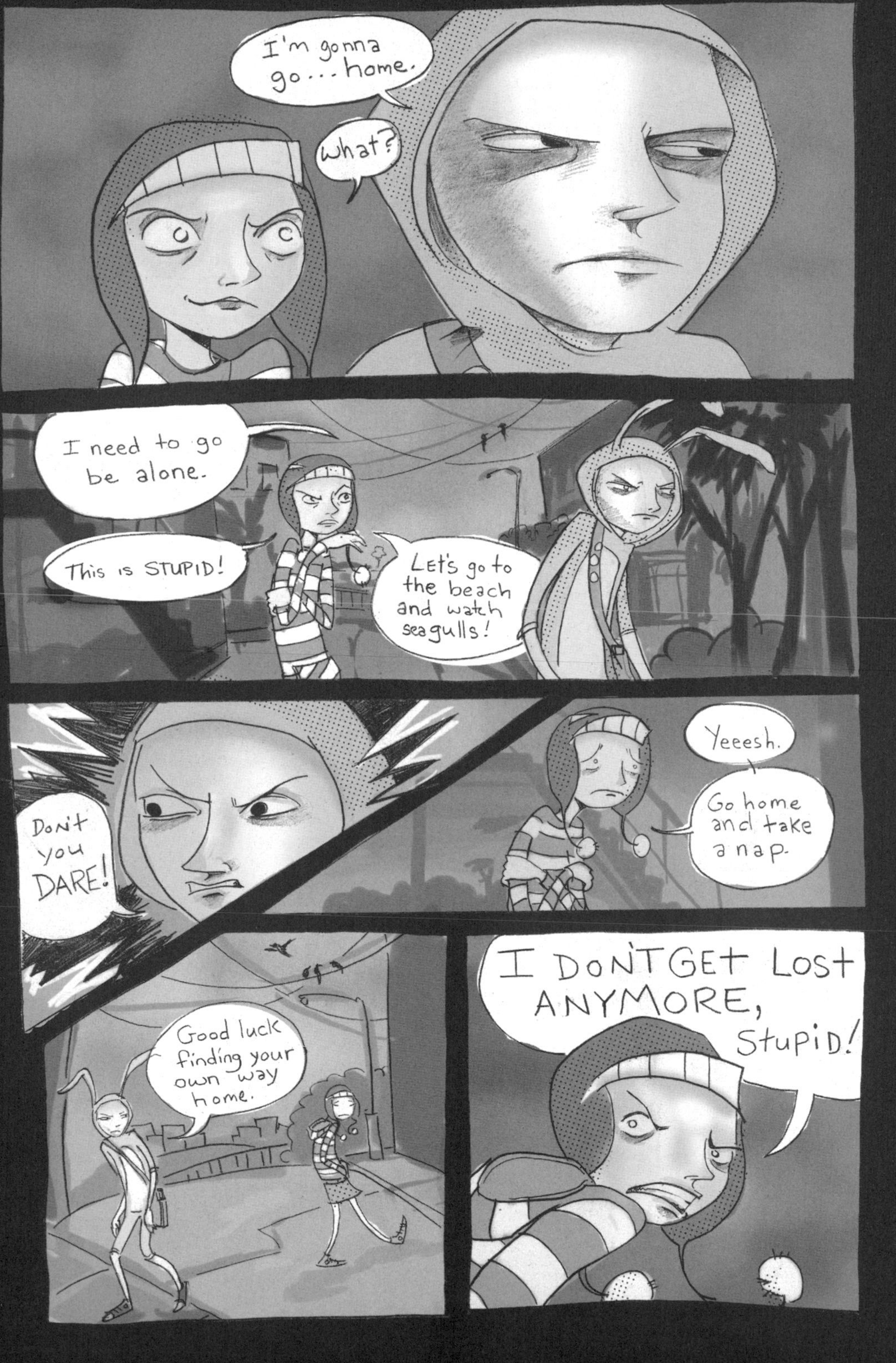
I'm gonna go... home.
What?
I need to go be alone.
This is STUPID!
Let's go to the beach and watch seagulls!
Don't you DARE!
Yeeesh.
Go home and take a nap.
Good luck finding your own way home.
I DONT GET LOST ANYMORE, STUPID!

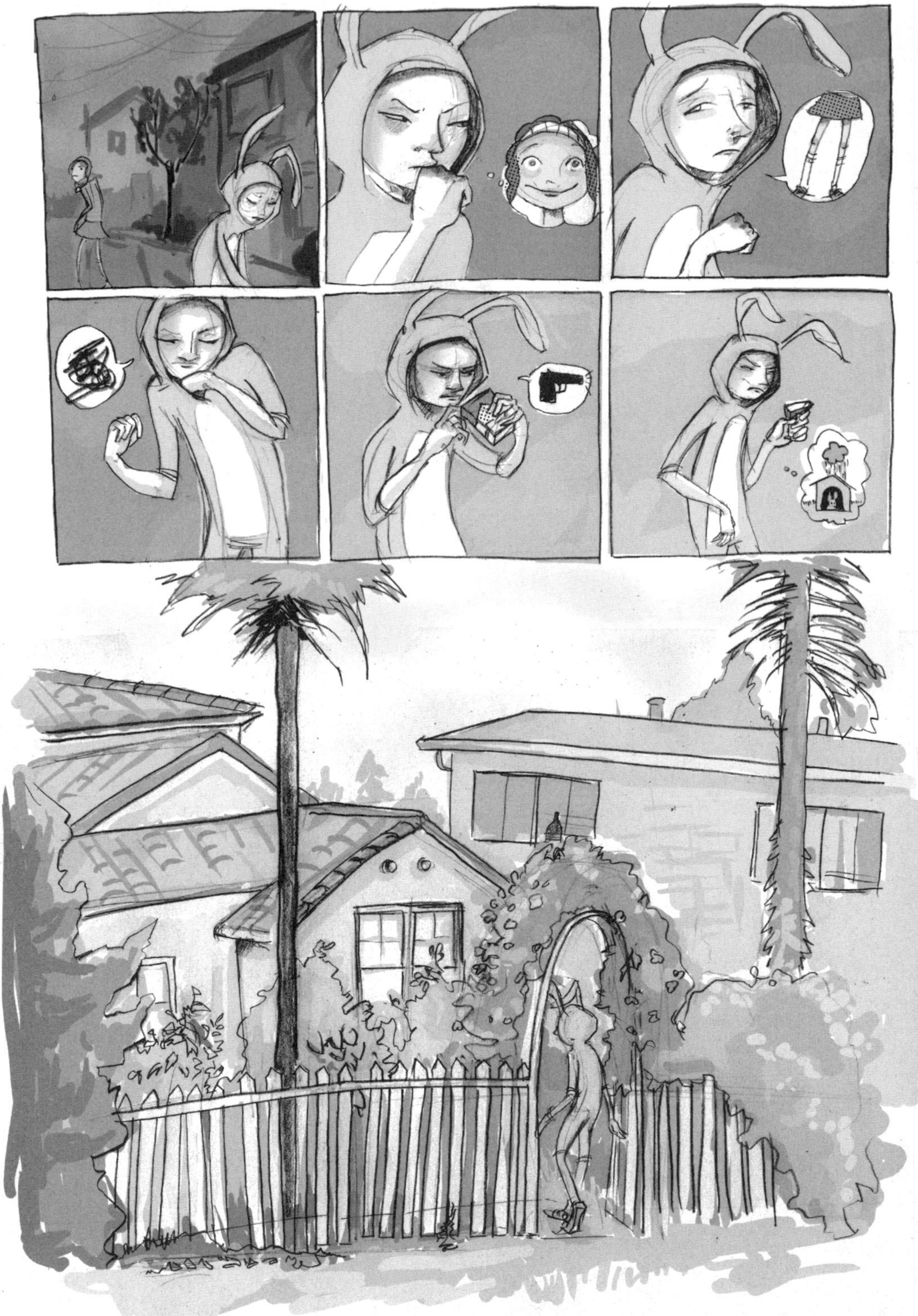

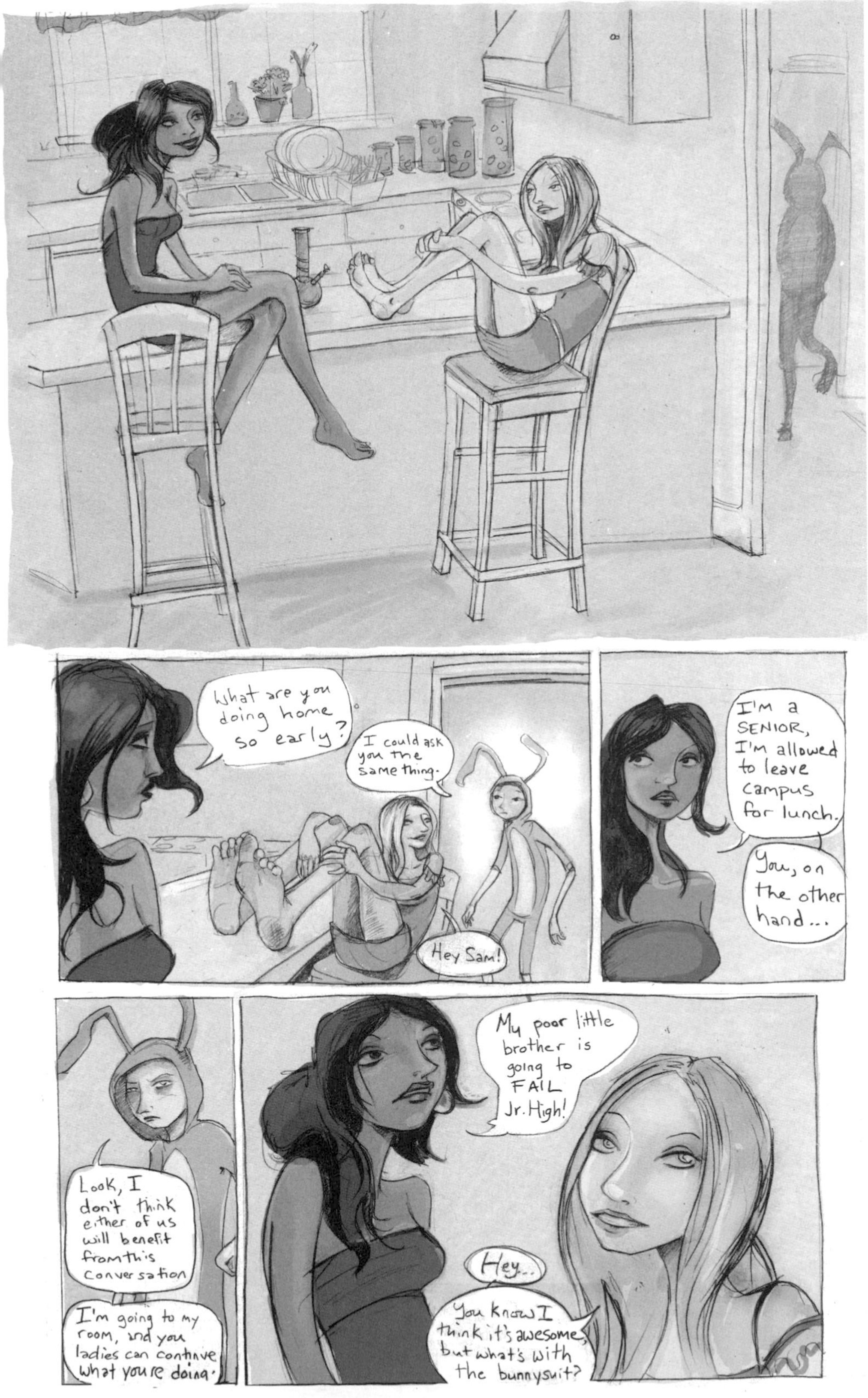
What are you doing home so early?
I could ask you the same thing.
Hey Sam!
I'm a SENIOR, I'm allowed to leave campus for lunch.
You, on the other hand...
Look, I don't think either of us will benefit from this conversation
I'm going to my room, and you ladies can continue what you're doing.
My poor little brother is going to FAIL Jr. High!
Hey...
You know I think it's awesome, but what's with the bunnysuit?

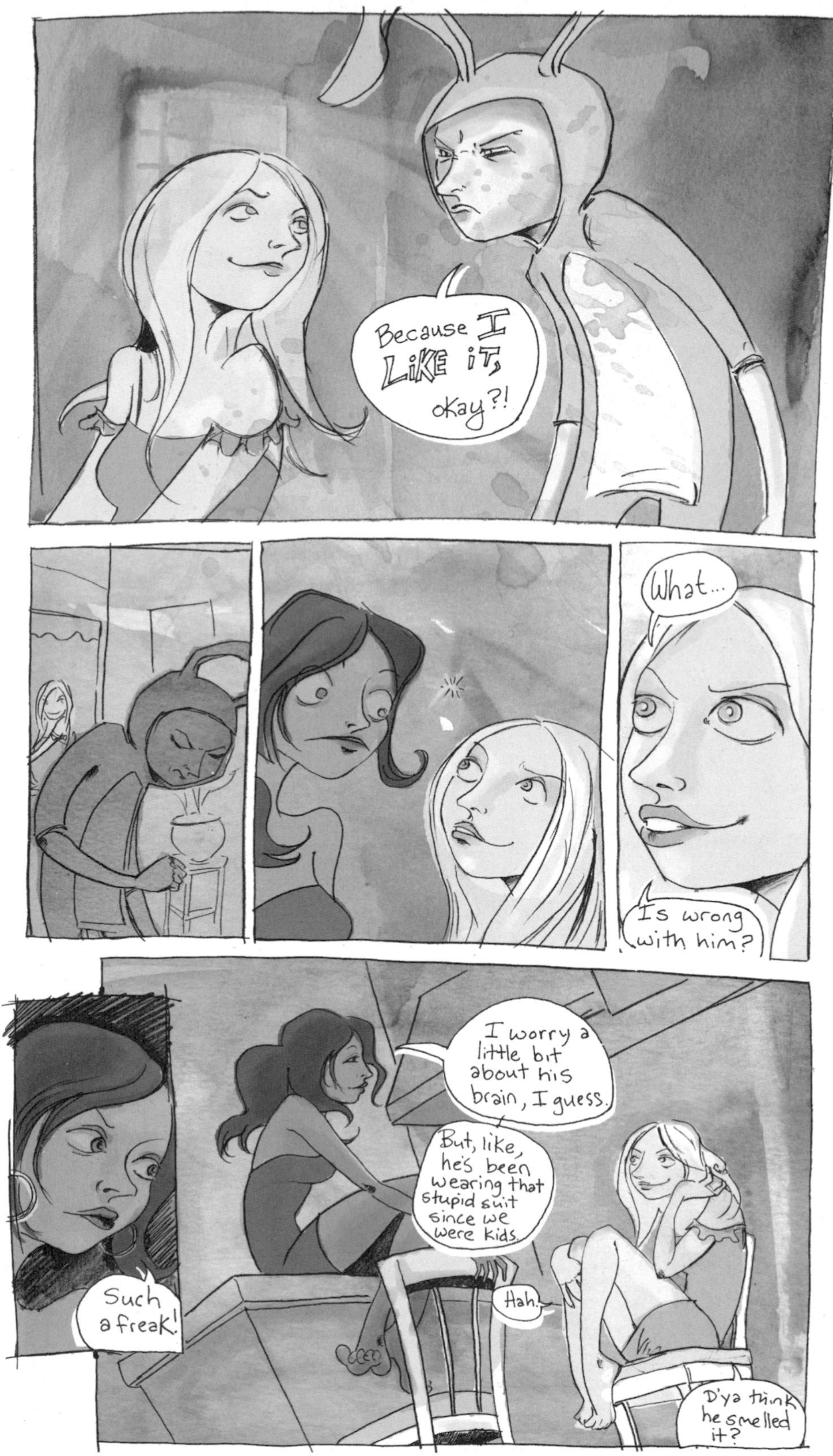
Because I LIKE IT, okay?!
What...
Is wrong with him?
I worry a little bit about his brain, I guess.
But, like, he's been wearing that stupid suit since we were kids.
Such a freak!
Hah!
D'ya think he smelled it?

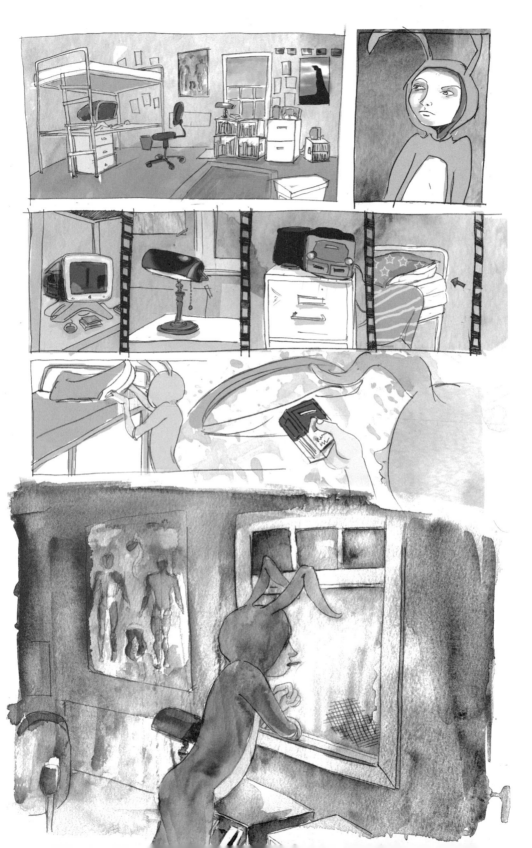

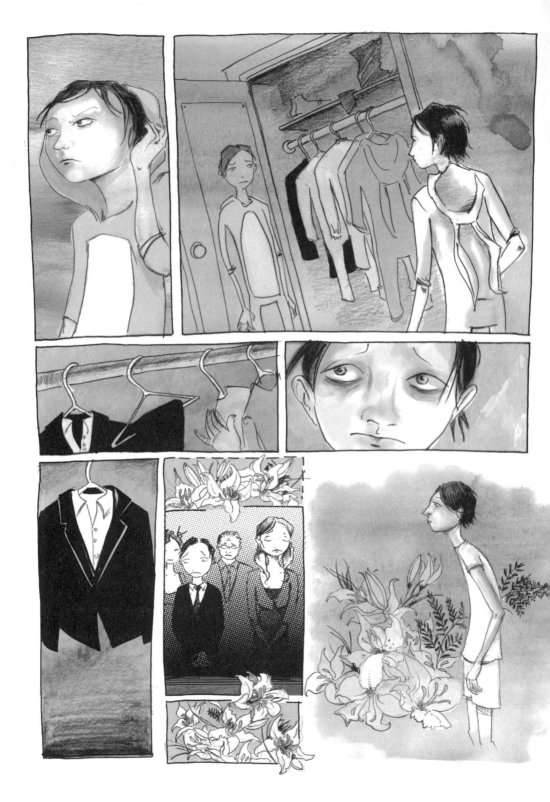

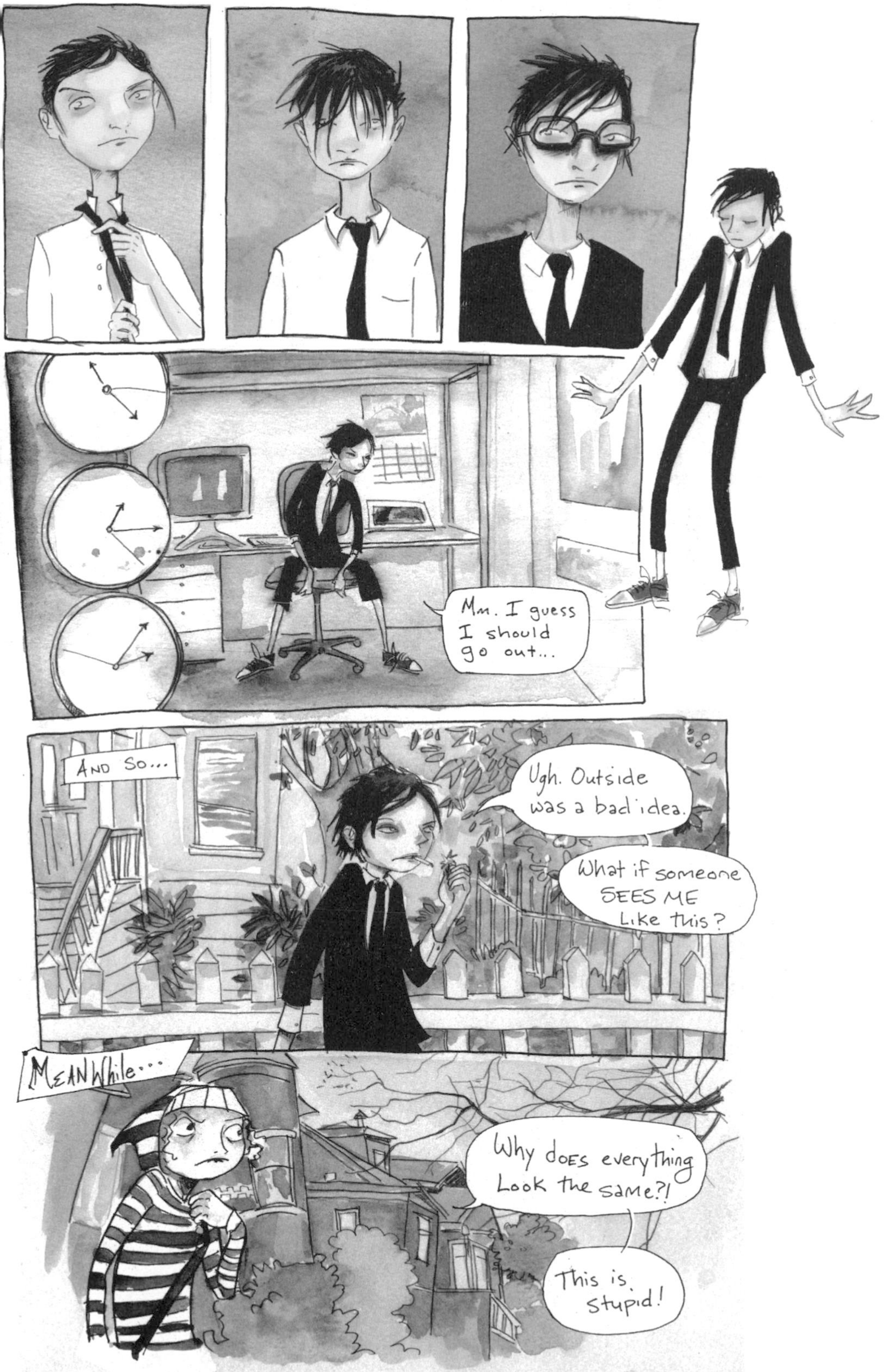
Mm. I guess I should go out...
And so...
Ugh. Outside was a bad idea.
What if someone SEES ME like this?
Meanwhile...
Why does everything look the same?!
This is stupid!

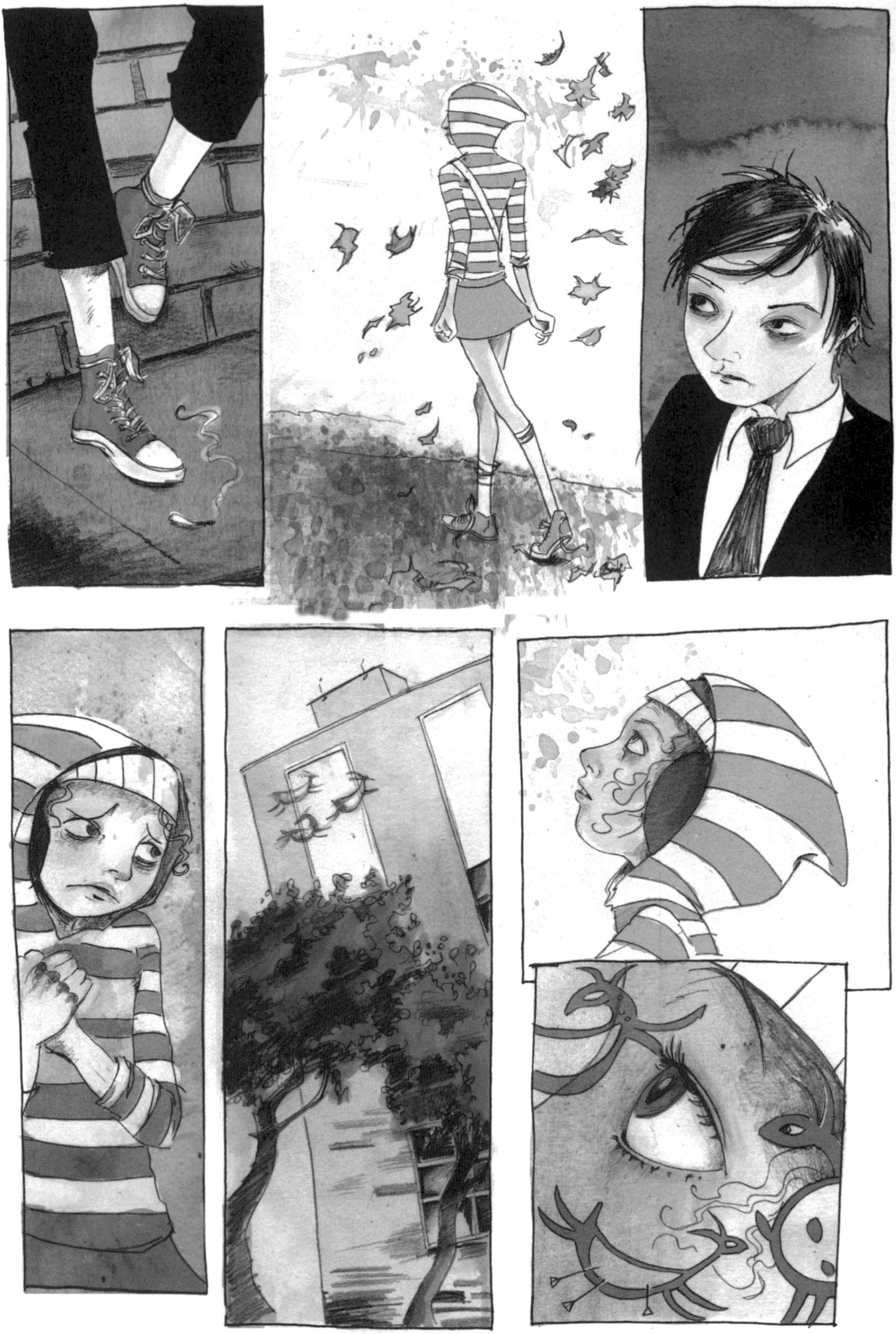

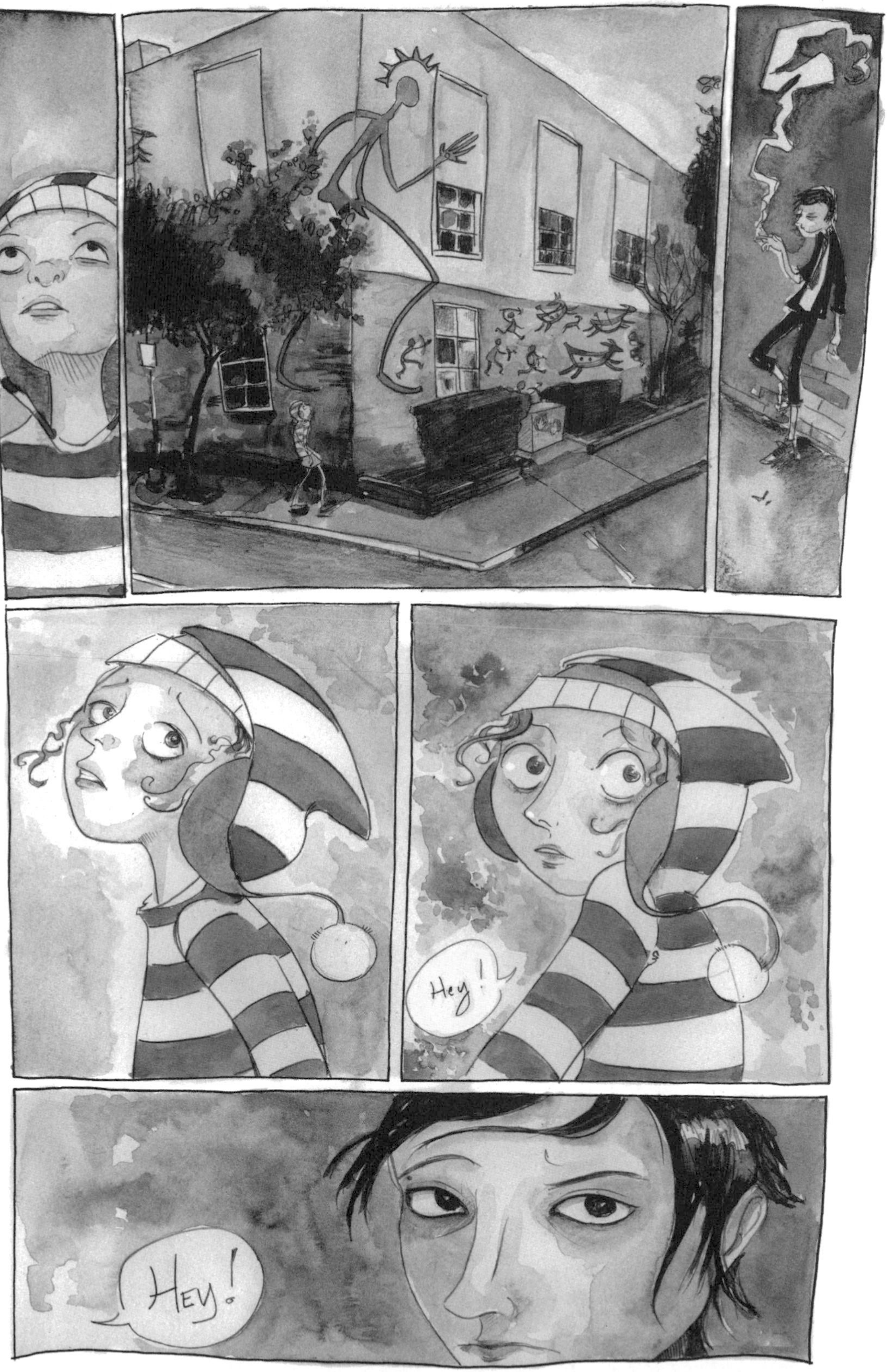
Hey!
Hey!

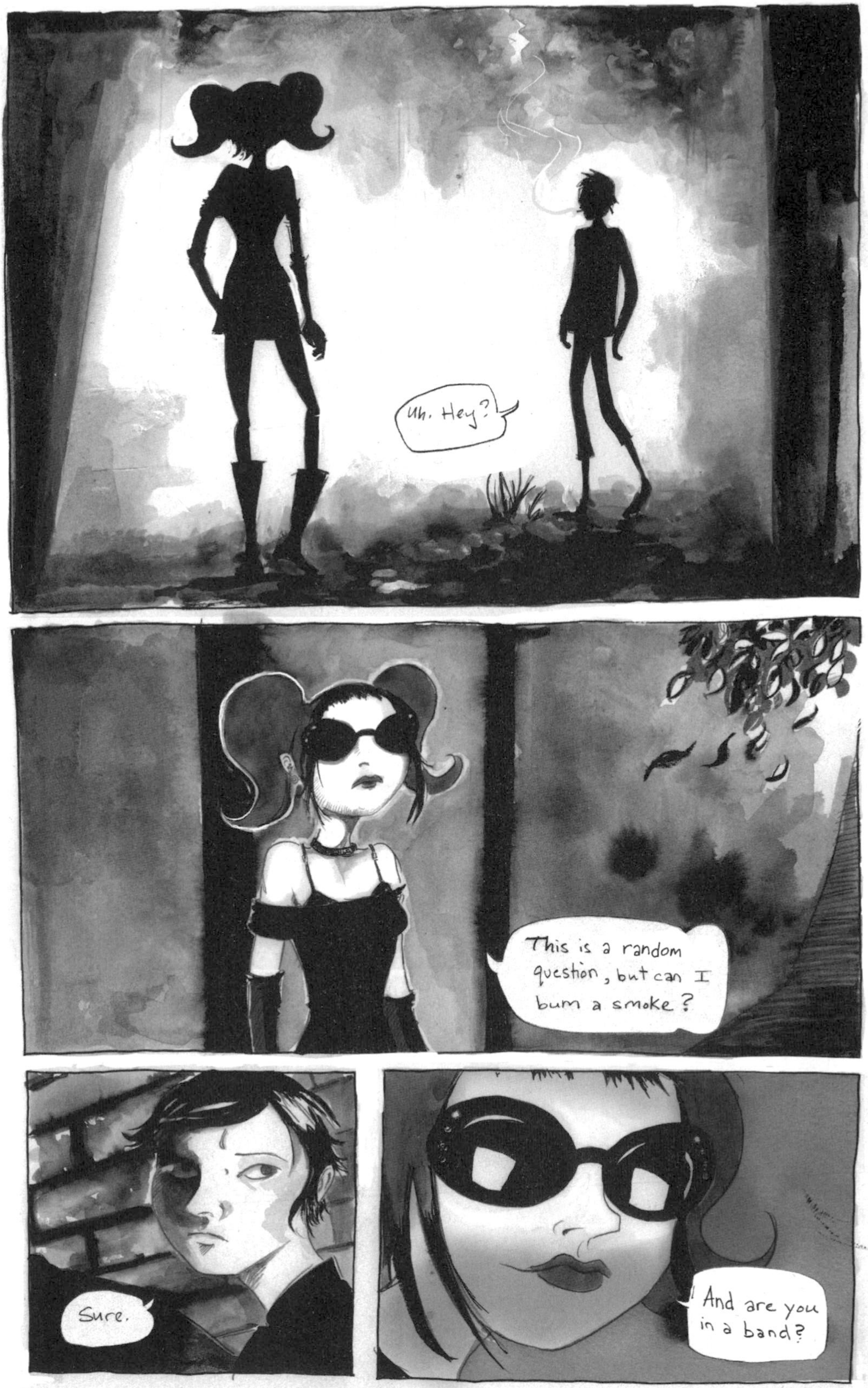
Uh. Hey?
This is a random question, but can I bum a smoke?
Sure.
And are you in a band?

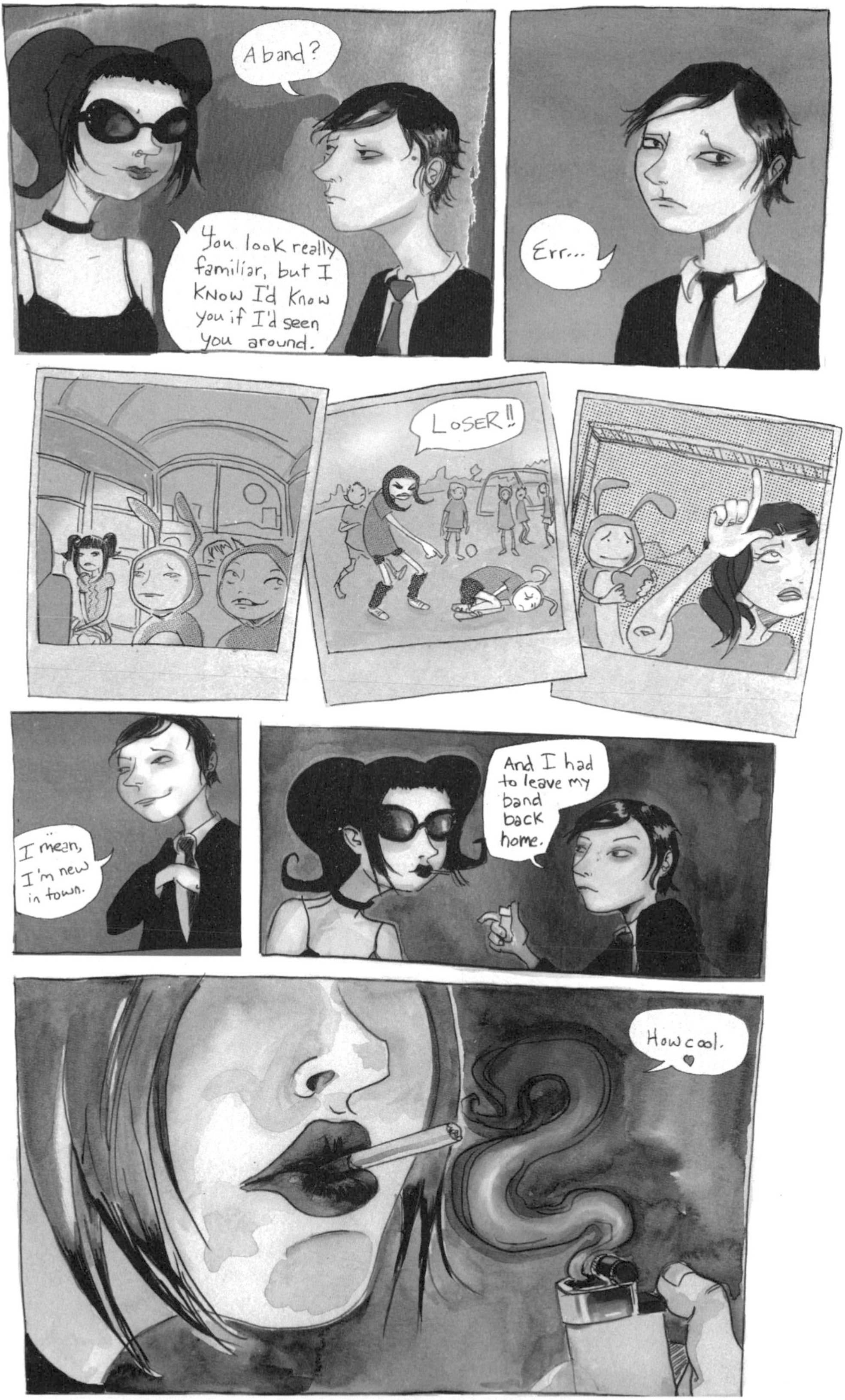
A band?
You look really familiar, but I KNOW I'd know you if I'd seen you around.
Err...
LOSER!!
I mean, I'm new in town.
And I had to leave my band back home.
How cool.

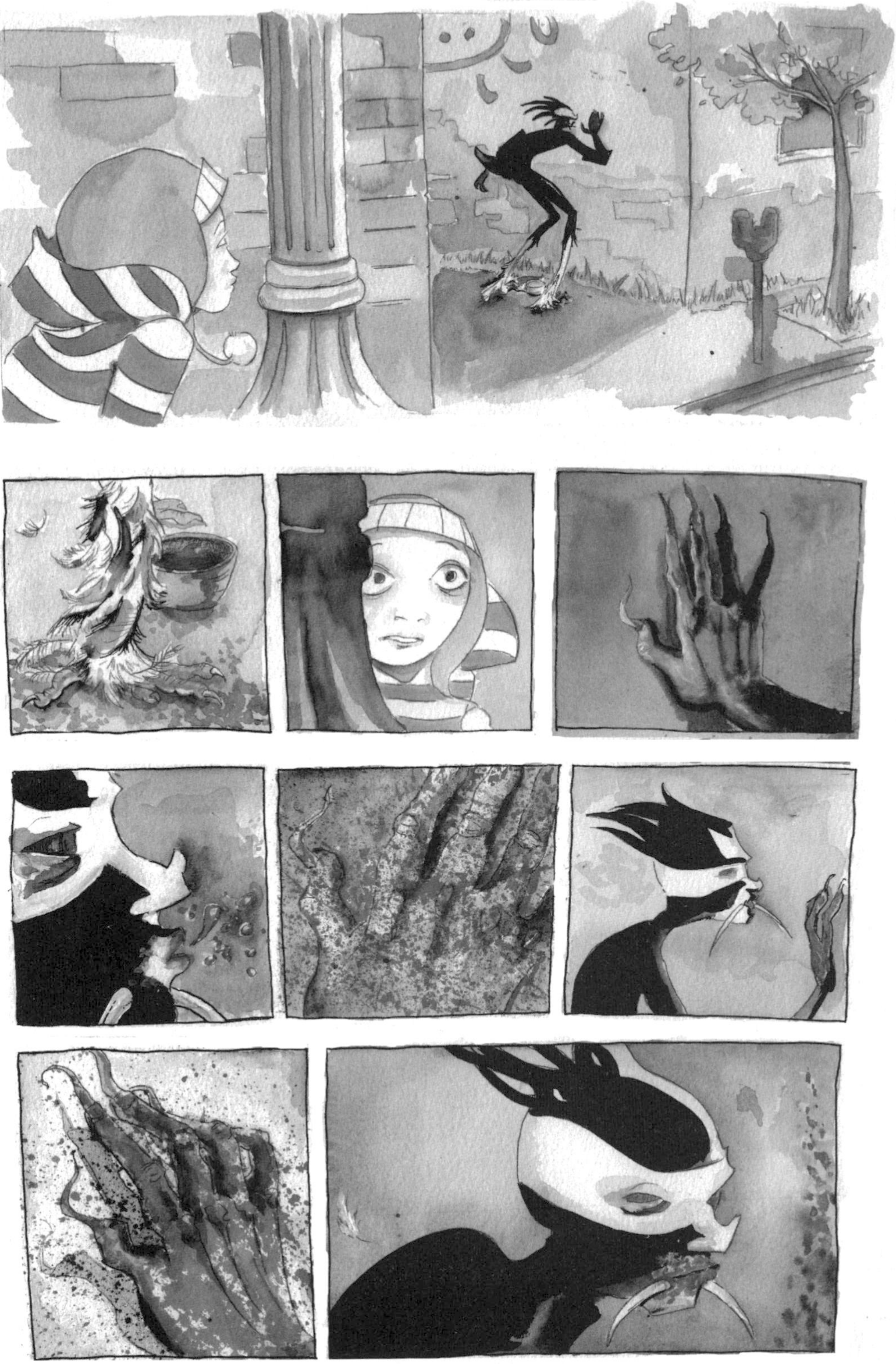

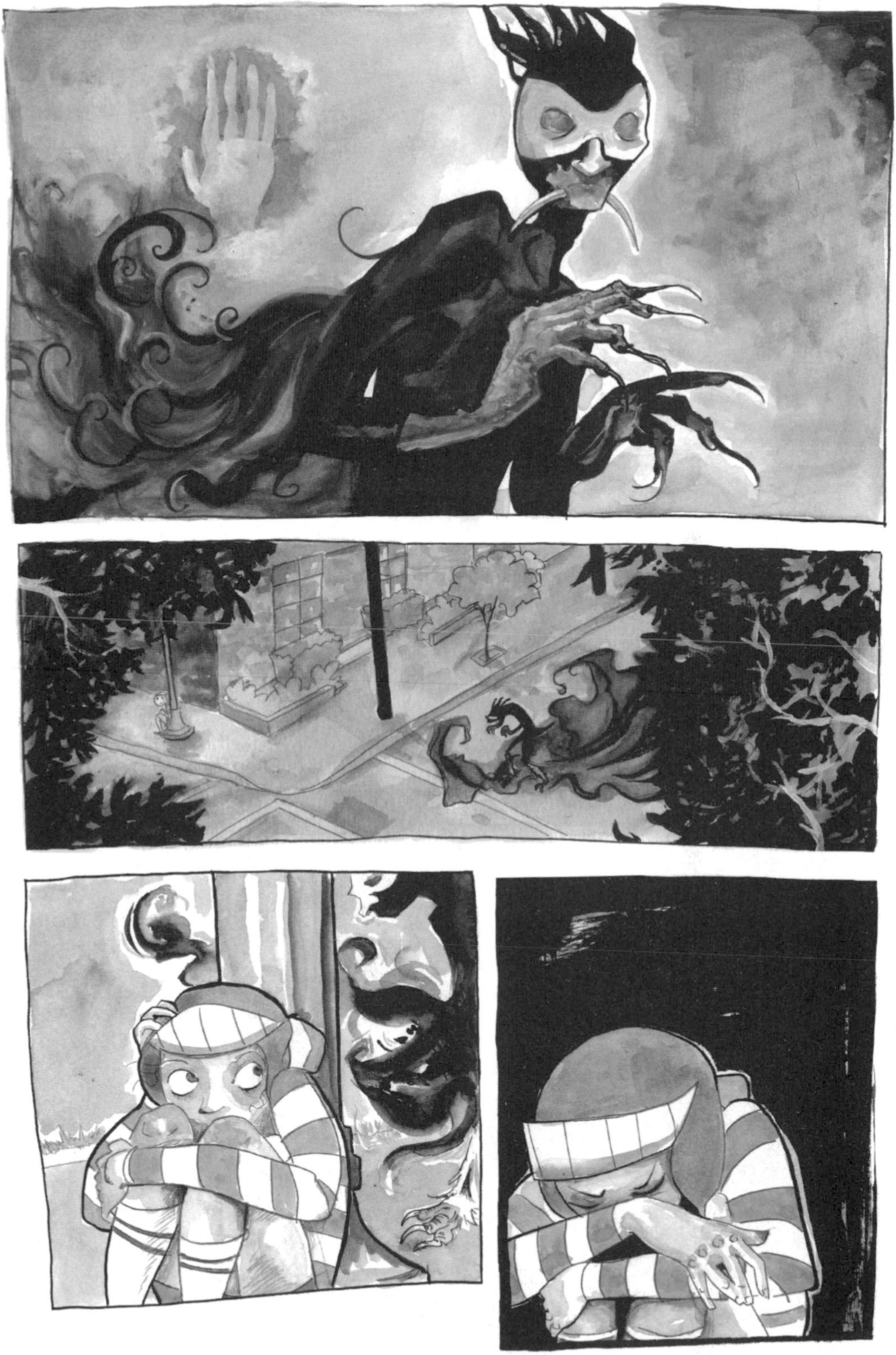

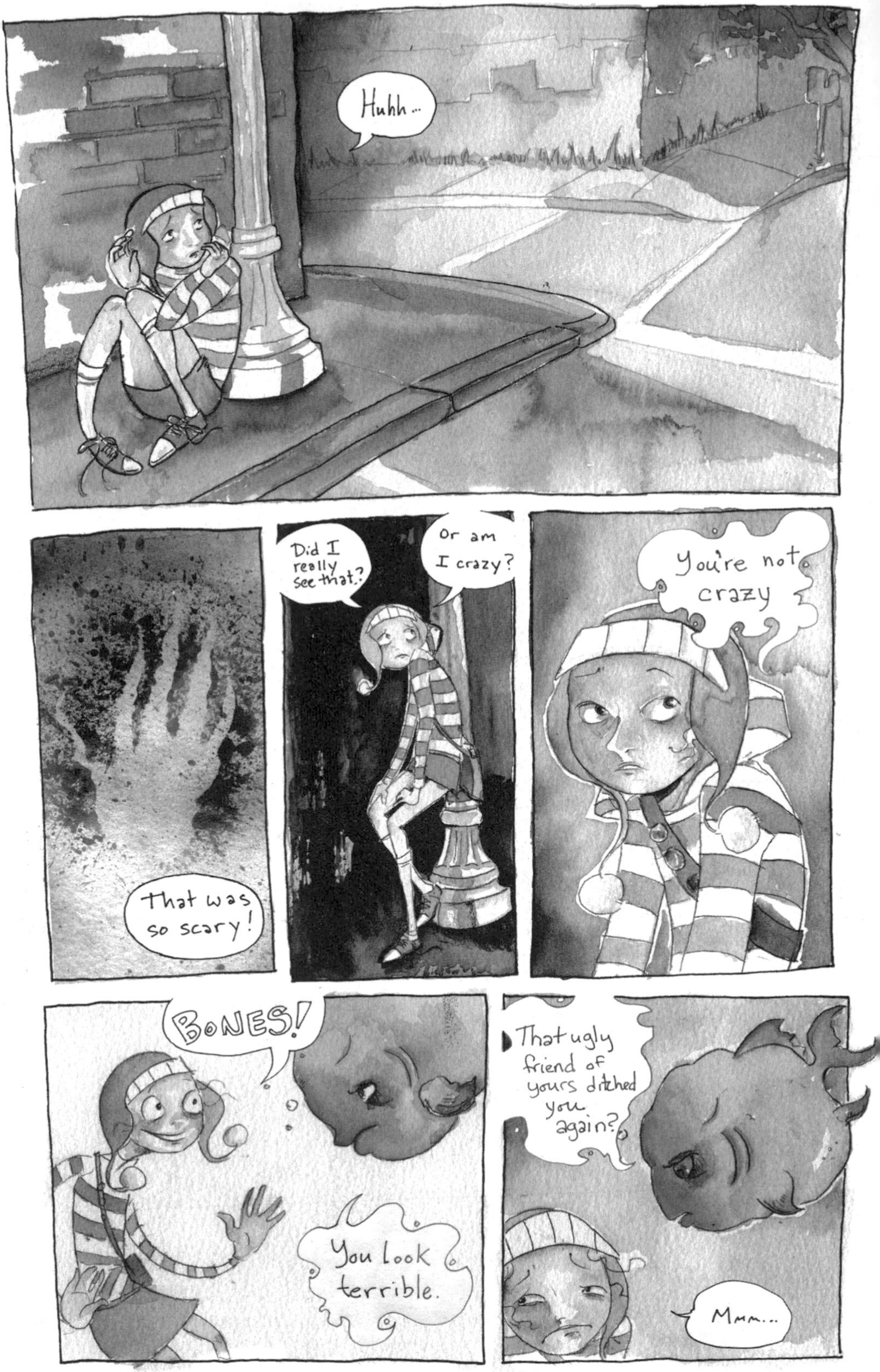
Huhh...
That was so scary!
Did I really see that?
Or am I crazy?
You're not crazy
BONES!
You look terrible.
That ugly friend of yours ditched you again?
Mmm...

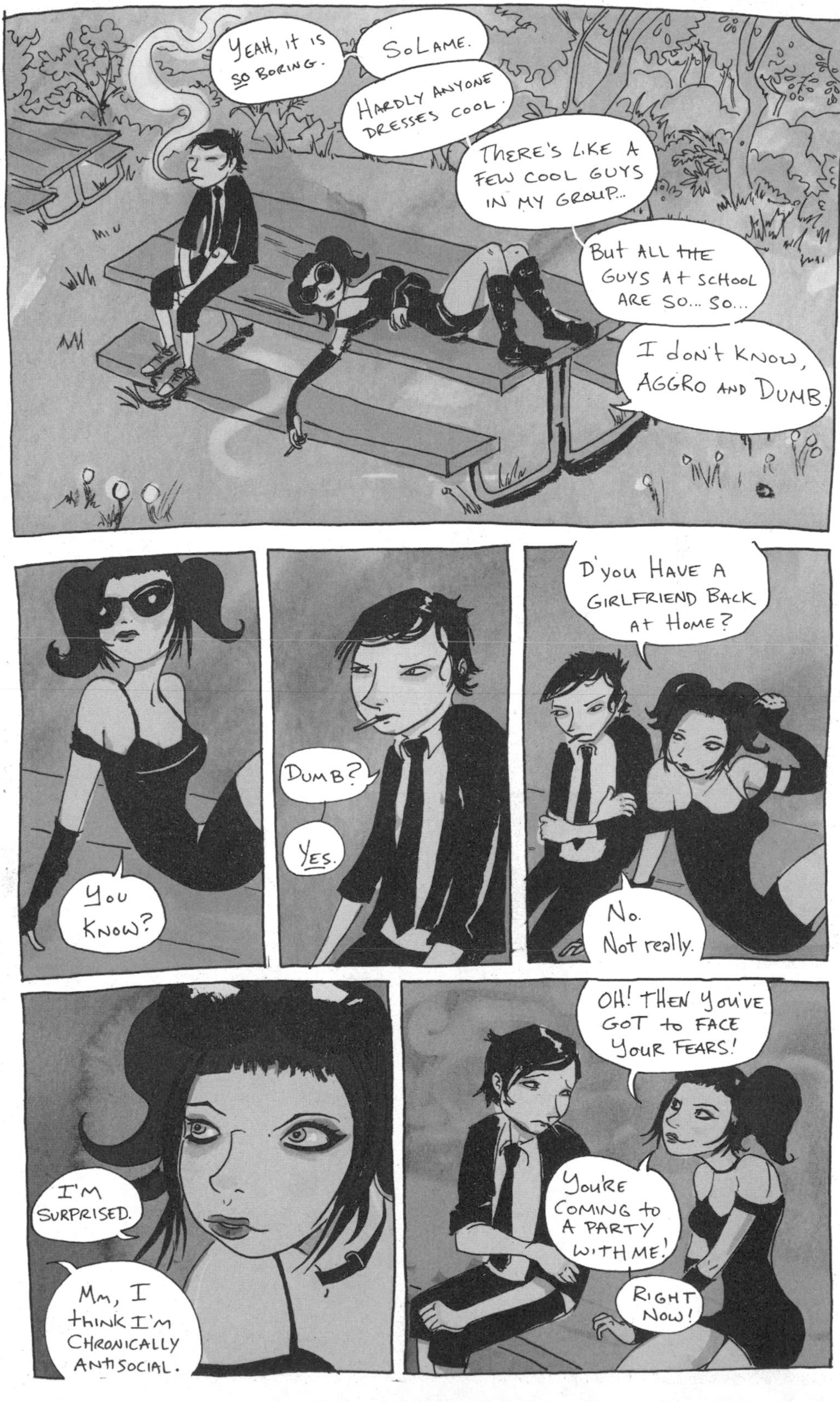
YEAH, IT IS SO BORING.
SO LAME.
HARDLY ANYONE DRESSES COOL.
THERE'S LIKE A FEW COOL GUYS IN MY GROUP...
But ALL THE GUYS AT SCHOOL ARE SO... SO...
I don't KNOW, AGGRO AND DUMB.
YOU KNOW?
DUMB?
YES.
D'you HAVE A GIRLFRIEND BACK AT HOME?
No. Not really.
I'M SURPRISED.
Mm, I think I'm CHRONICALLY ANTISOCIAL.
OH! THEN YOU'VE GOT to FACE YOUR FEARS!
YOU'RE COMING to A PARTY WITH ME!
RIGHT NOW!

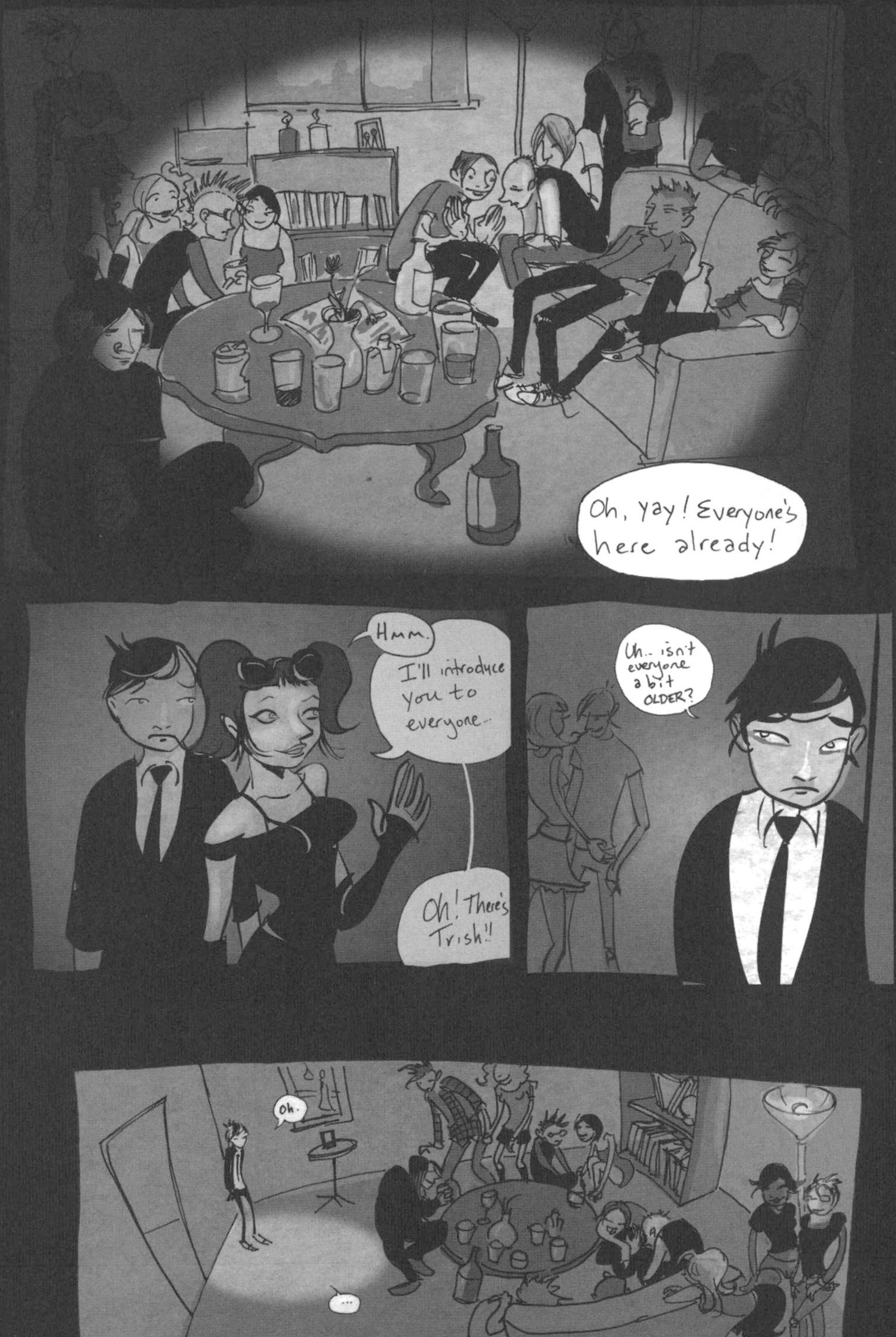
Oh, yay! Everyone's here already!
Hmm.
I'll introduce you to everyone...
Oh! There's Trish!!
Uh.. isn't everyone a bit OLDER?
Oh.
...

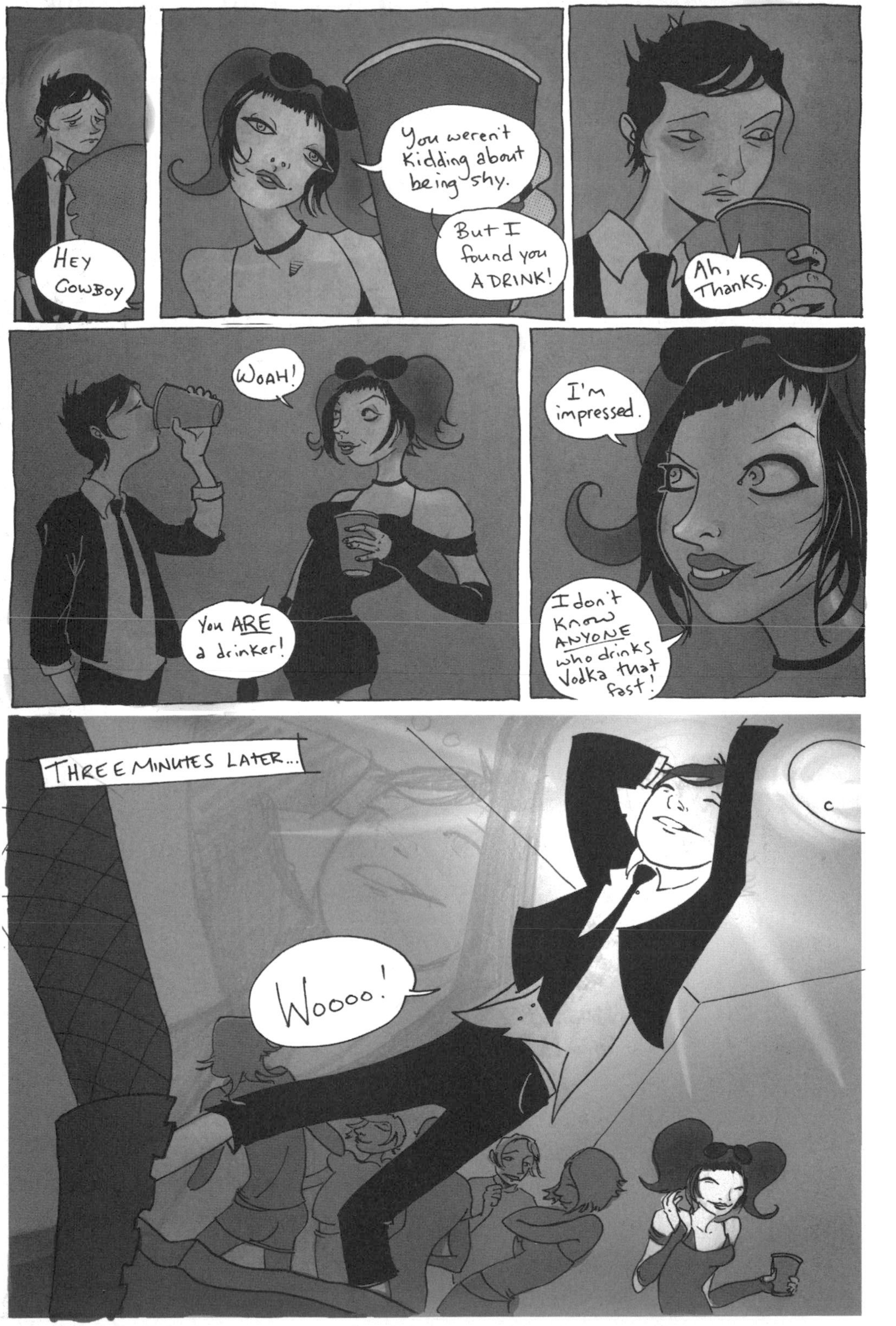
HEY COWBOY
You weren't kidding about being shy.
But I found you A DRINK!
Ah, Thanks.
WOAH!
You ARE a drinker!
I'm impressed.
I don't know ANYONE who drinks Vodka that fast!
THREE MINUTES LATER...
Woooo!

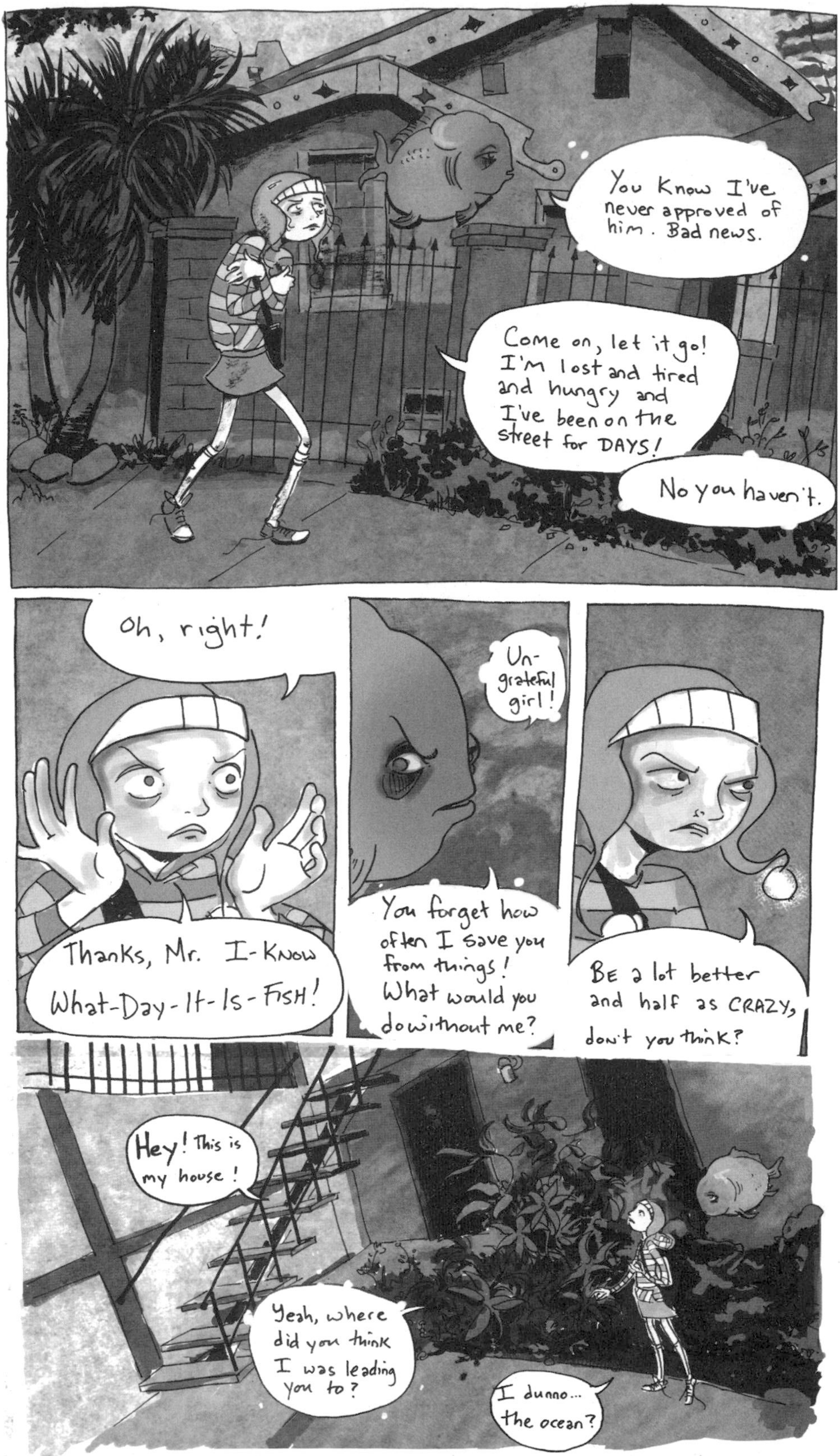
You Know I've never approved of him. Bad news.
Come on, let it go! I'm lost and tired and hungry and I've been on the street for DAYS!
No you haven't.
Oh, right!
Thanks, Mr. I-Know What-Day-It-Is-Fish!
Un-grateful girl!
You forget how often I save you from things! What would you do without me?
Be a lot better and half as CRAZY, don't you think?
Hey! This is my house!
Yeah, where did you think I was leading you to?
I dunno... the ocean?

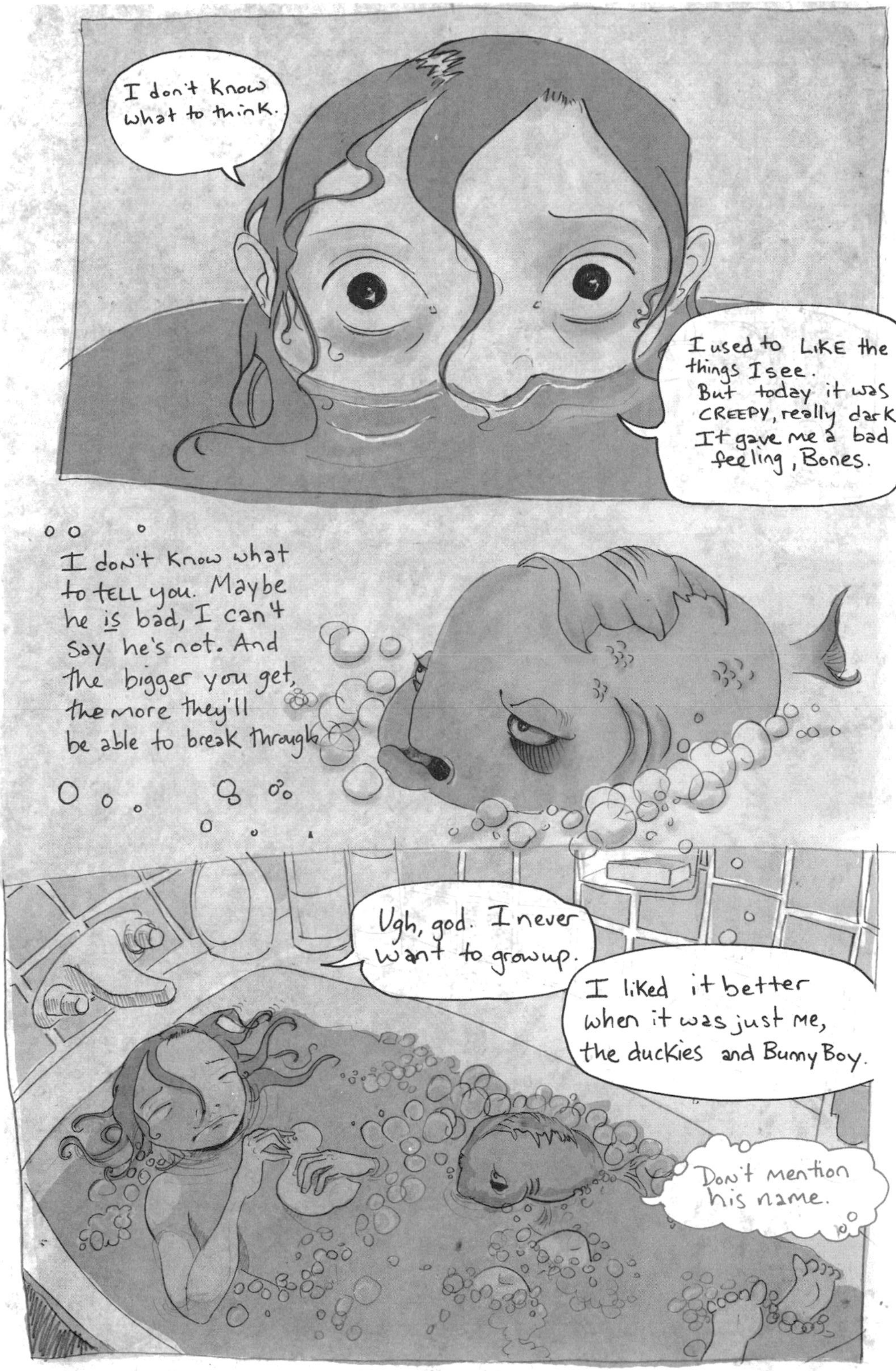
I don't Know what to think.
I used to LIKE the things I see. But today it was CREEPY, really dark. It gave me a bad feeling, Bones.
I don't Know what to TELL you. Maybe he is bad, I can't say he's not. And the bigger you get, the more they'll be able to break through.
Ugh, god. I never want to grow up.
I liked it better when it was just me, the duckies and Bunny Boy.
Don't mention his name.

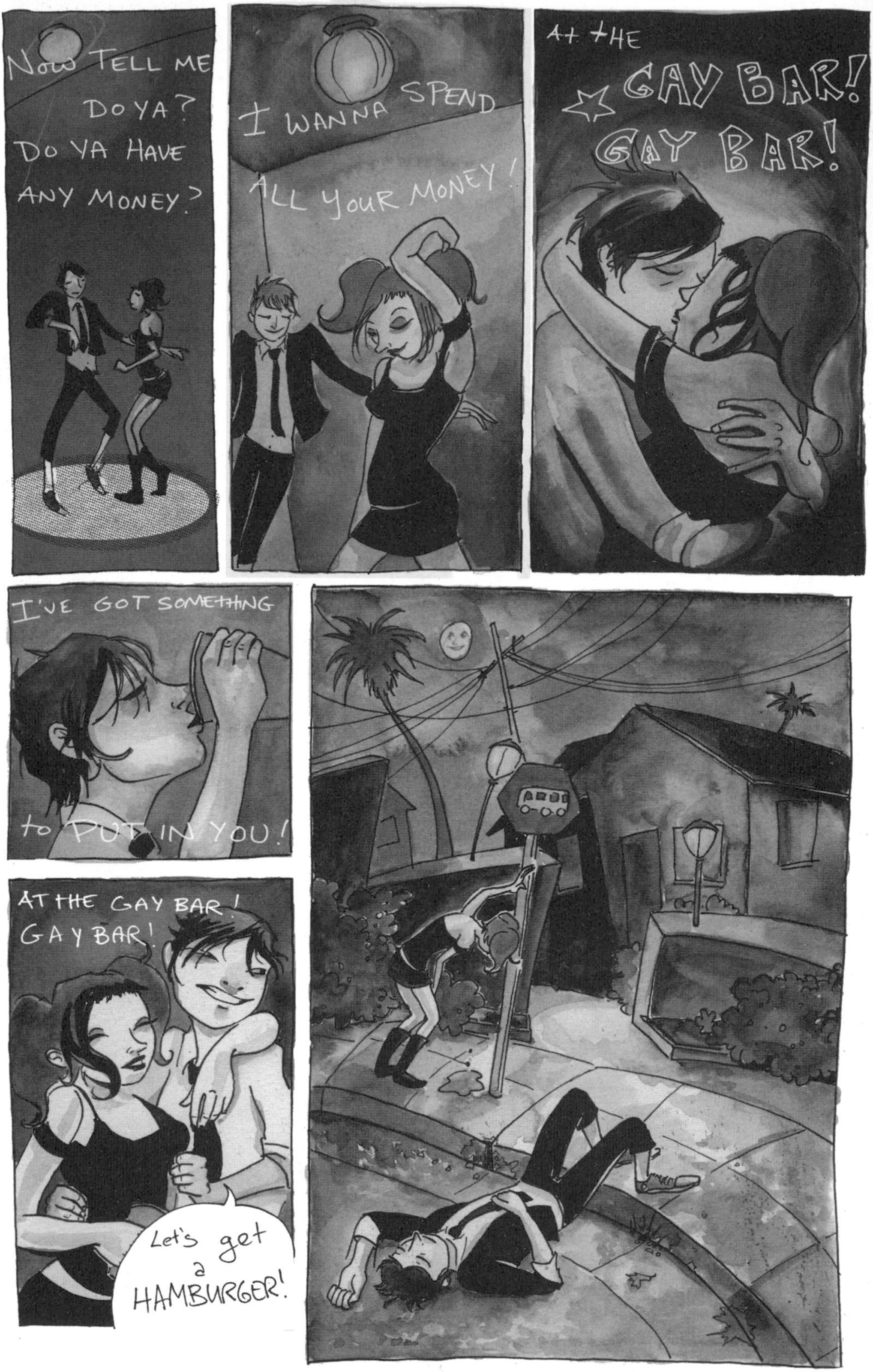
Now TELL ME
DO YA?
DO YA HAVE
ANY MONEY?
I WANNA SPEND
ALL YOUR MONEY!
At the
GAY BAR!
GAY BAR!
I'VE GOT SOMETHING
to PUT IN YOU!
AT THE GAY BAR!
GAY BAR!
Let's get a HAMBURGER!

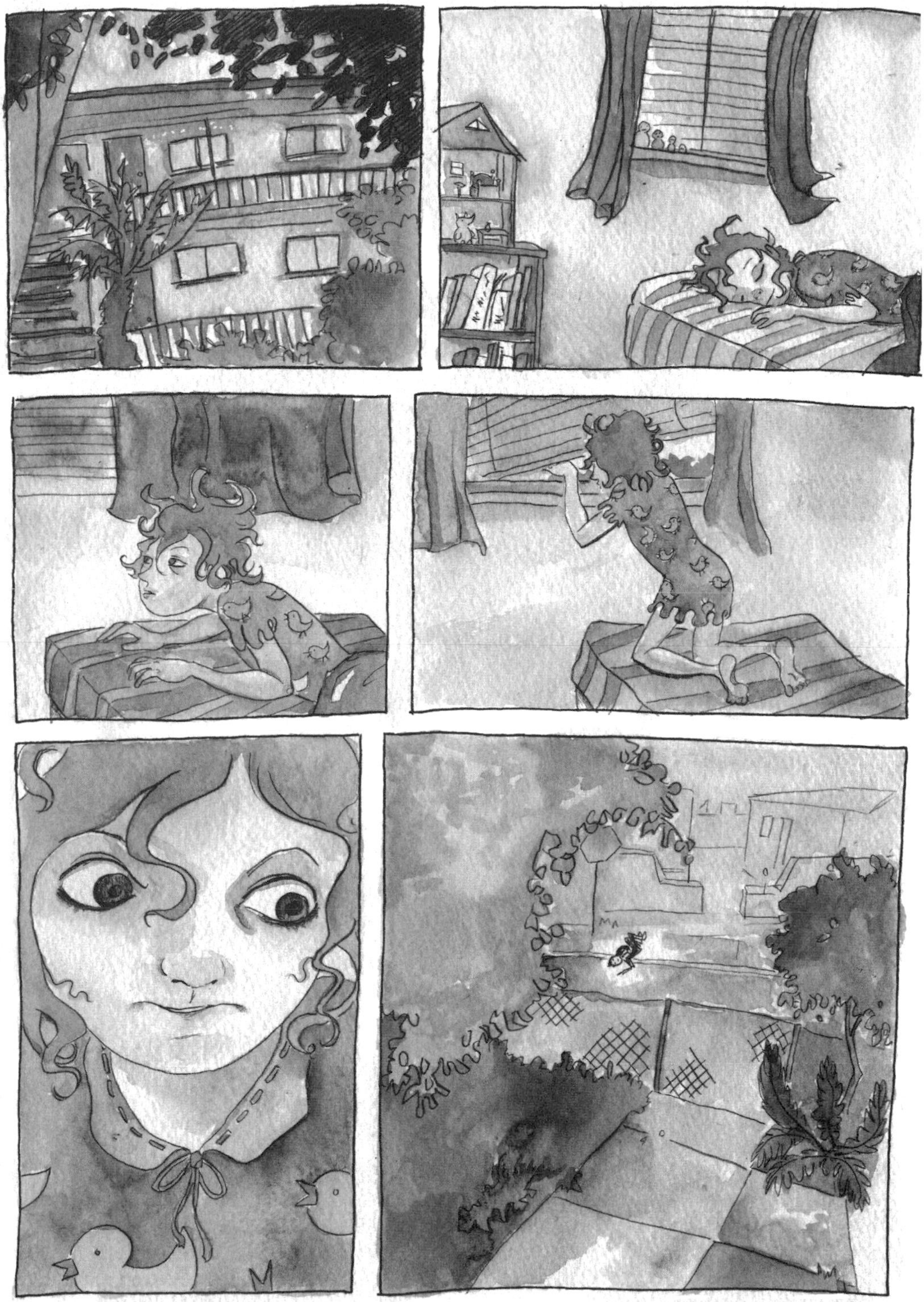

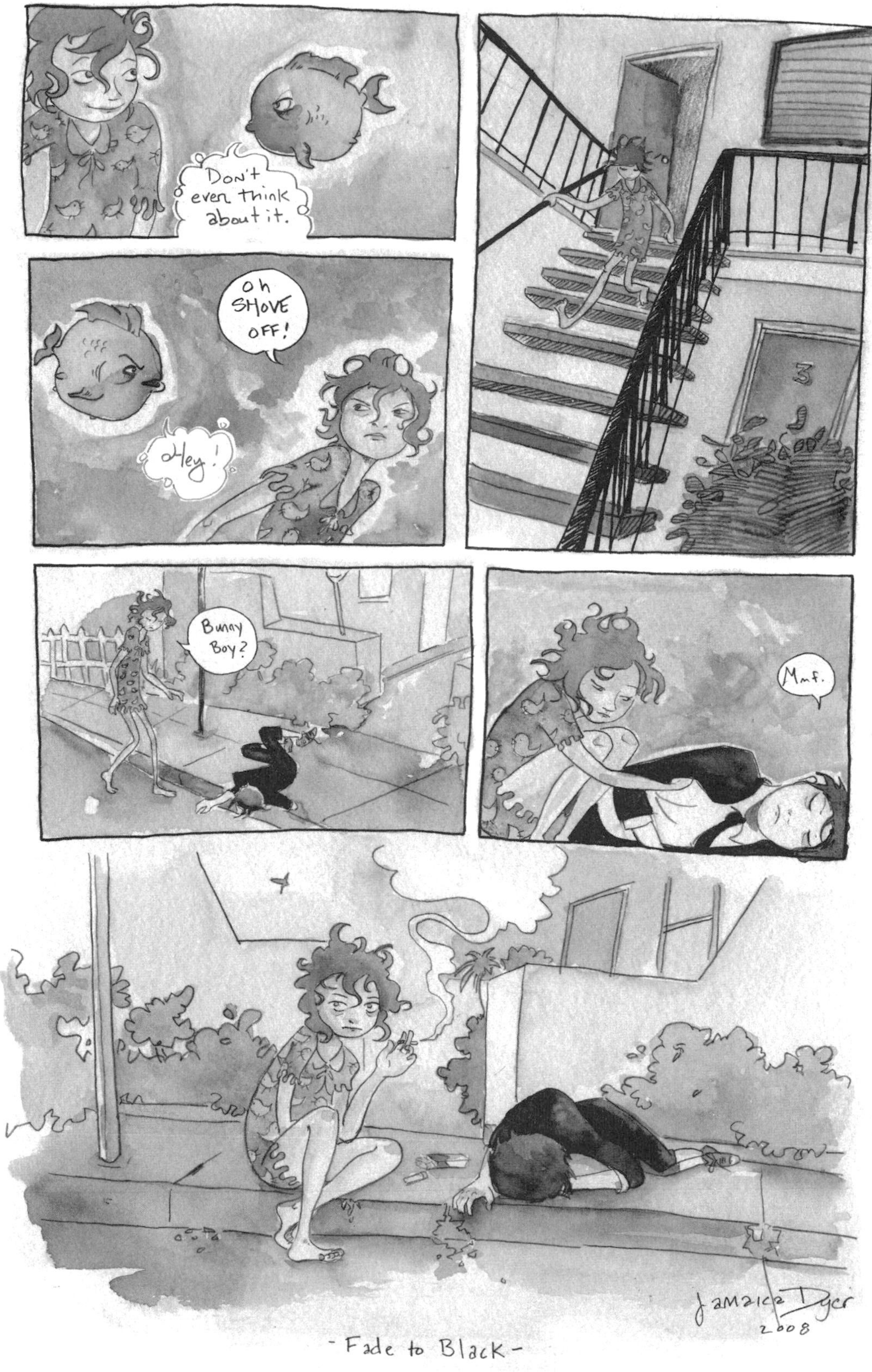
Don't even think about it.
Oh SHOVE OFF!
Hey!
Bunny Boy?
Mmf.
Jamaica Dyer 2008

- Fade to Black -

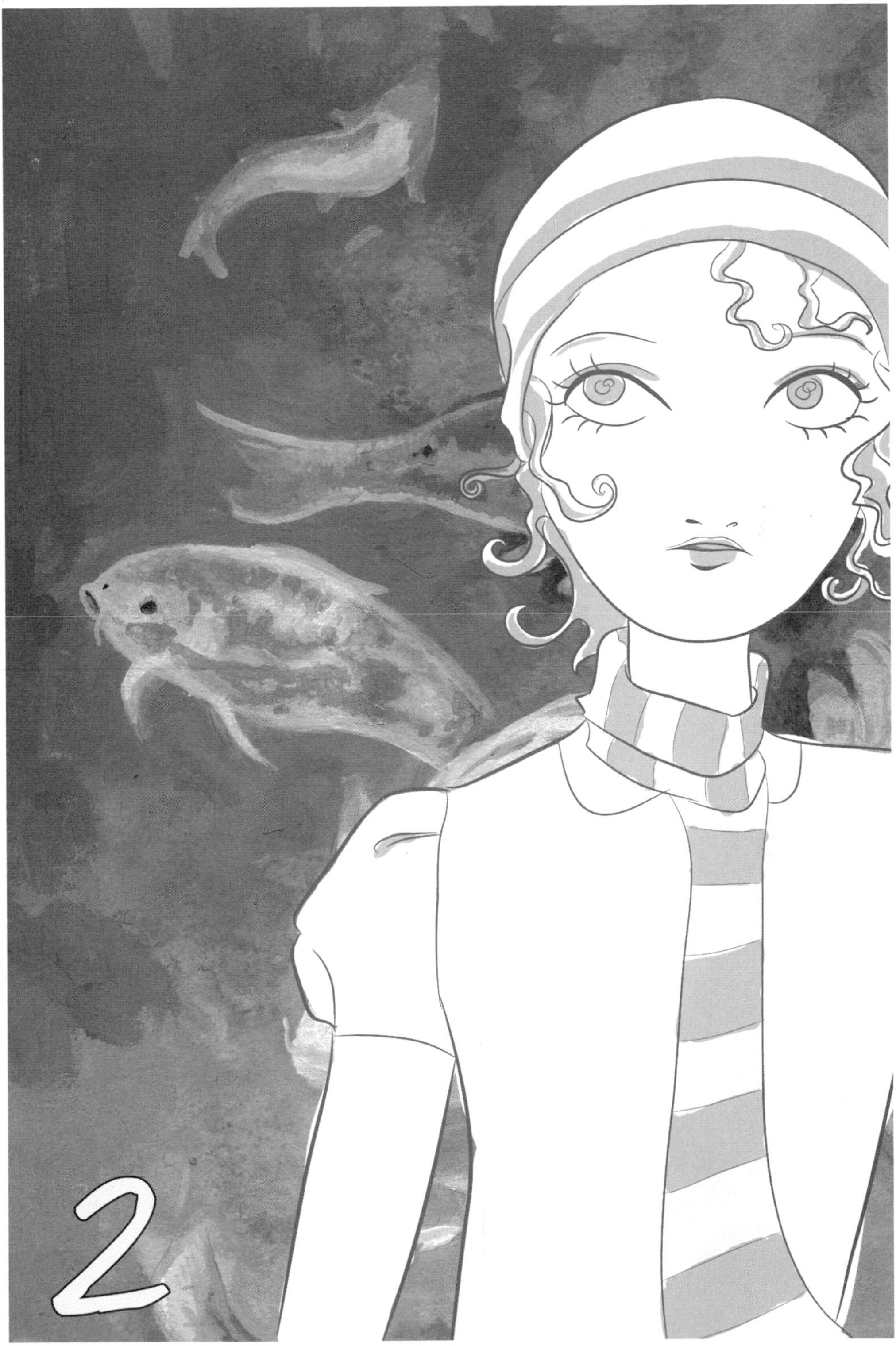
2

SOCIAL LINKS

Chapter 2

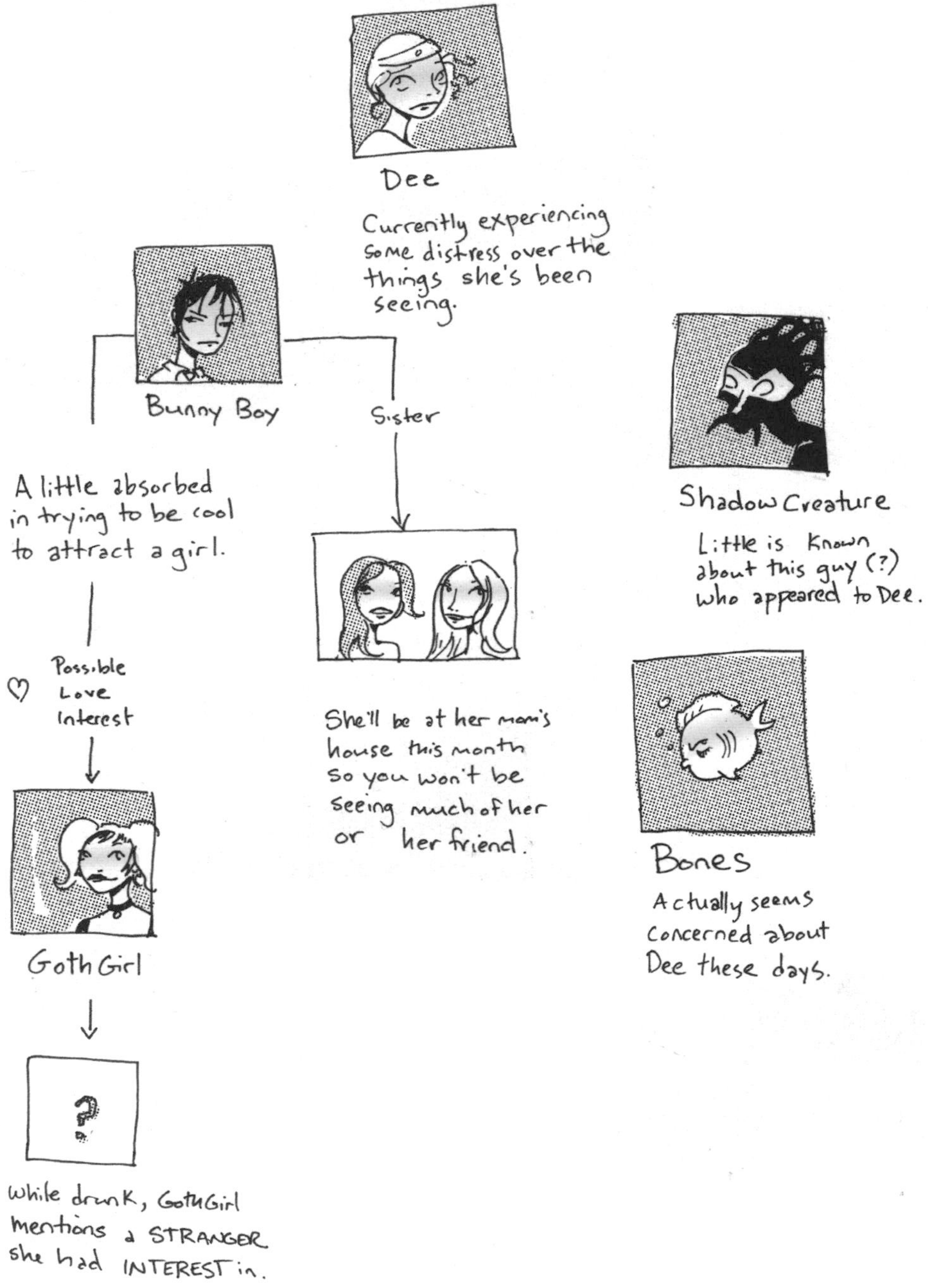
Dee
Currently experiencing some distress over the things she's been seeing.
Bunny Boy
A little absorbed in trying to be cool to attract a girl.
Sister
She'll be at her mom's house this month so you won't be seeing much of her or her friend.
Possible Love Interest
Goth Girl
?
While drunk, GothGirl mentions a STRANGER she had INTEREST in.
Shadow Creature
Little is known about this guy (?) who appeared to Dee.
Bones
Actually seems concerned about Dee these days.

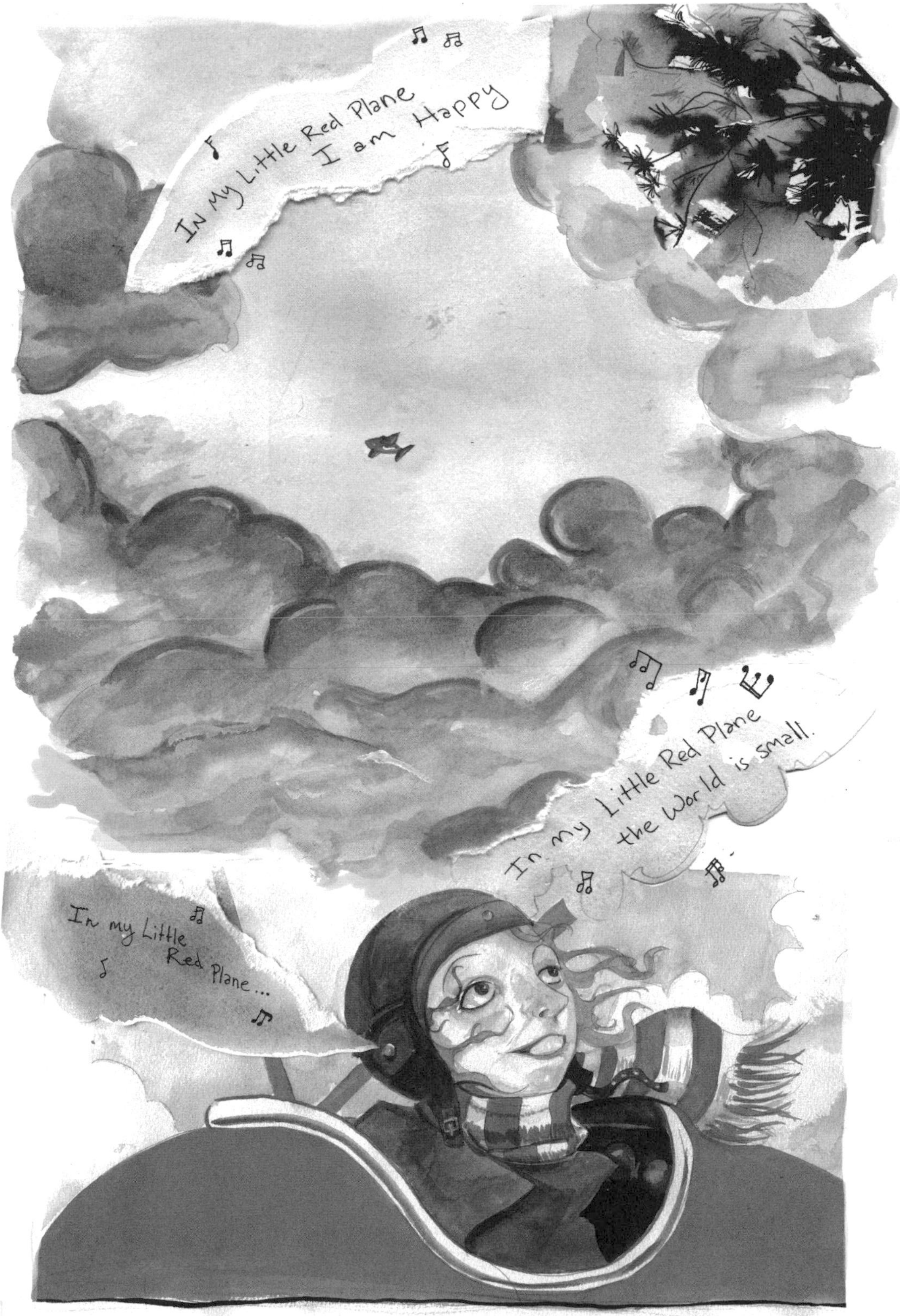
In My Little Red Plane
I am Happy
In my Little Red Plane
the World is small.
In my Little
Red Plane...

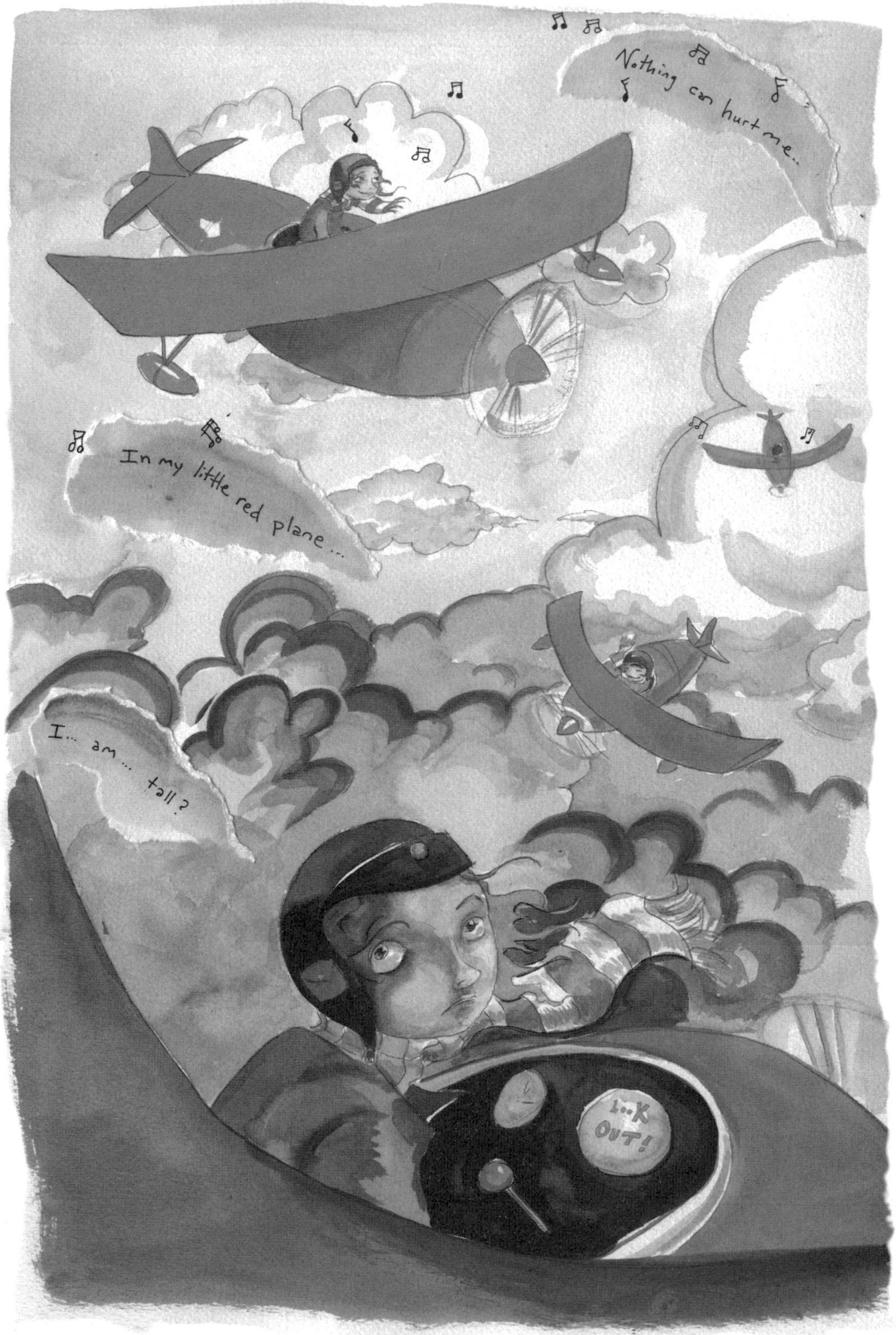

Nothing can hurt me...
In my little red plane...
I... am... tall?
LooK OUT!

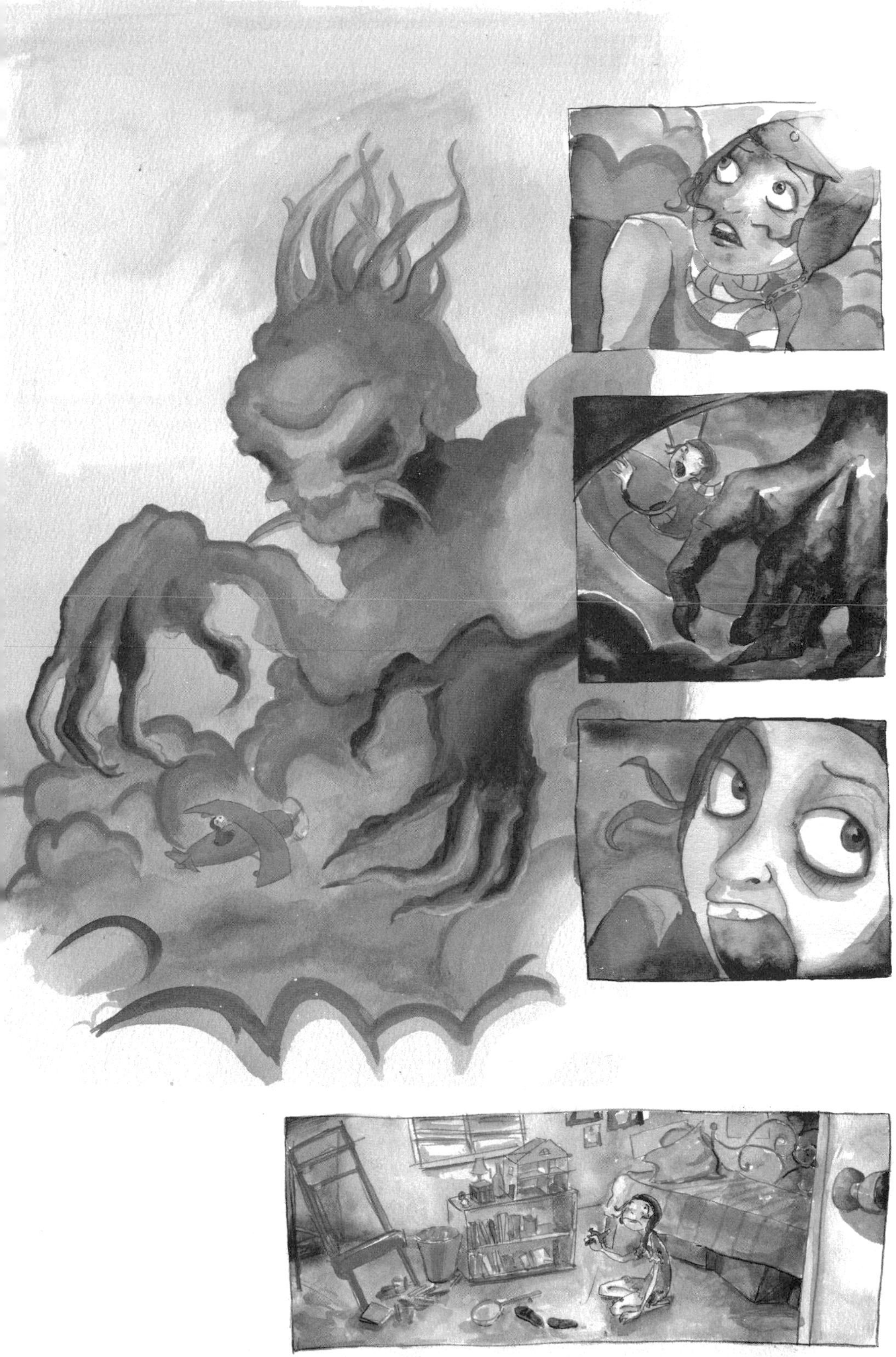

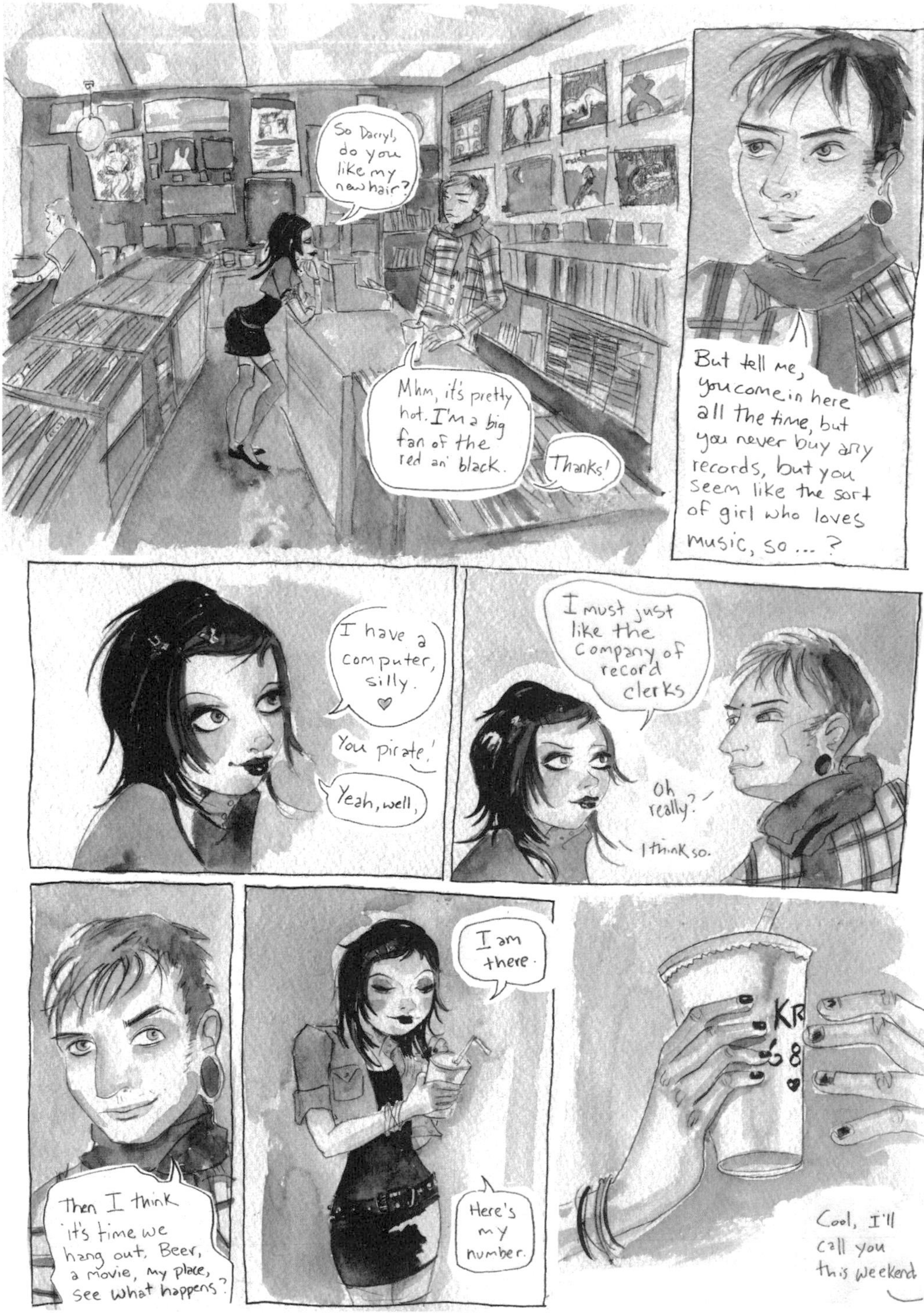

So Darryl, do you like my new hair?
Mhm, it's pretty hot. I'm a big fan of the red an' black.
Thanks!
But tell me, you come in here all the time, but you never buy any records, but you seem like the sort of girl who loves music, so...?
I have a computer, silly.
You pirate!
Yeah, well,
I must just like the company of record clerks
Oh really?
I think so.
Then I think it's time we hang out. Beer, a movie, my place, see what happens?
I am there.
Here's my number.
Cool, I'll call you this weekend

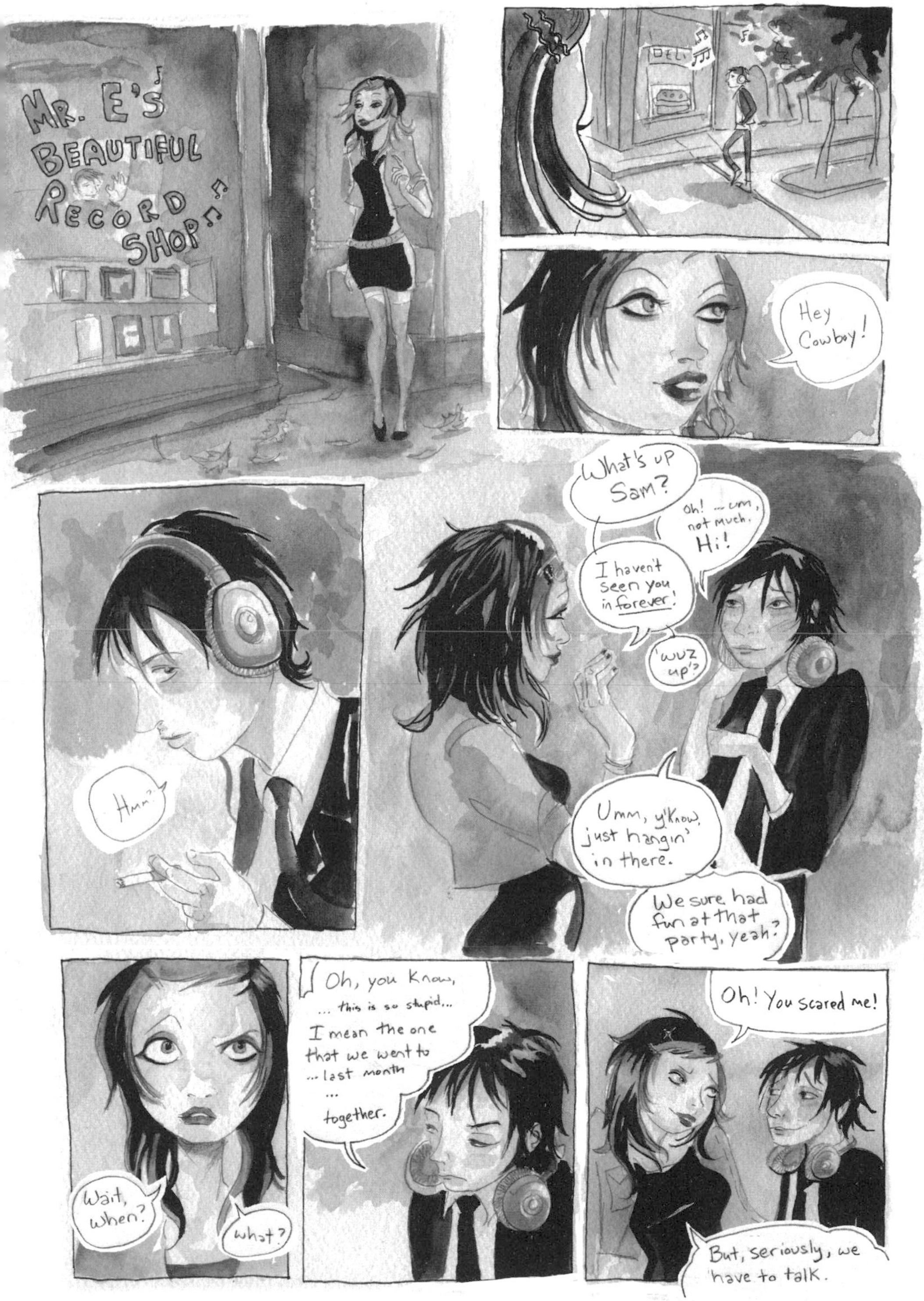
MR. E's BEAUTIFUL RECORD SHOP
DELI
Hey Cowboy!
Hmm?
What's up Sam?
I haven't seen you in forever!
'wuz up?
Oh! ...um, not much. Hi!
Umm, y'know, just hangin' in there.
We sure had fun at that party, yeah?
Wait, when?
what?
Oh, you know,
... this is so stupid...
I mean the one that we went to ...last month ... together.
Oh! You scared me!
But, seriously, we have to talk.

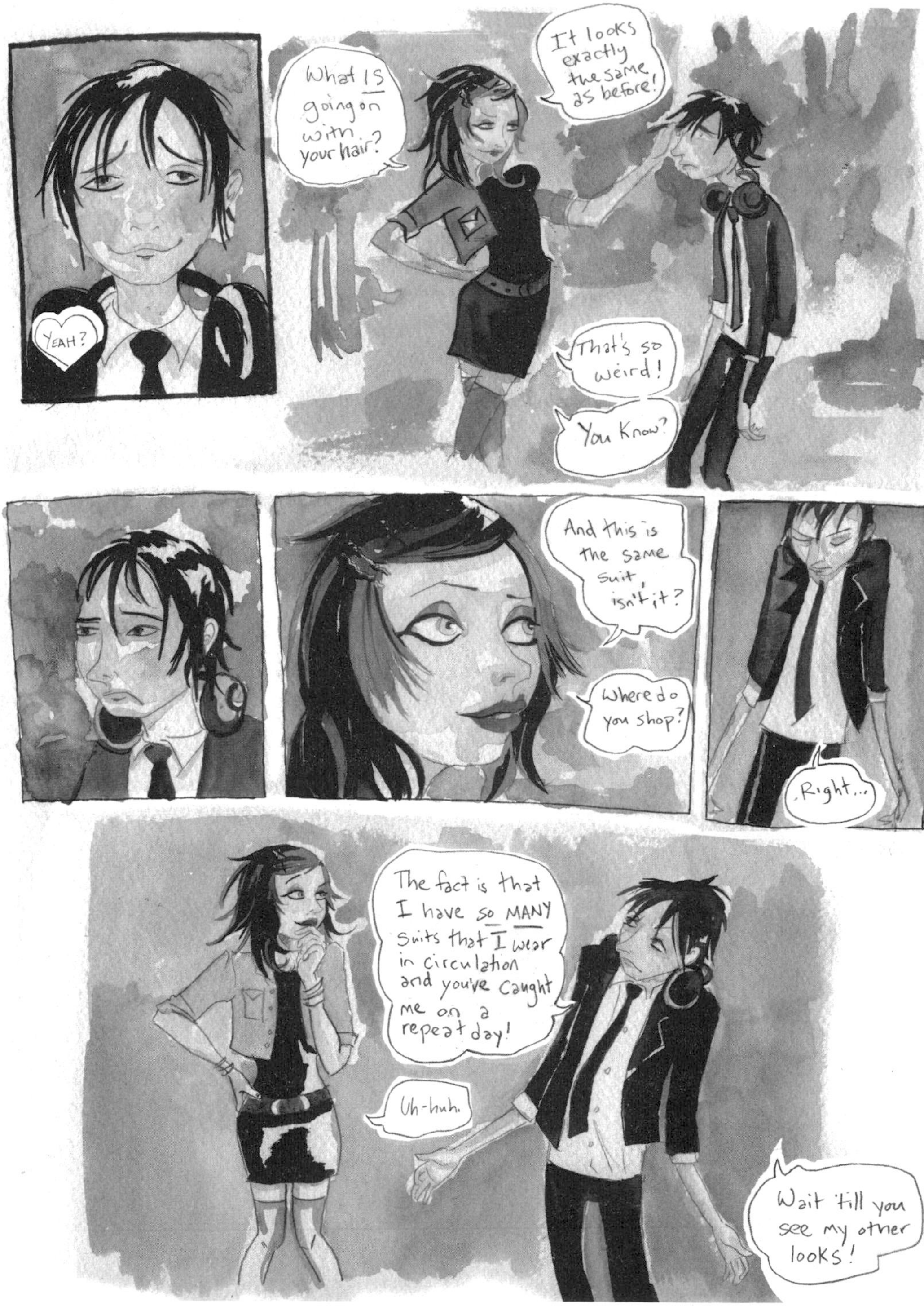
YEAH?
What IS going on with your hair?
It looks exactly the same as before!
That's so weird!
You Know?
And this is the same suit, isn't it?
Where do you shop?
Right...
The fact is that I have SO MANY suits that I wear in circulation and you've caught me on a repeat day!
Uh-huh.
Wait 'till you see my other looks!

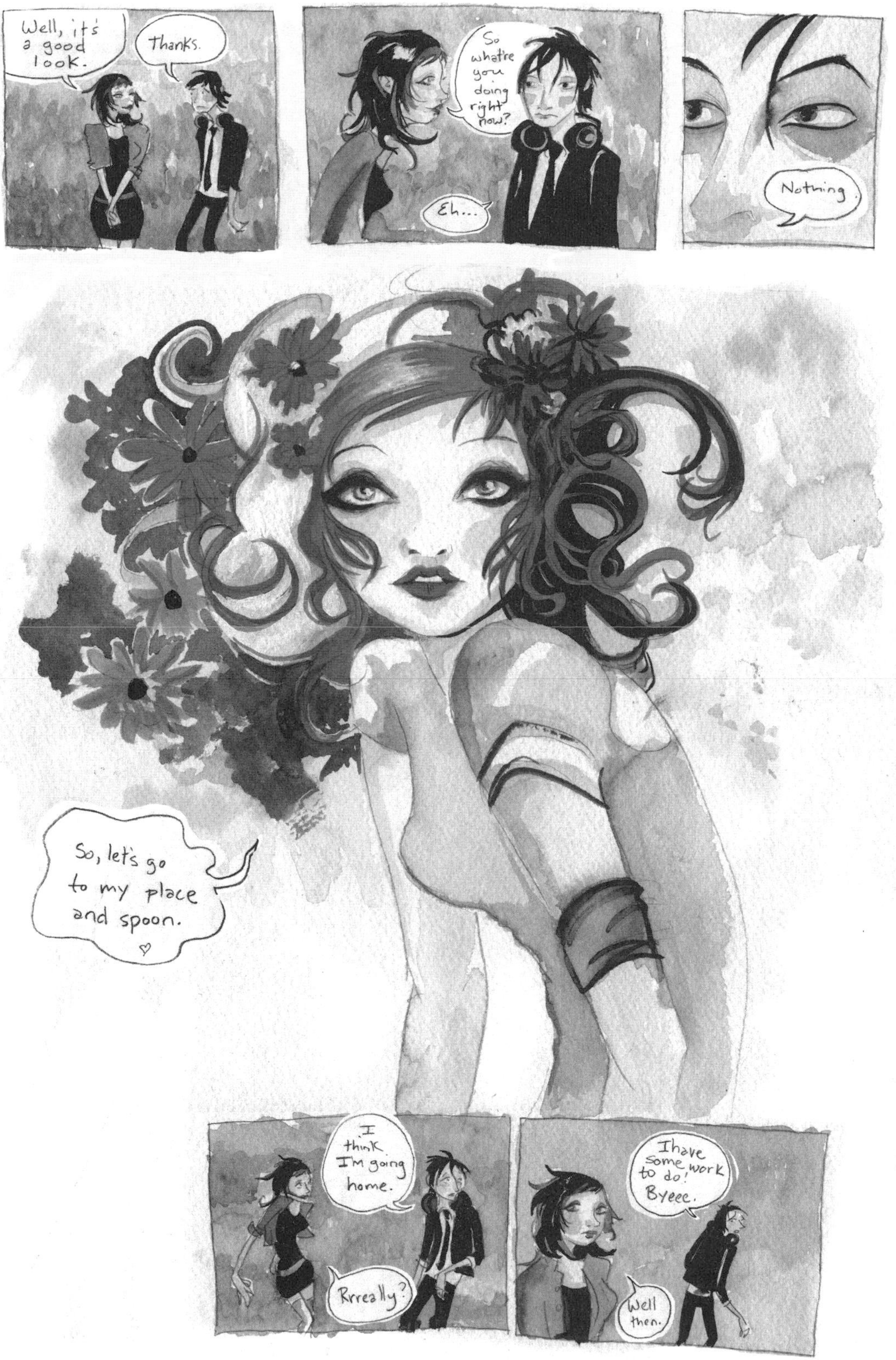
Well, it's a good look.
Thanks.
So what're you doing right now?
Eh...
Nothing.
So, let's go to my place and spoon.
I think I'm going home.
Rrreally?
I have some work to do! Byeee.
Well then.

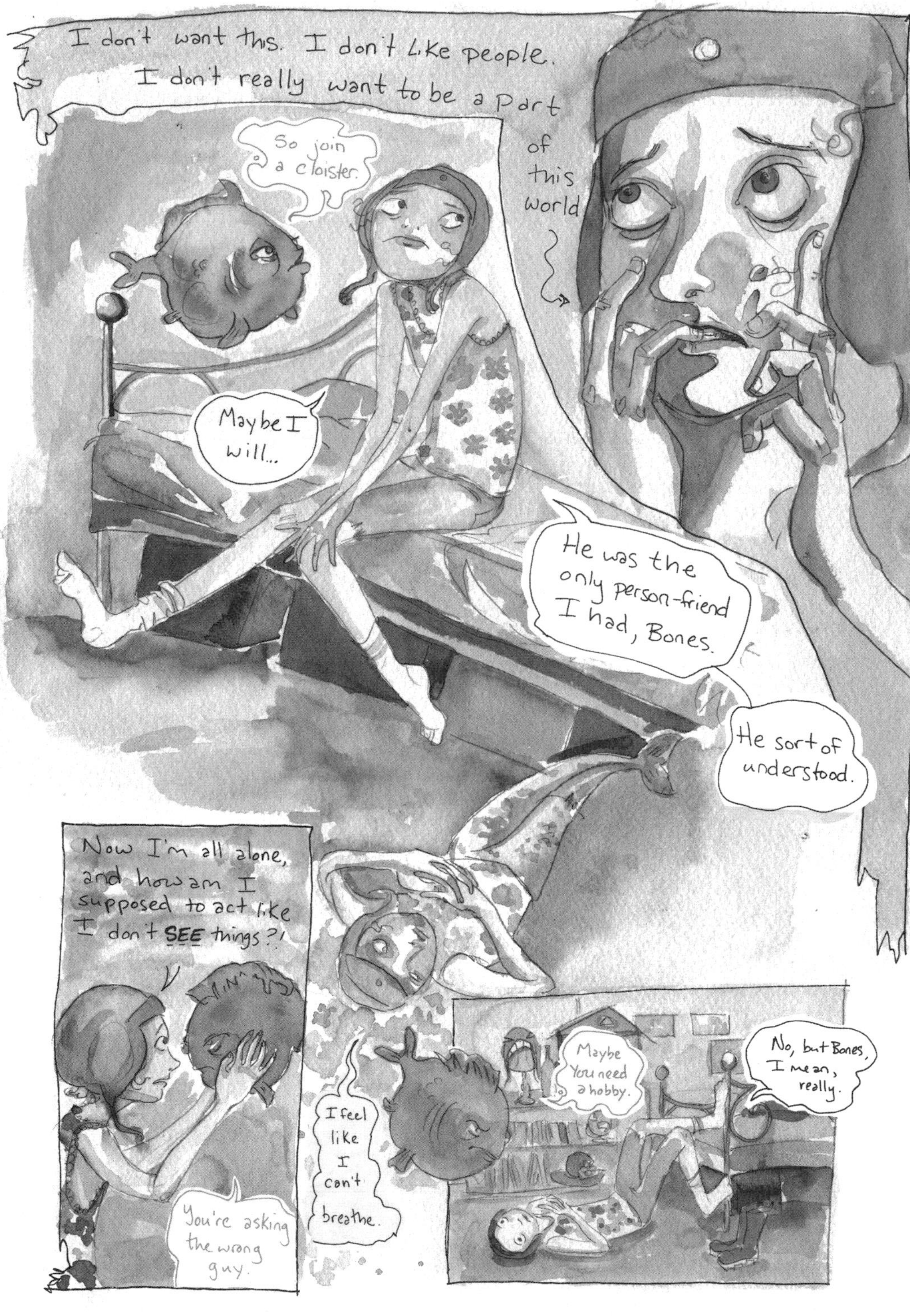
I don't want this. I don't like people. I don't really want to be a part of this world
So join a cloister.
Maybe I will...
He was the only person-friend I had, Bones.
He sort of understood.
Now I'm all alone, and how am I supposed to act like I don't SEE things?!
You're asking the wrong guy.
I feel like I can't breathe.
Maybe you need a hobby.
No, but Bones, I mean, really.

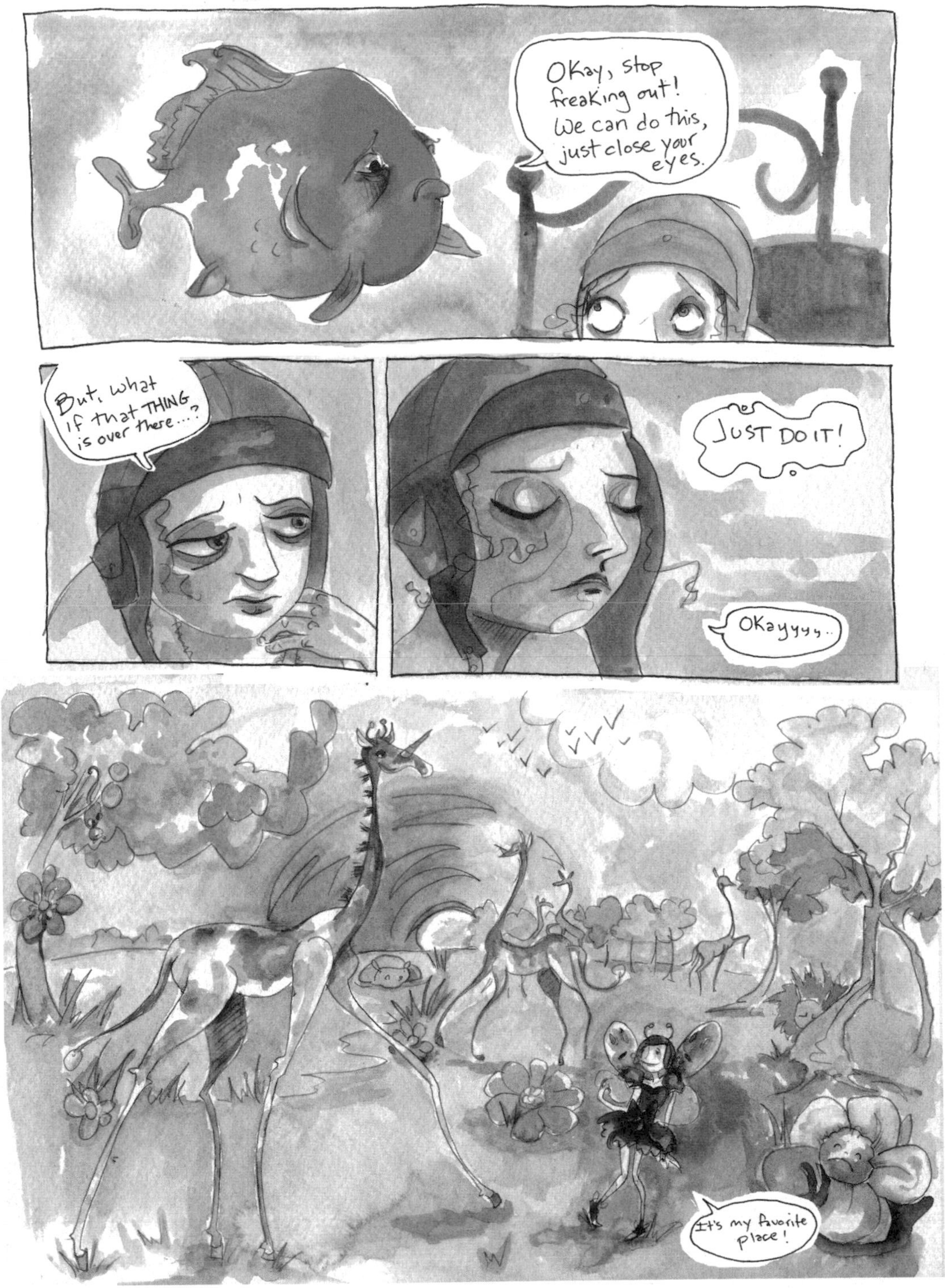
OKay, stop freaking out! We can do this, just close your eyes.
But, what if that THING is over there...?
JUST DO IT!
OKayyyy..
It's my favorite place!

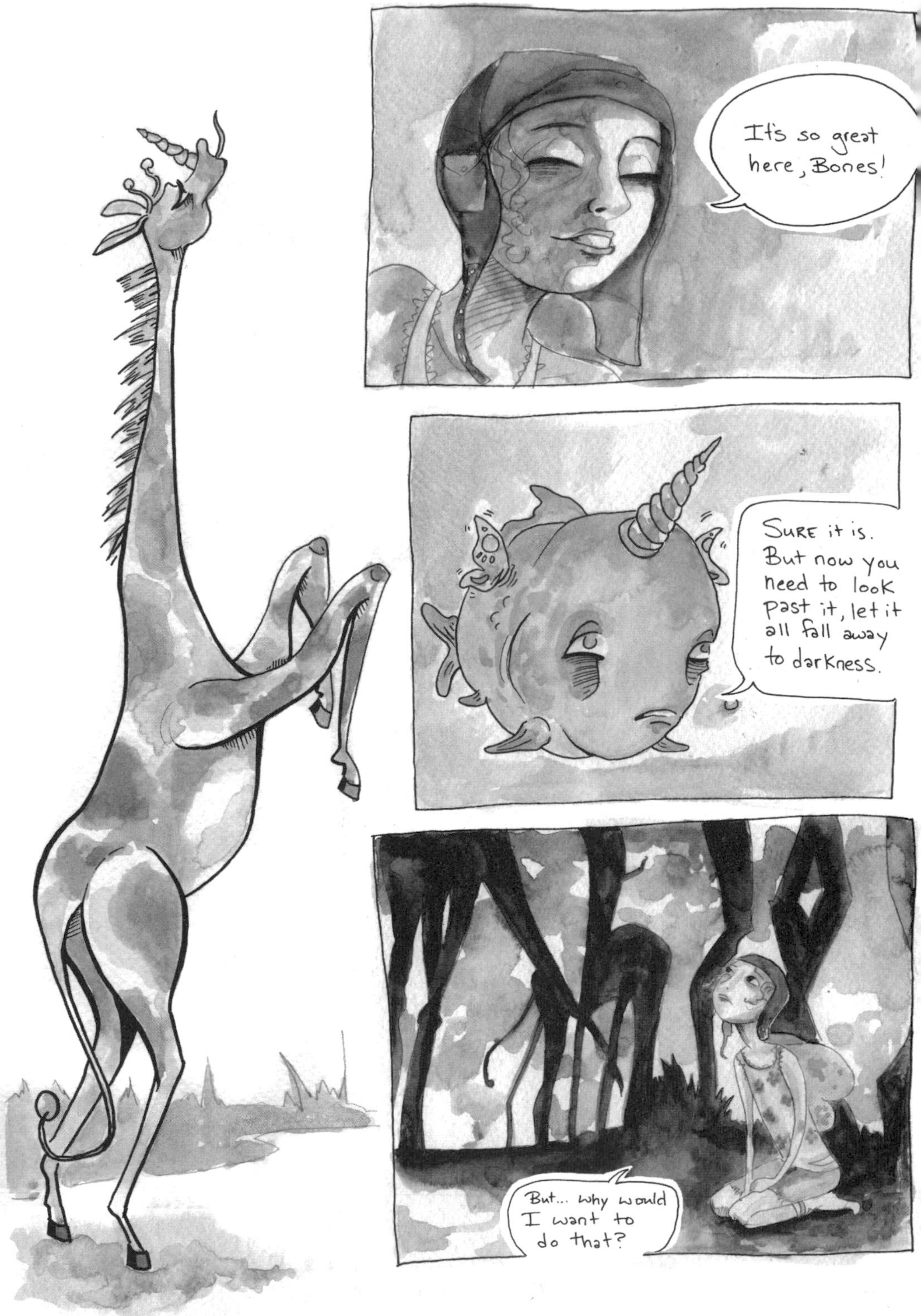
It's so great here, Bones!
Sure it is. But now you need to look past it, let it all fall away to darkness.
But... why would I want to do that?

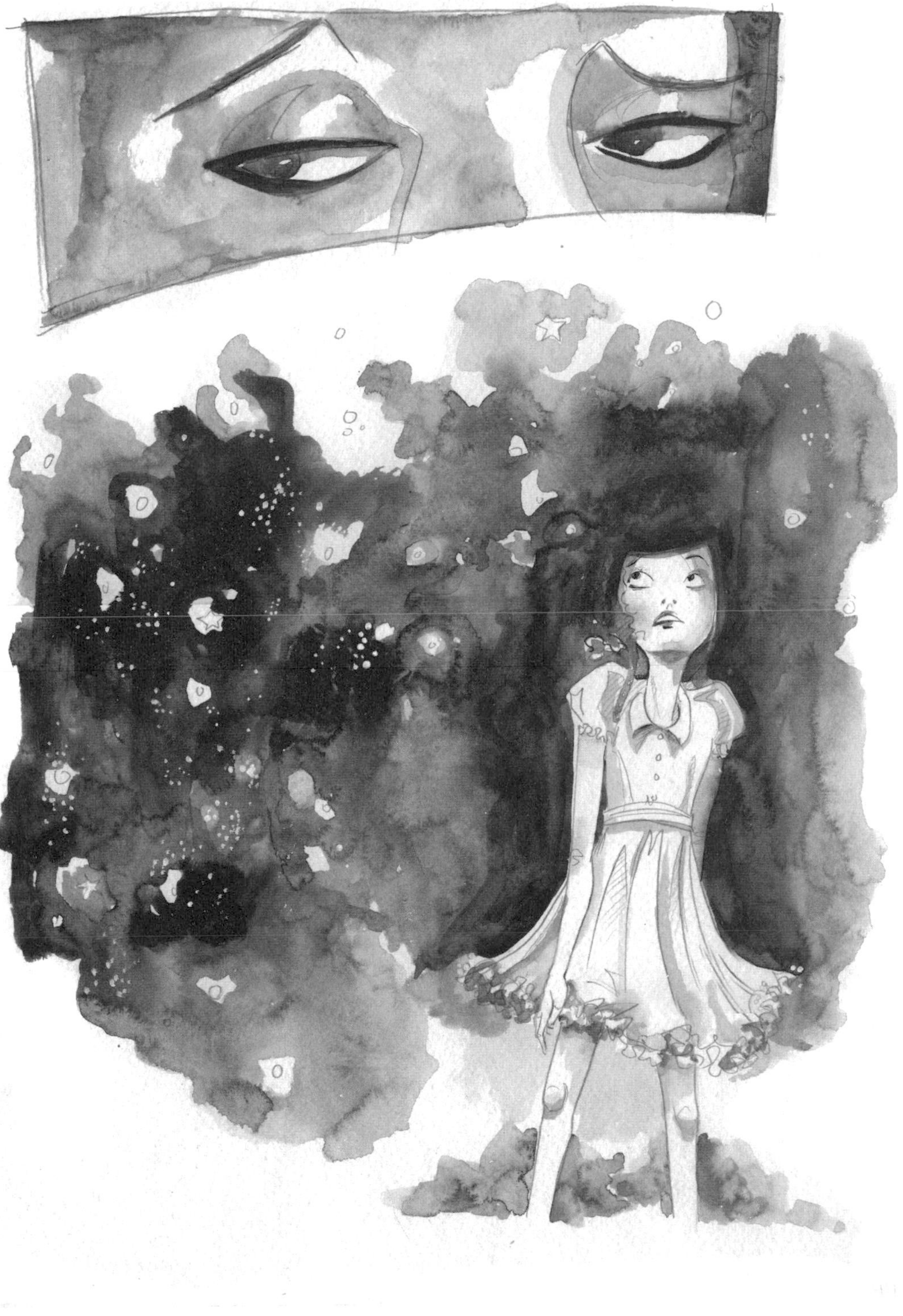

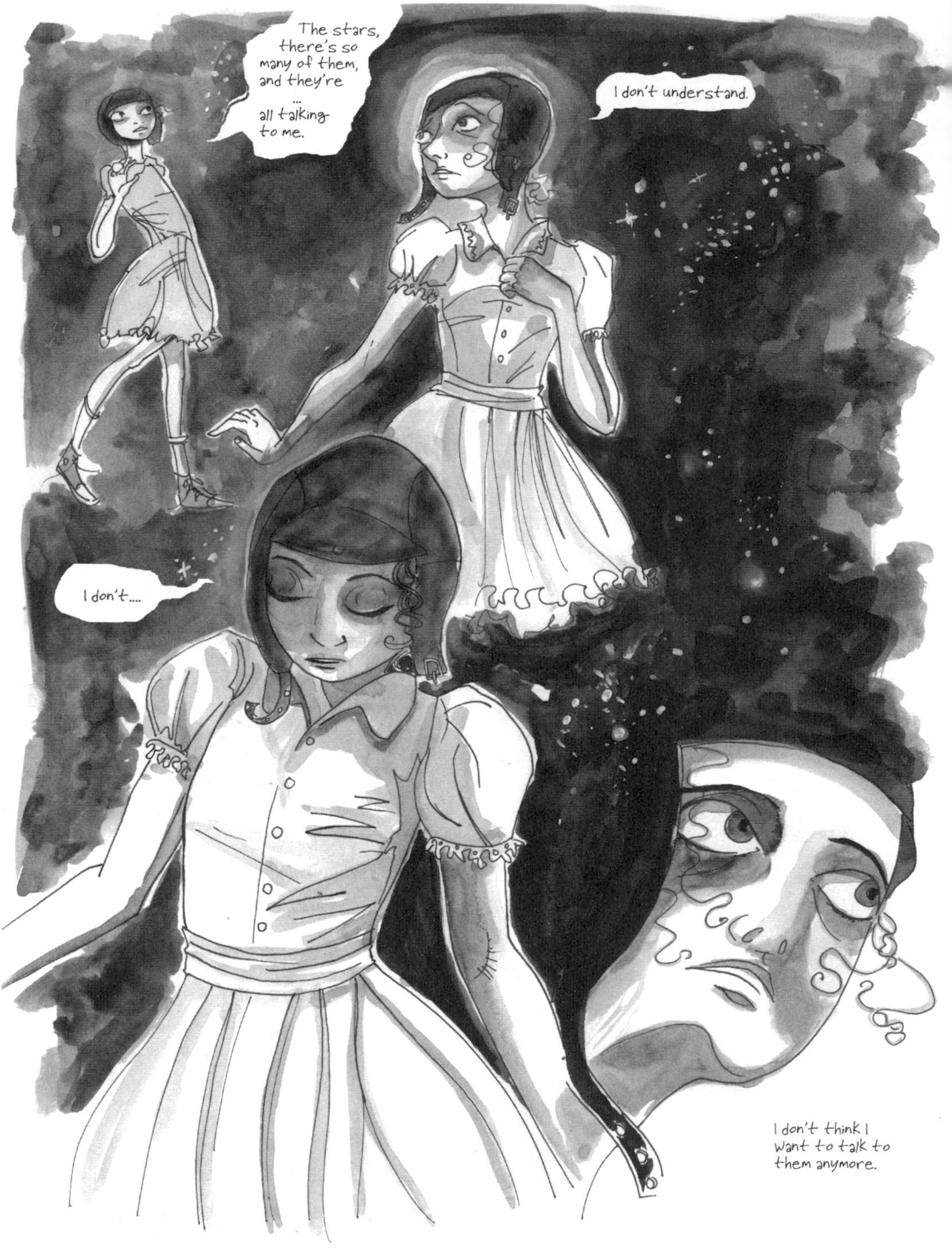
The stars, there's so many of them, and they're ... all talking to me.
I don't understand.
I don't....
I don't think I want to talk to them anymore.

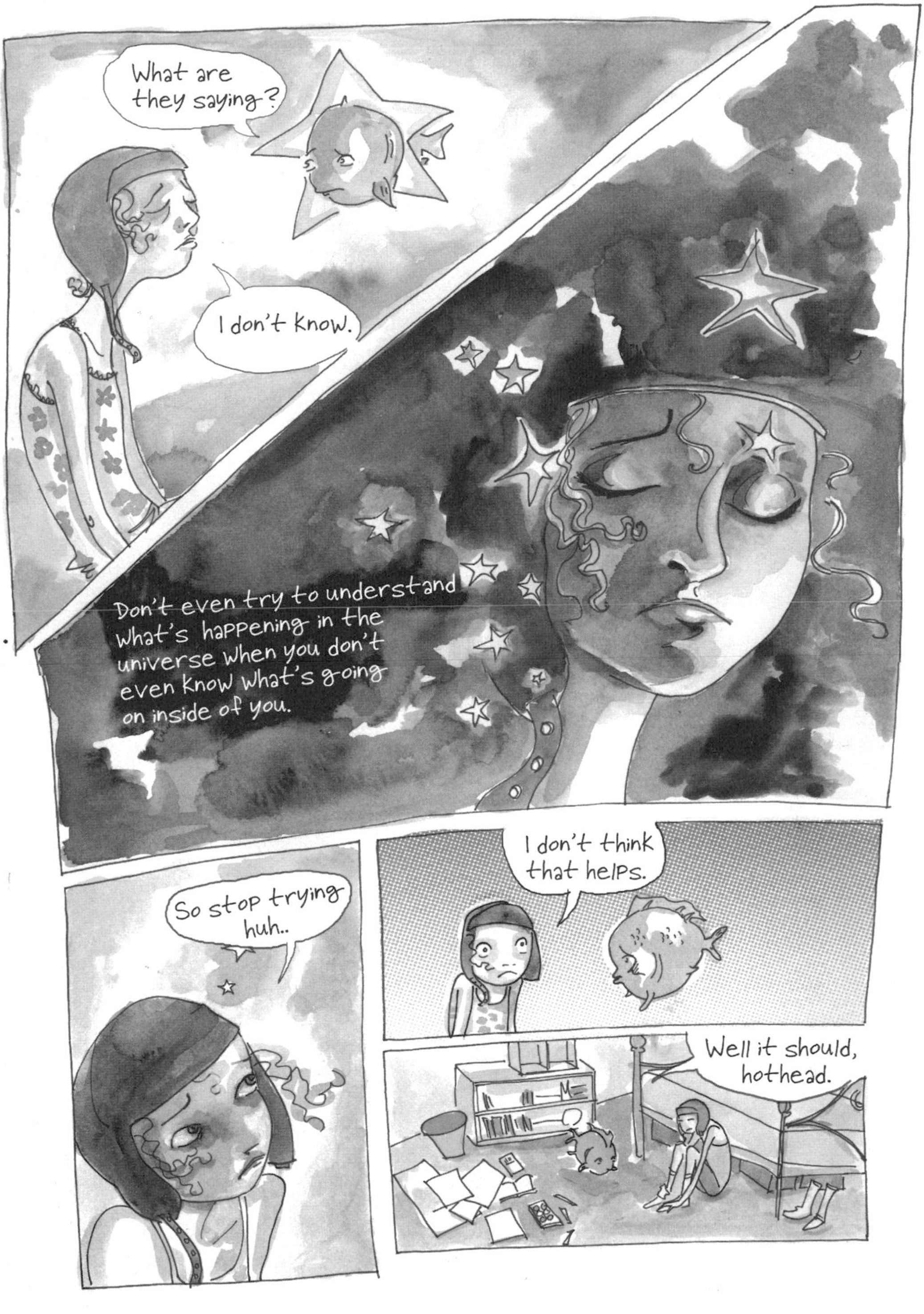
What are they saying?
I don't know.
Don't even try to understand what's happening in the universe when you don't even know what's going on inside of you.
So stop trying huh..
I don't think that helps.
Well it should, hothead.

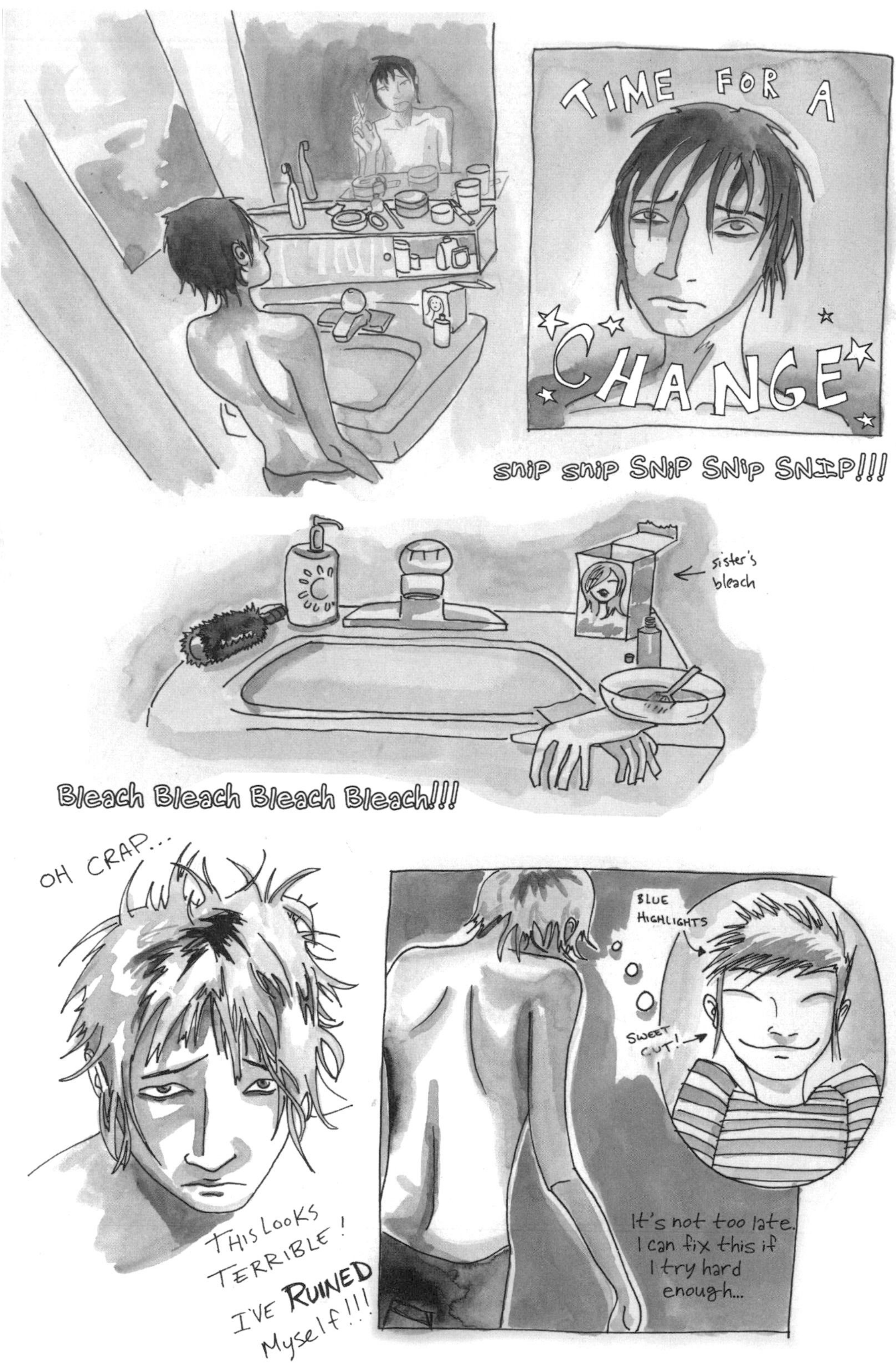
TIME FOR A CHANGE
snip snip SNiP SNiP SNIP!!!
sister's bleach
Bleach Bleach Bleach Bleach!!!
OH CRAP...
THIS LOOKS TERRIBLE!
I'VE RUINED MYSELF!!!
BLUE HIGHLIGHTS
SWEET CUT!
It's not too late. I can fix this if I try hard enough...

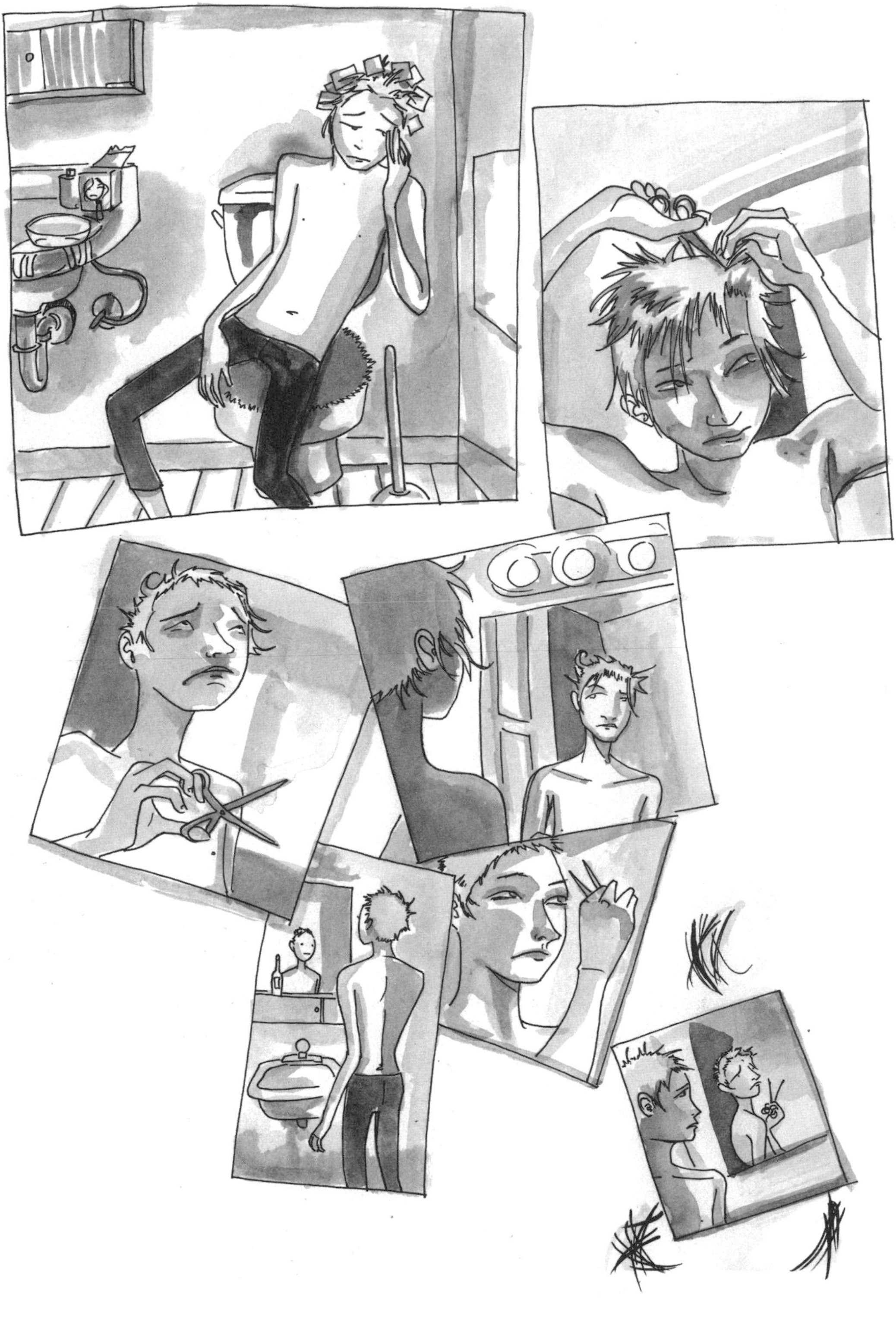

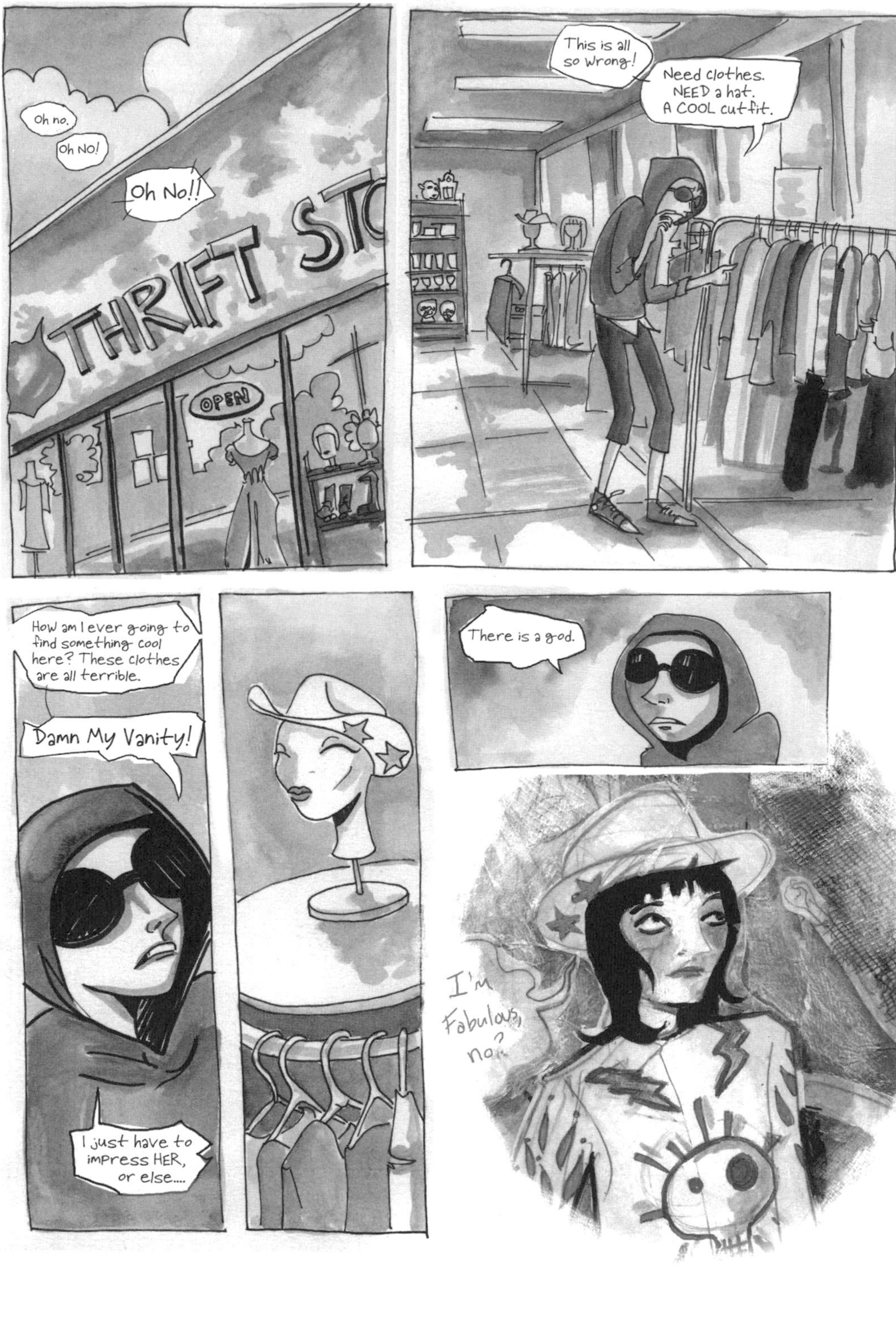
Oh no.
Oh NO!
Oh No!!
THRIFT STO
OPEN
This is all so wrong!
Need clothes. NEED a hat. A COOL cutfit.
How am I ever going to find something cool here? These clothes are all terrible.
Damn My Vanity!
I just have to impress HER, or else....
There is a god.
I'm Fabulous, no?

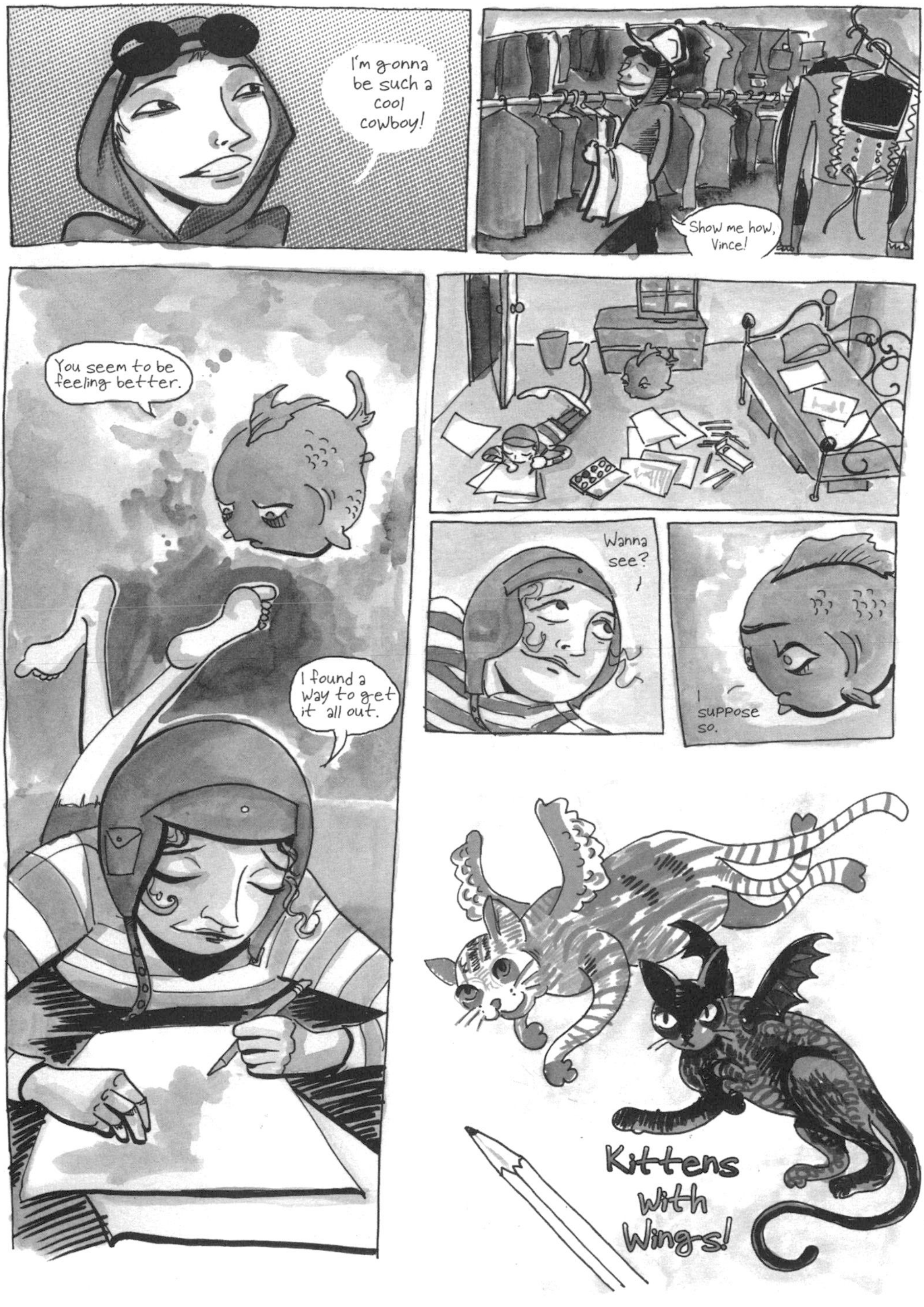
I'm gonna be such a cool cowboy!
Show me how, Vince!
You seem to be feeling better.
I found a way to get it all out.
Wanna see?
I suppose so.
Kittens With Wings!

MORNING...

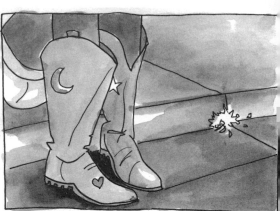

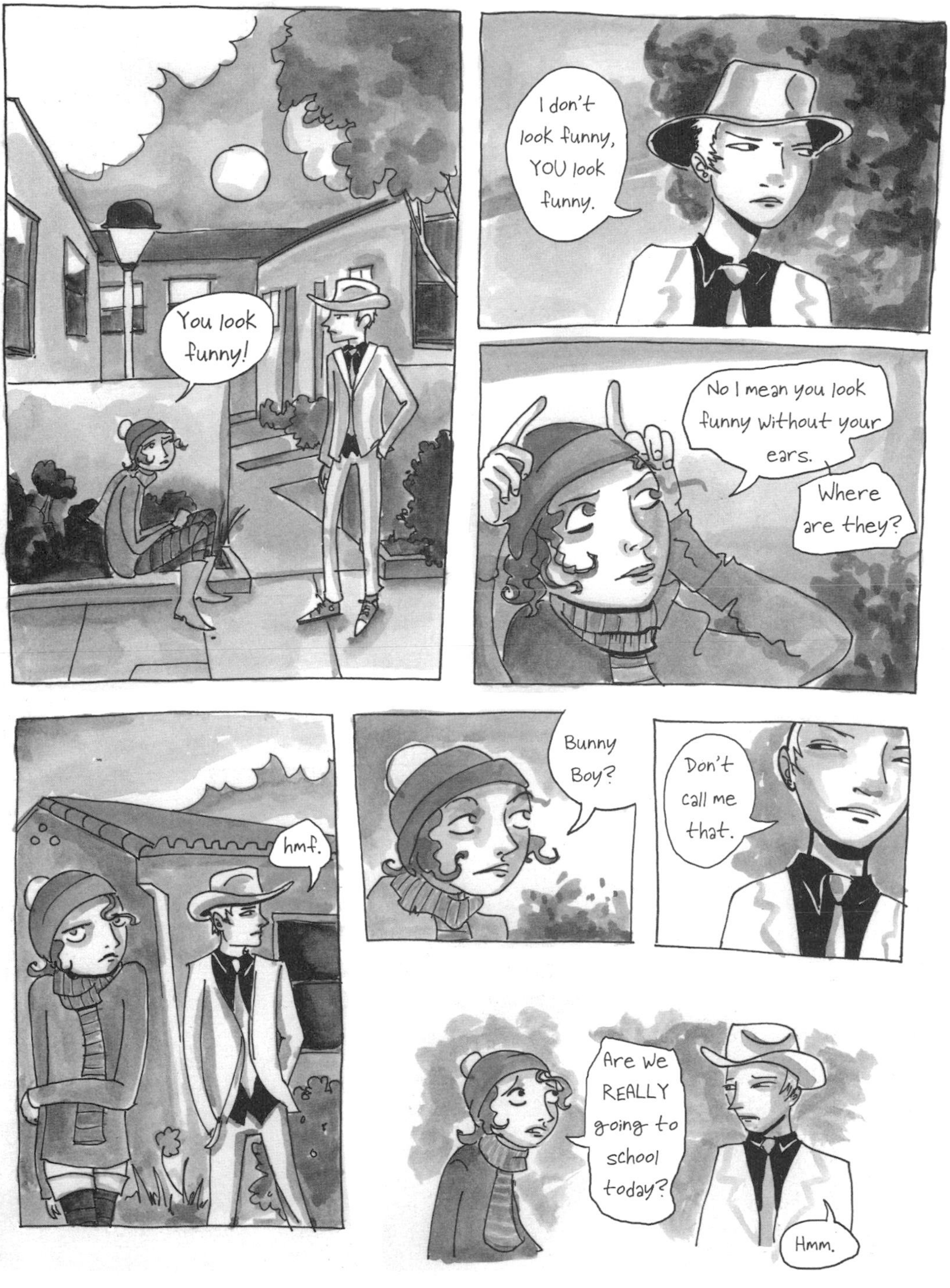
You look funny!
I don't look funny, YOU look funny.
No I mean you look funny without your ears.
Where are they?
hmf.
Bunny Boy?
Don't call me that.
Are we REALLY going to school today?
Hmm.

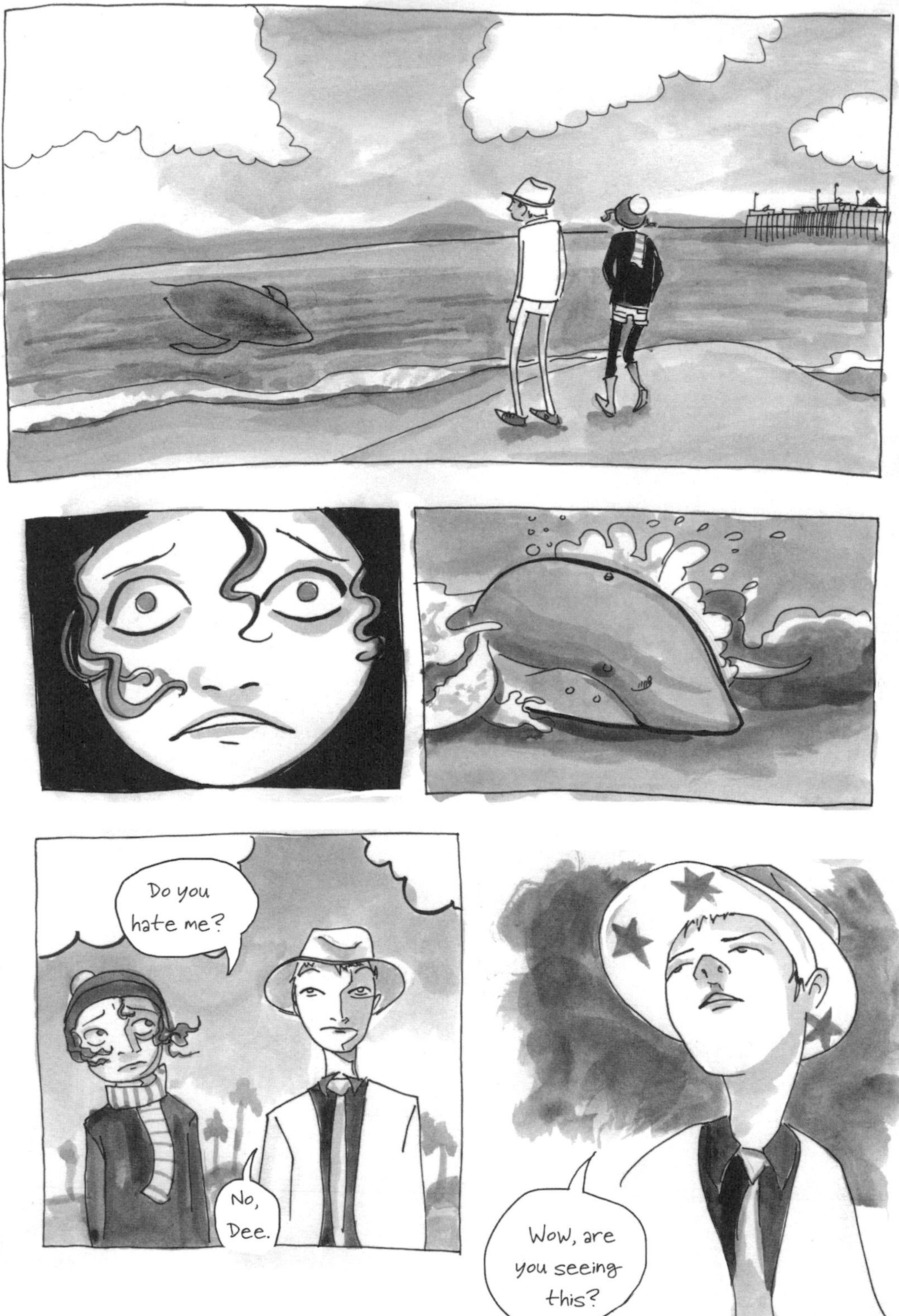
Do you hate me?
No, Dee.
Wow, are you seeing this?

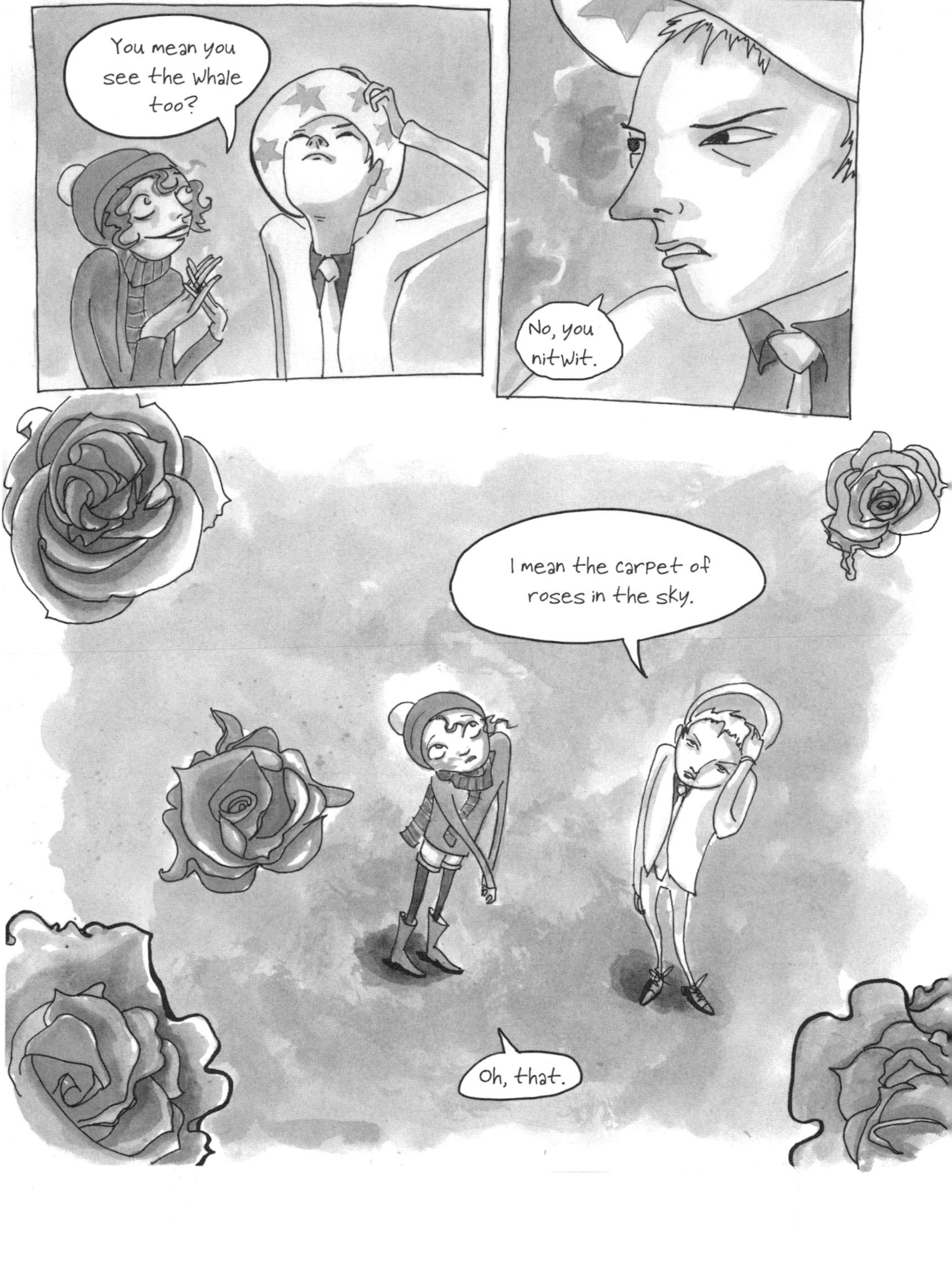
You mean you see the whale too?
No, you nitwit.
I mean the carpet of roses in the sky.
Oh, that.

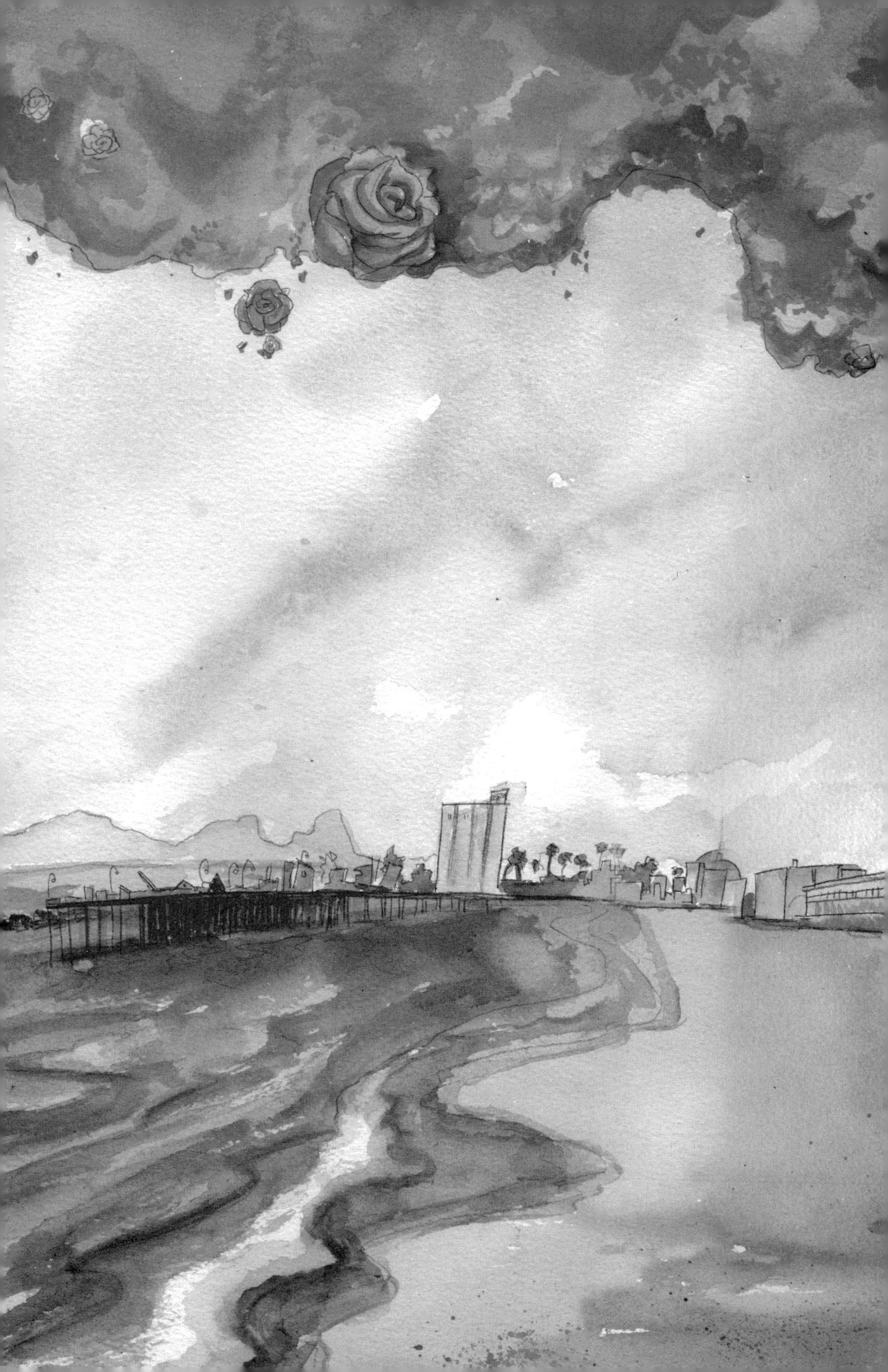

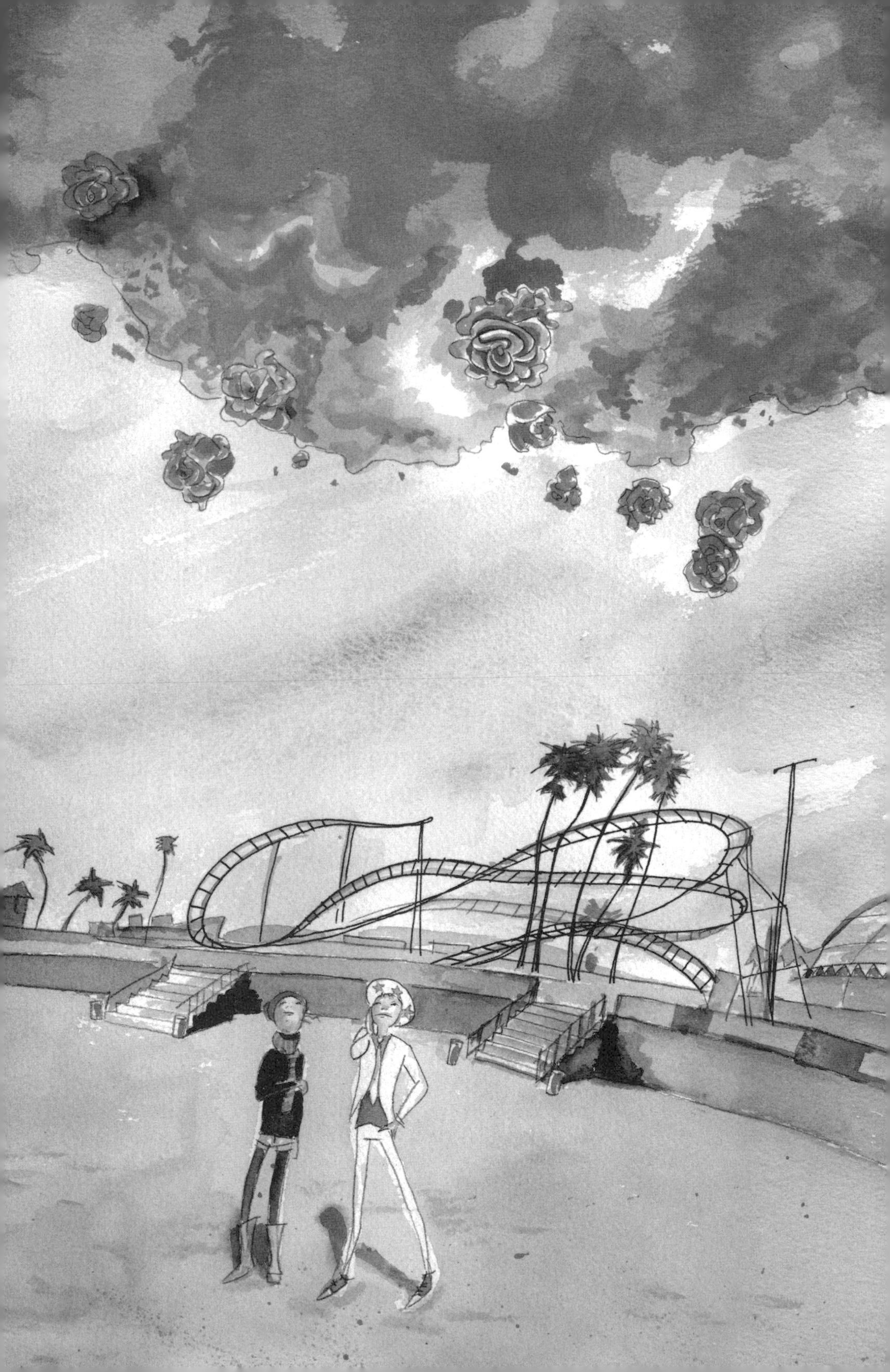

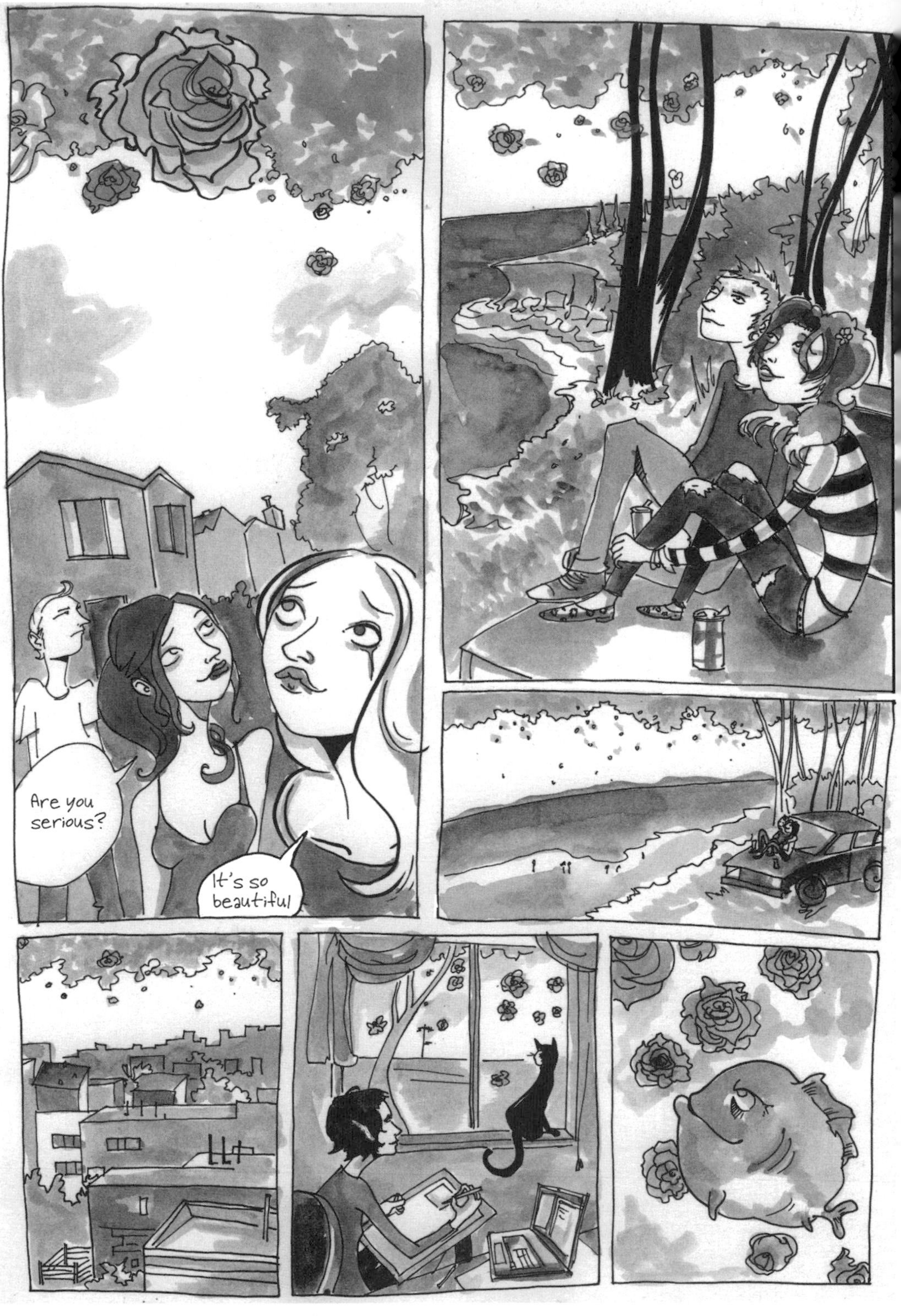
Are you serious?
It's so beautiful

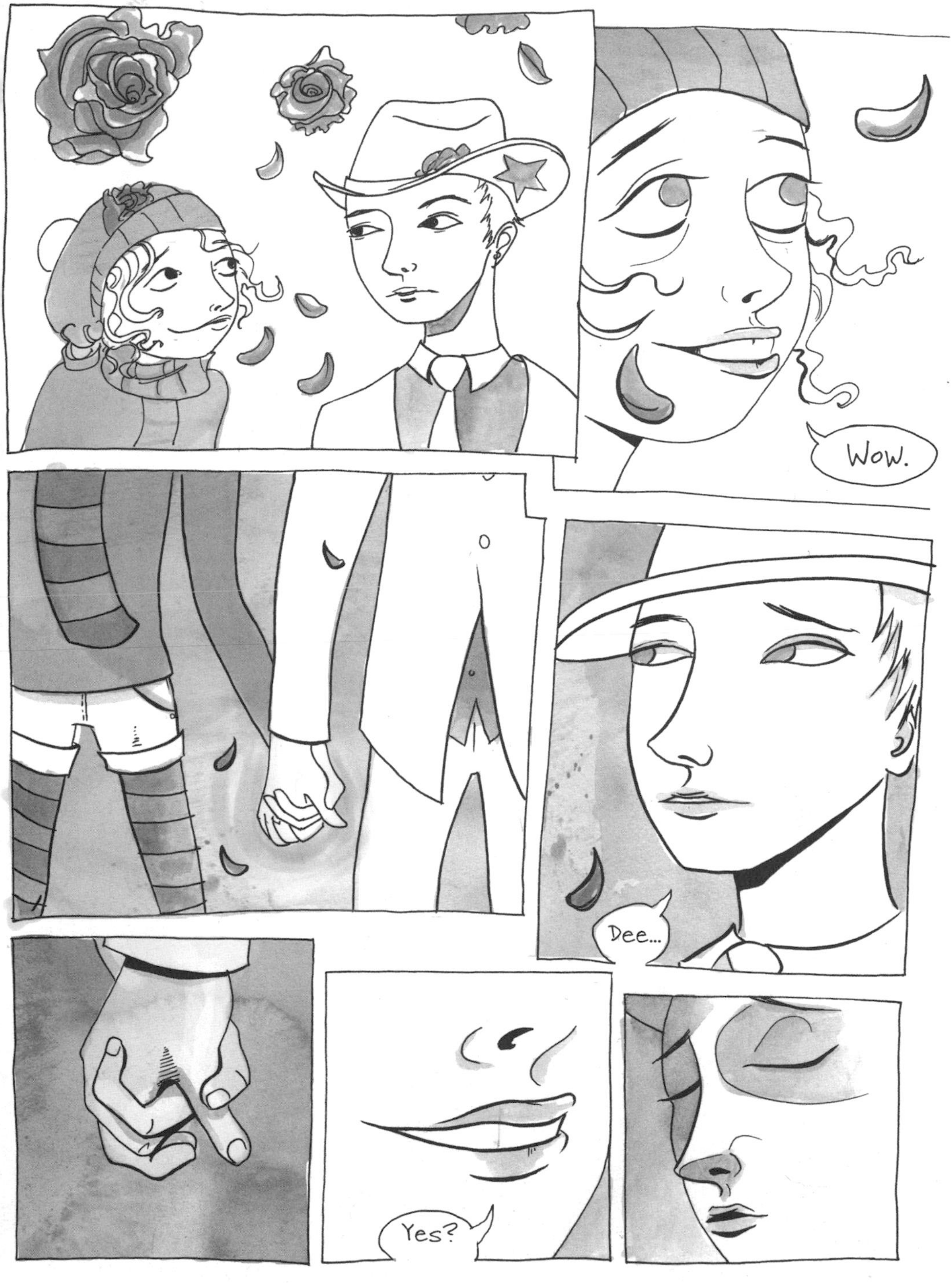
Wow.
Dee...
Yes?

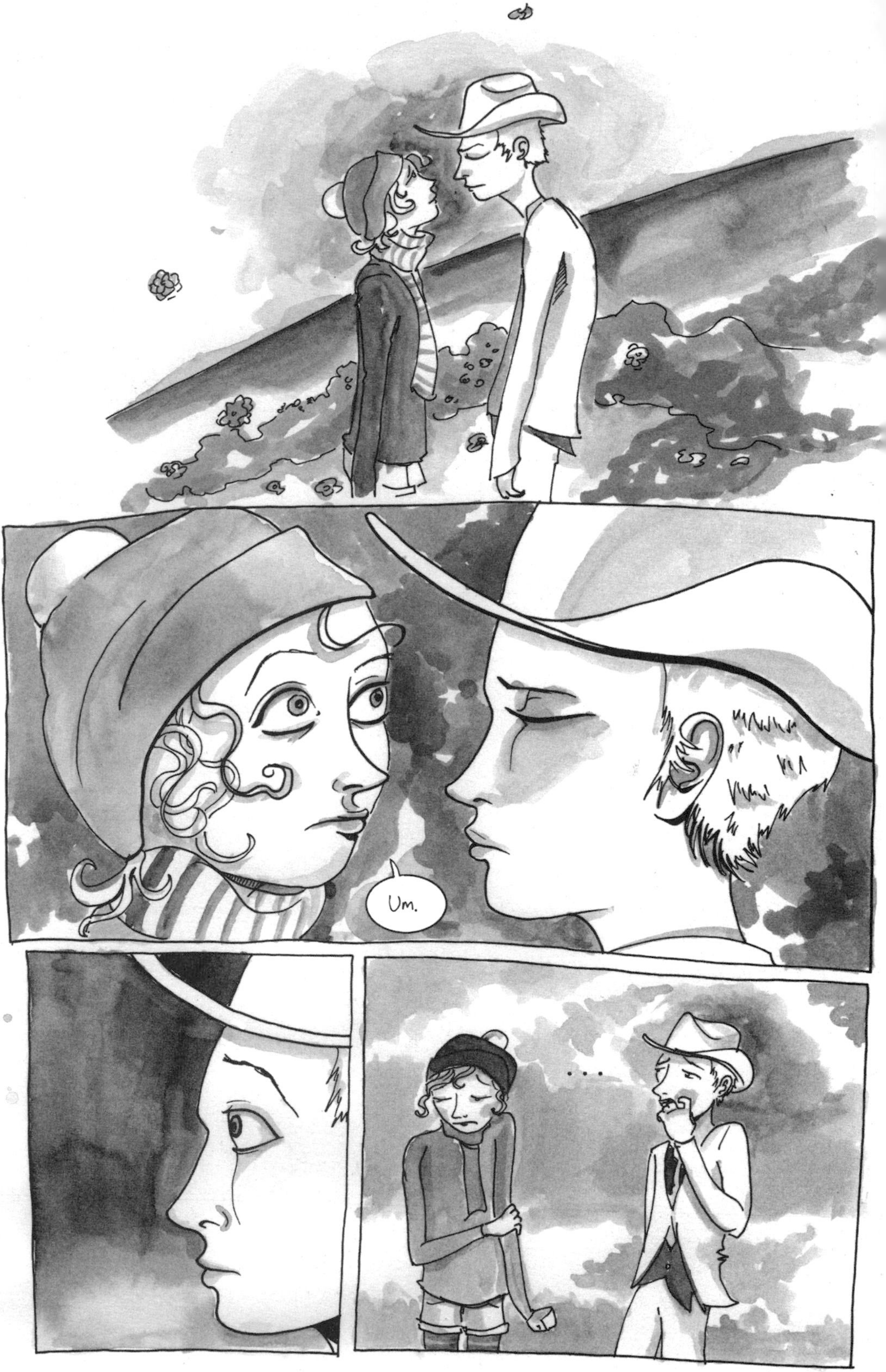
Um.
...

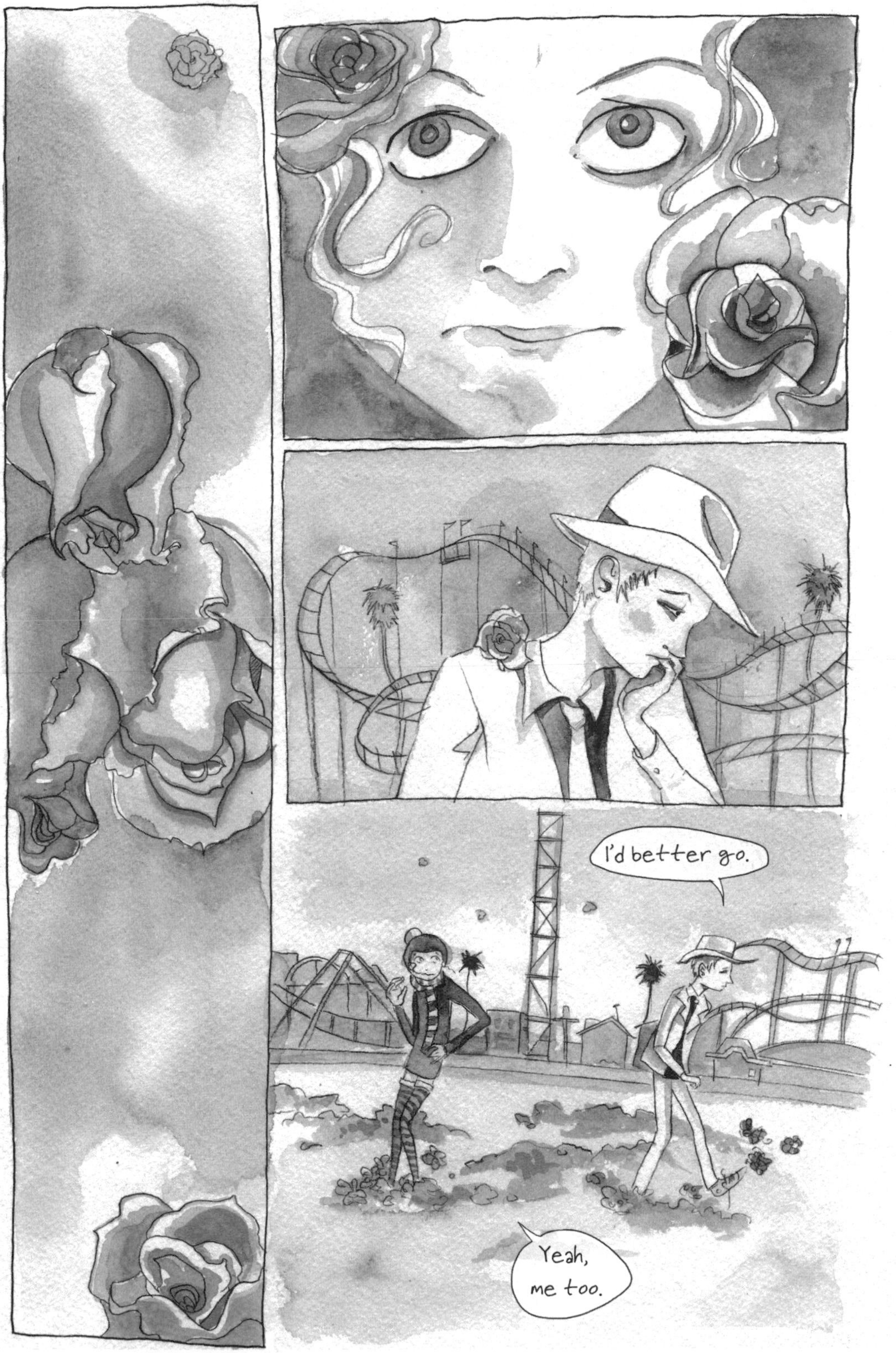
I'd better go.
Yeah, me too.

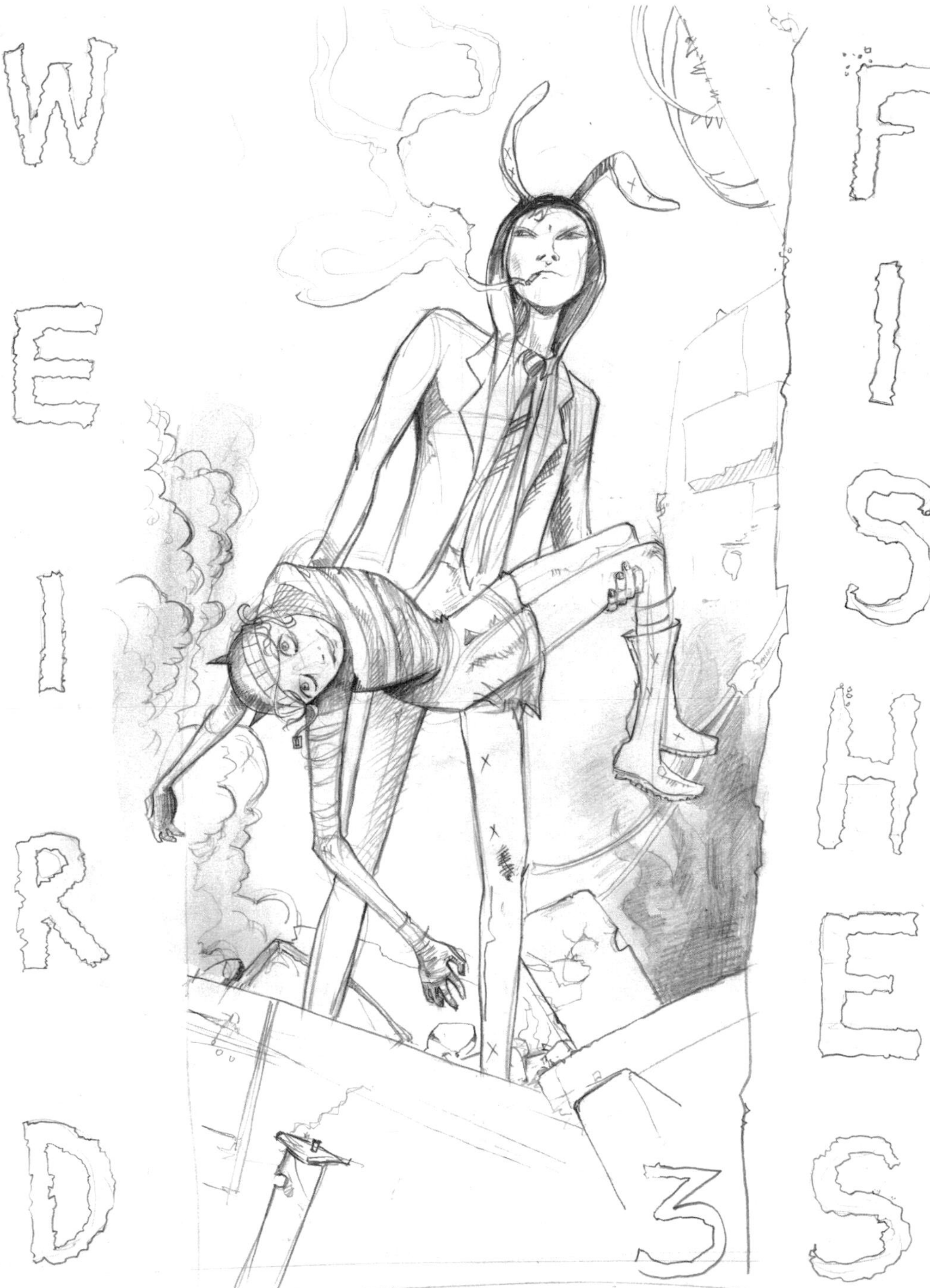
WEIRD
FISHES
3

Social Links

Chapter 3

since the rose event there's been a lot of changes in the characters of Weird Fishes!

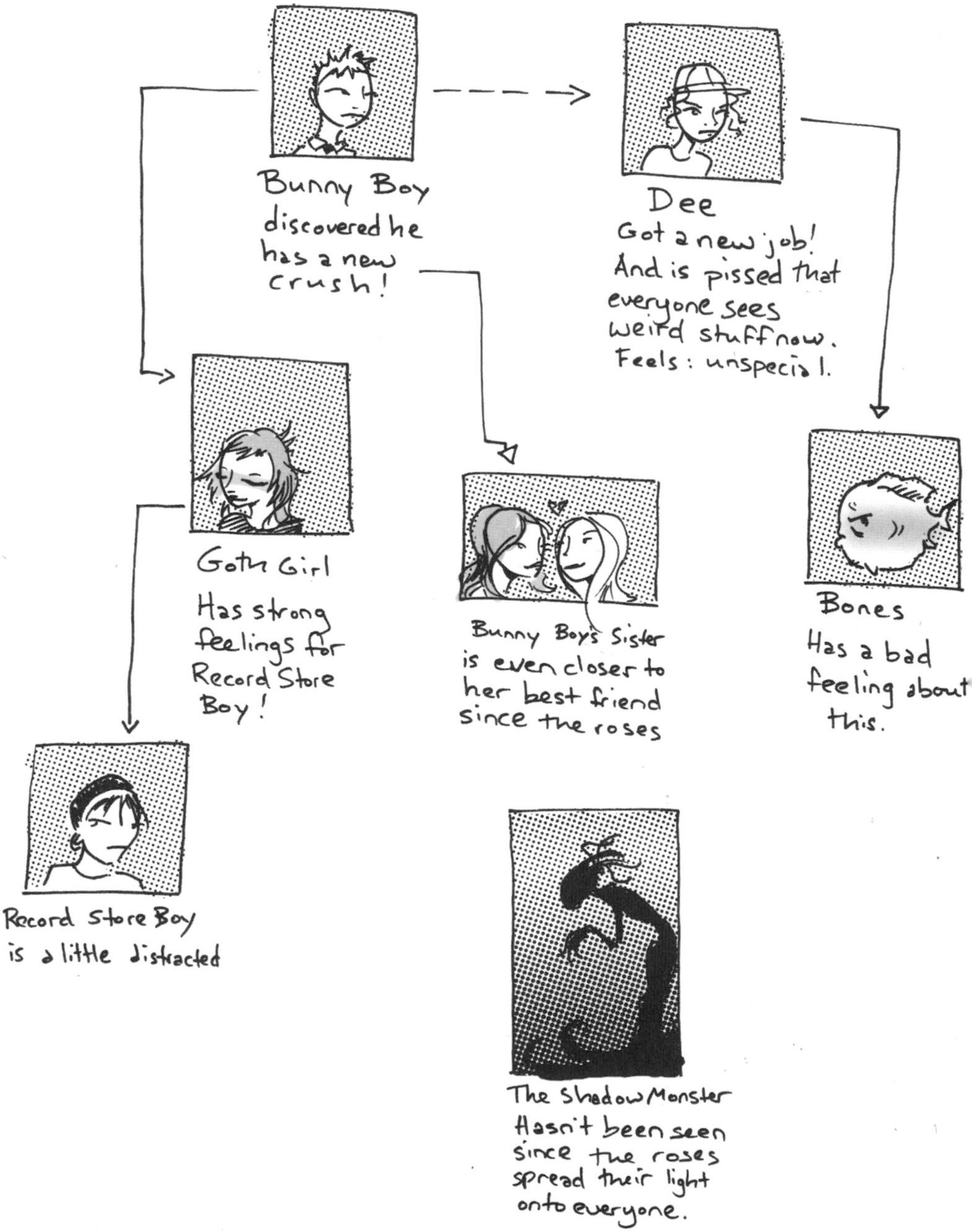
Bunny Boy
discovered he has a new crush!
Dee
Got a new job! And is pissed that everyone sees weird stuff now. Feels: unspecial.
Goth Girl
Has strong feelings for Record Store Boy!
Bunny Boy's Sister
is even closer to her best friend since the roses
Bones
Has a bad feeling about this.
Record Store Boy
is a little distracted
The Shadow Monster
Hasn't been seen since the roses spread their light onto everyone.

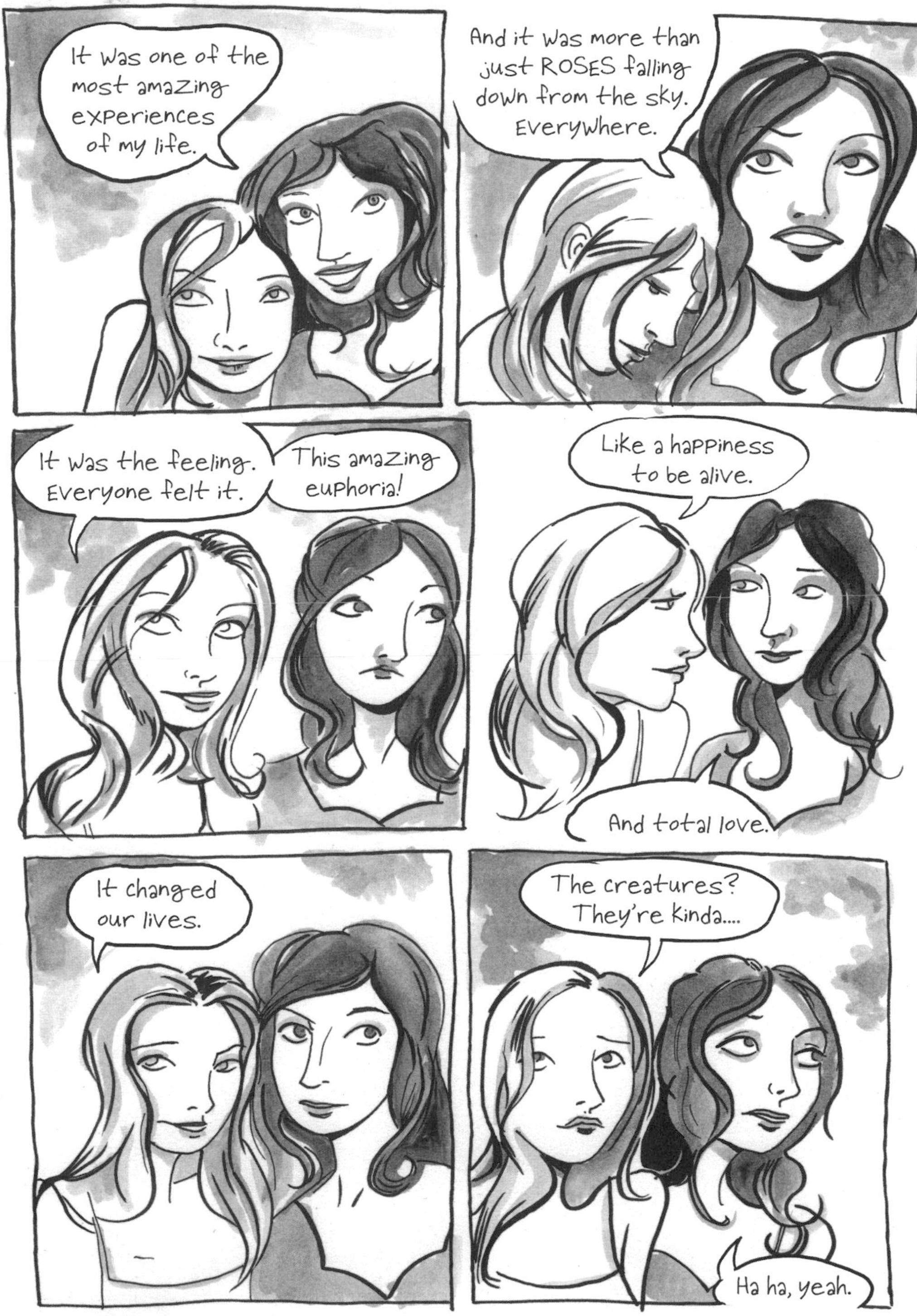
It was one of the most amazing experiences of my life.
And it was more than just ROSES falling down from the sky. Everywhere.
It was the feeling. Everyone felt it.
This amazing euphoria!
Like a happiness to be alive.
And total love.
It changed our lives.
The creatures? They're kinda....
Ha ha, yeah.

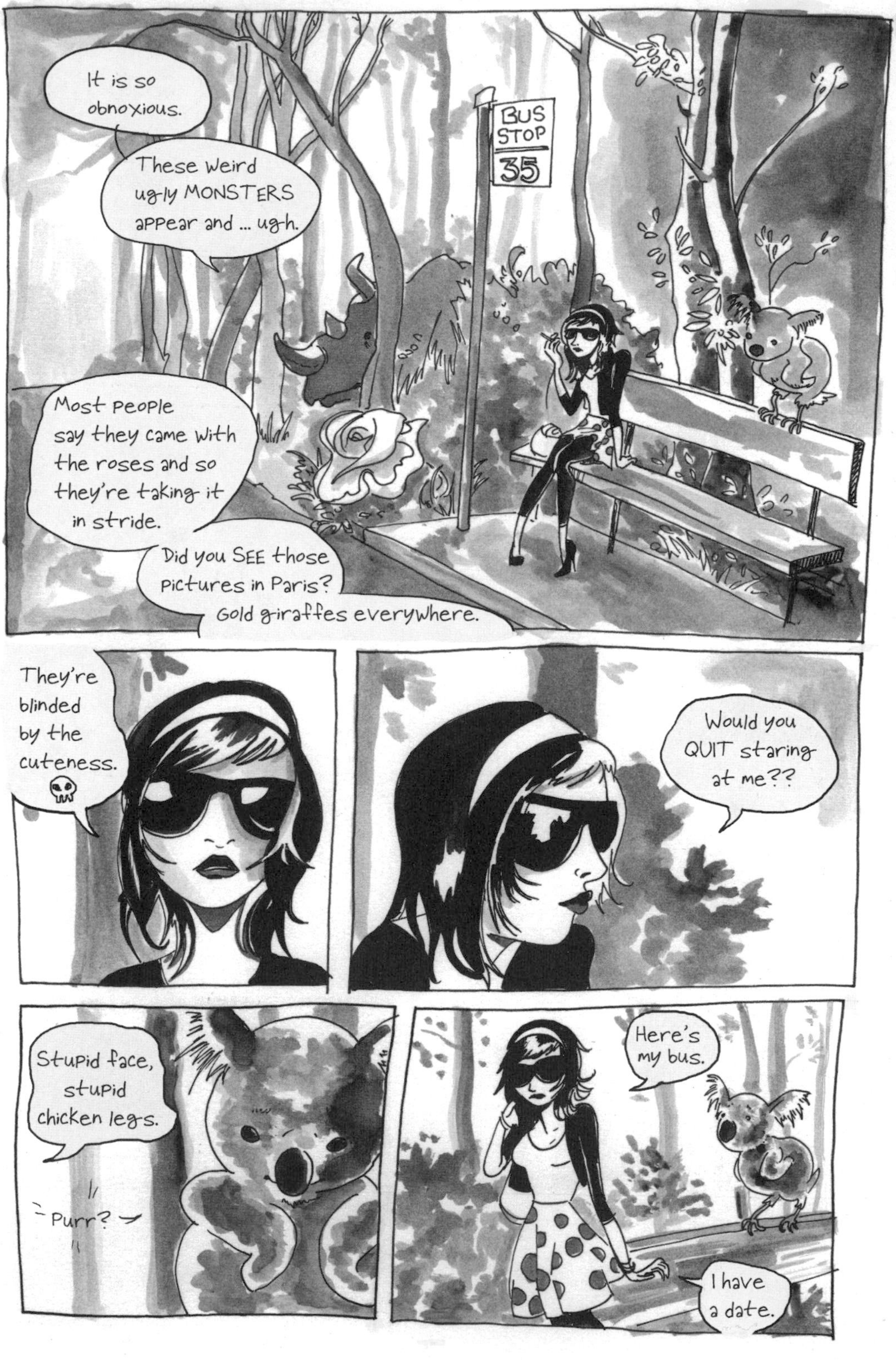
It is so obnoxious.
These weird ugly MONSTERS appear and ... ugh.
BUS STOP
35
Most people say they came with the roses and so they're taking it in stride.
Did you SEE those pictures in Paris? Gold giraffes everywhere.
They're blinded by the cuteness.
Would you QUIT staring at me??
Stupid face, stupid chicken legs.
Purr?
Here's my bus.
I have a date.

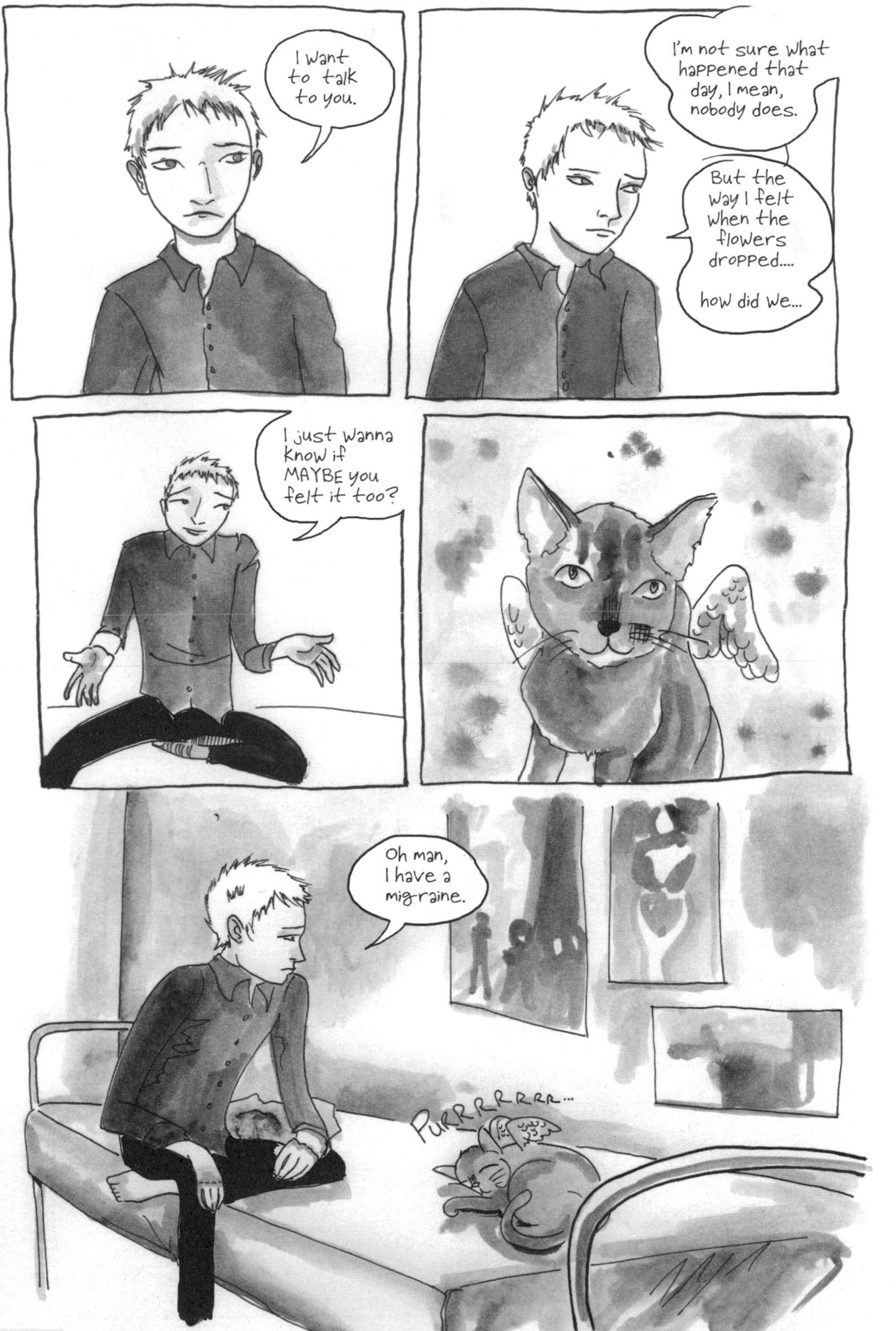
I want to talk to you.
I'm not sure what happened that day, I mean, nobody does.
But the way I felt when the flowers dropped....
how did we...
I just wanna know if MAYBE you felt it too?
Oh man, I have a mig-raine.
PURRRRRRR...

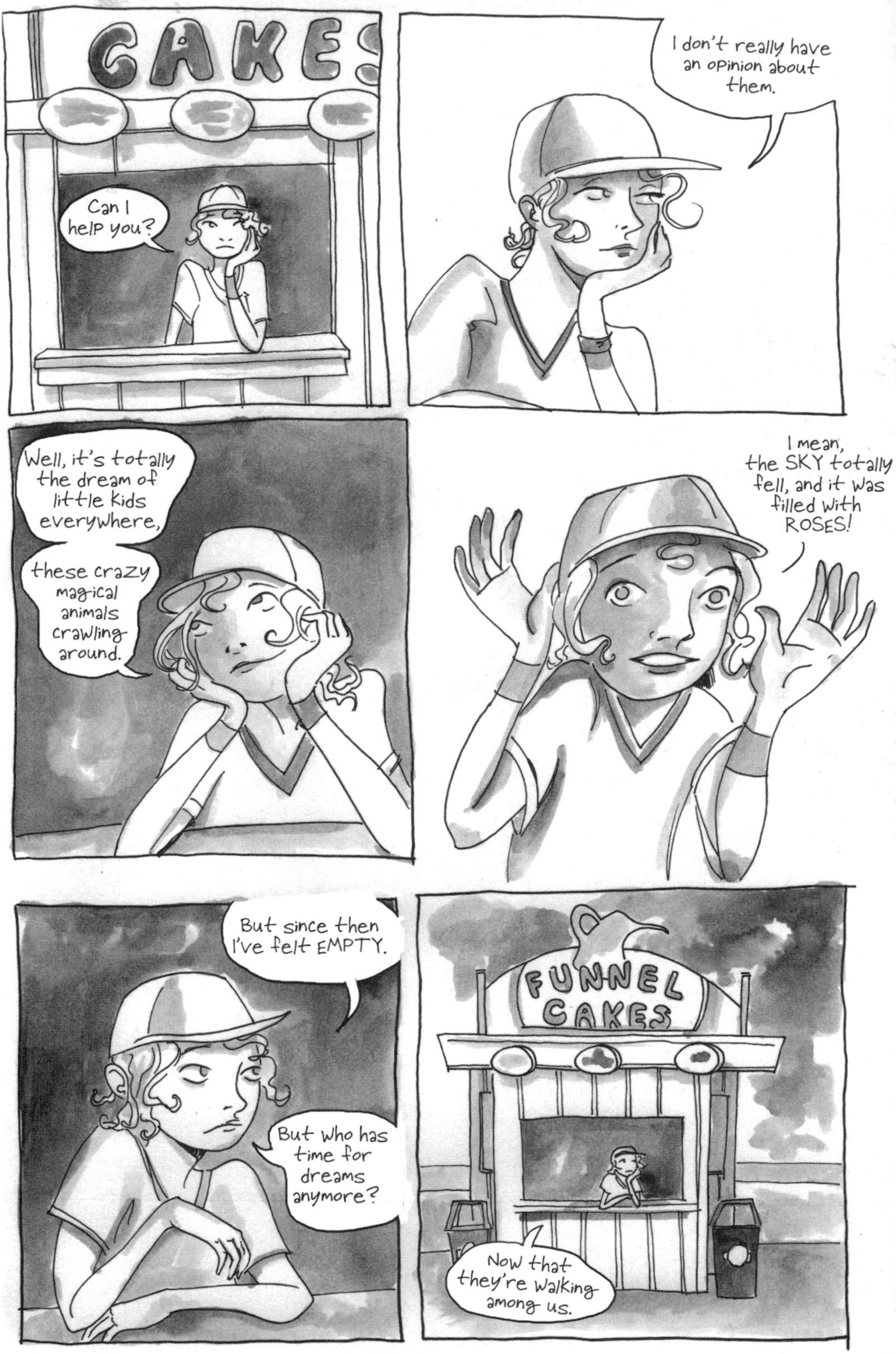
CAKES
Can I help you?
I don't really have an opinion about them.
Well, it's totally the dream of little kids everywhere,
these crazy magical animals crawling around.
I mean, the SKY totally fell, and it was filled with ROSES!
But since then I've felt EMPTY.
But who has time for dreams anymore?
FUNNEL CAKES
Now that they're walking among us.

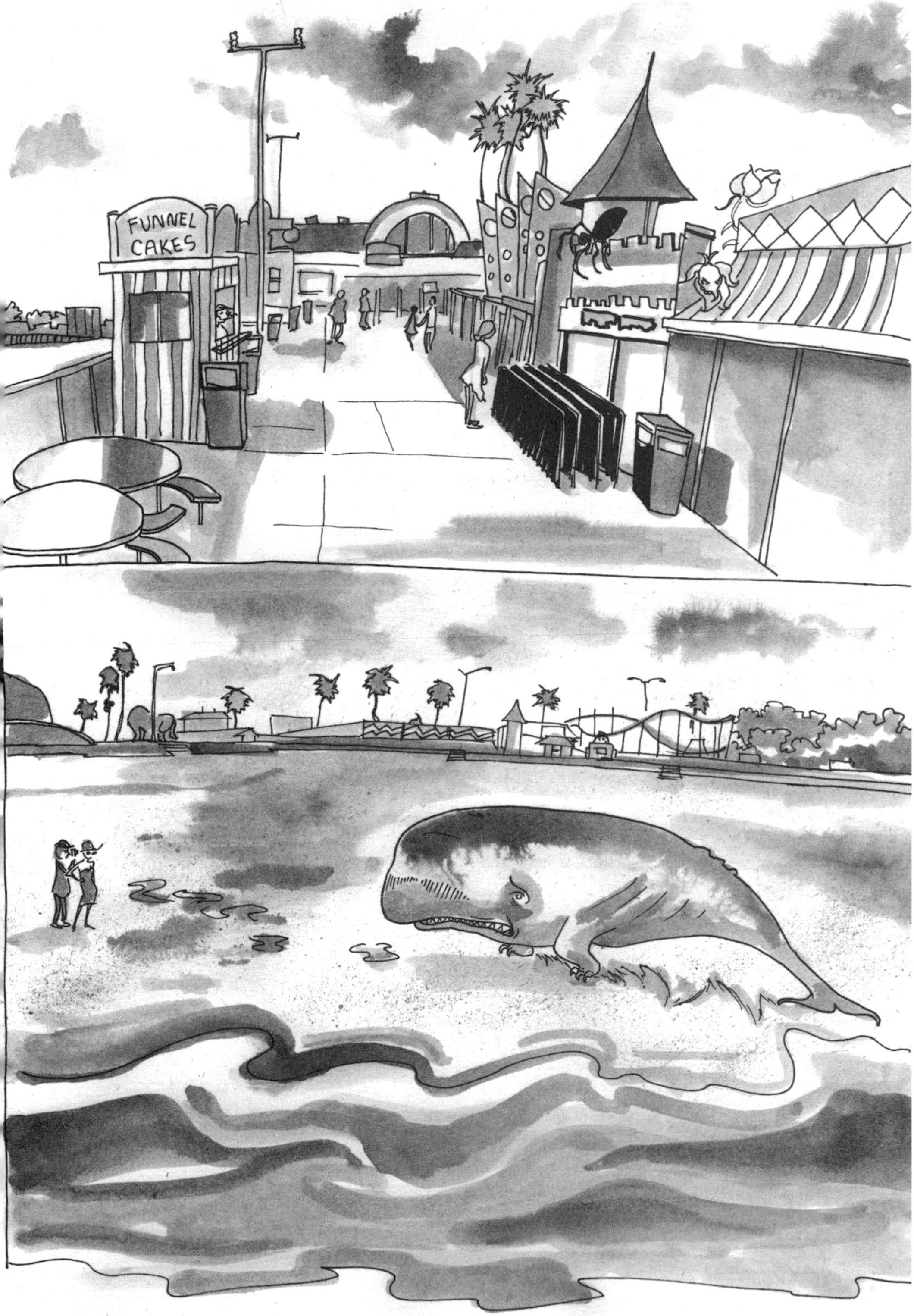
FUNNEL CAKES

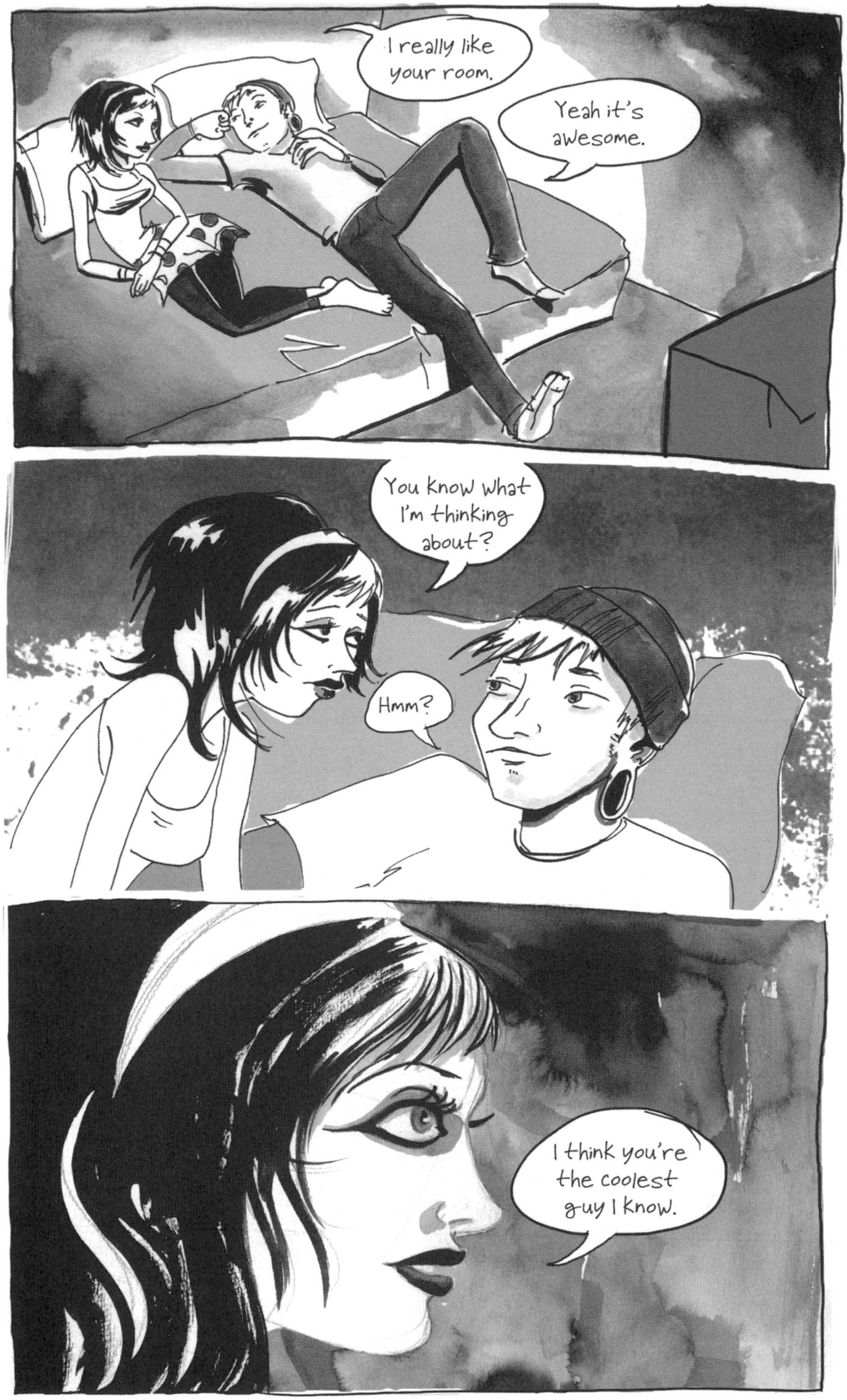
I really like your room.
Yeah it's awesome.
You know what I'm thinking about?
Hmm?
I think you're the coolest guy I know.

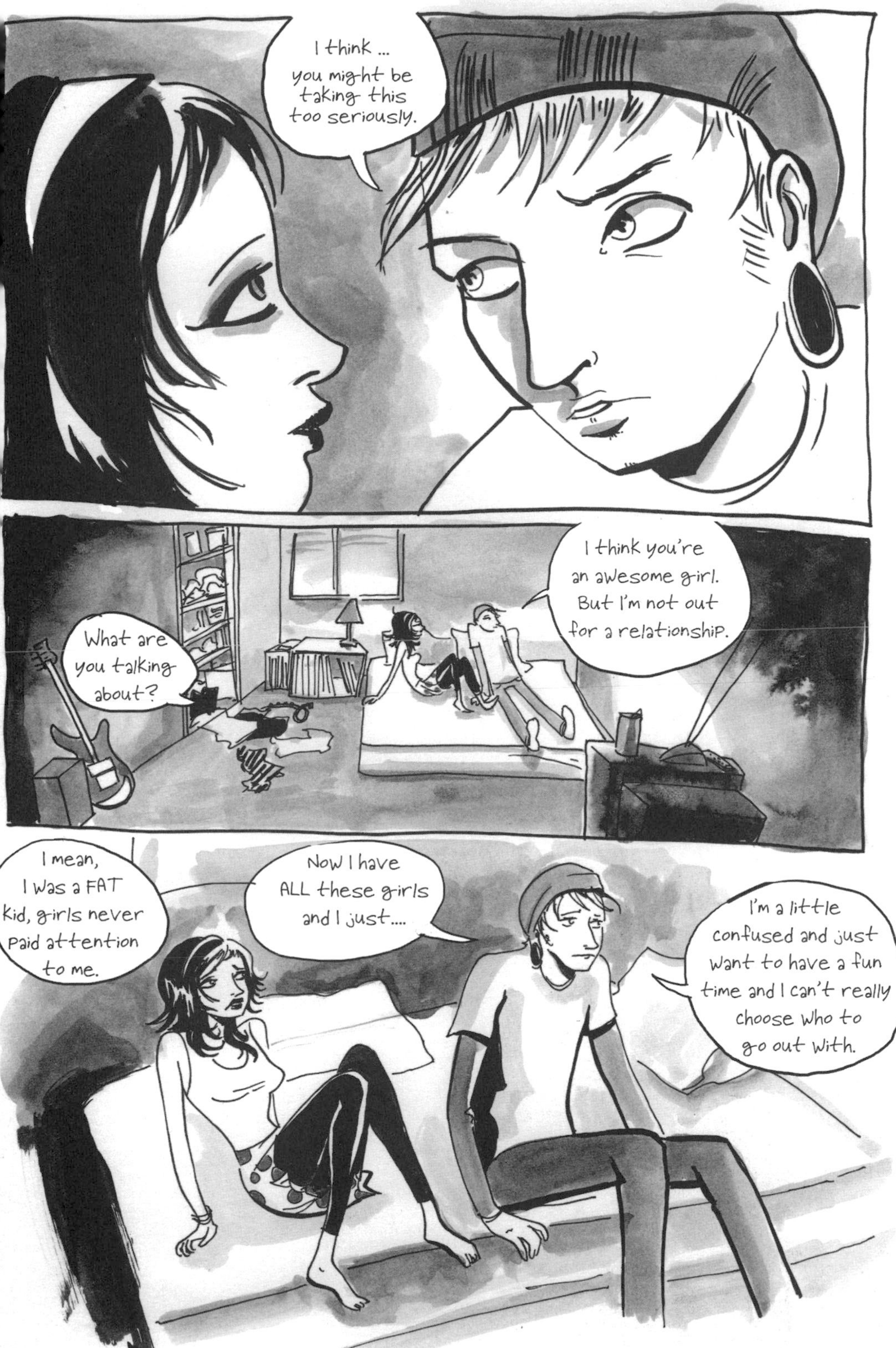
I think ... you might be taking this too seriously.
What are you talking about?
I think you're an awesome girl. But I'm not out for a relationship.
I mean, I was a FAT kid, girls never paid attention to me.
Now I have ALL these girls and I just....
I'm a little confused and just want to have a fun time and I can't really choose who to go out with.

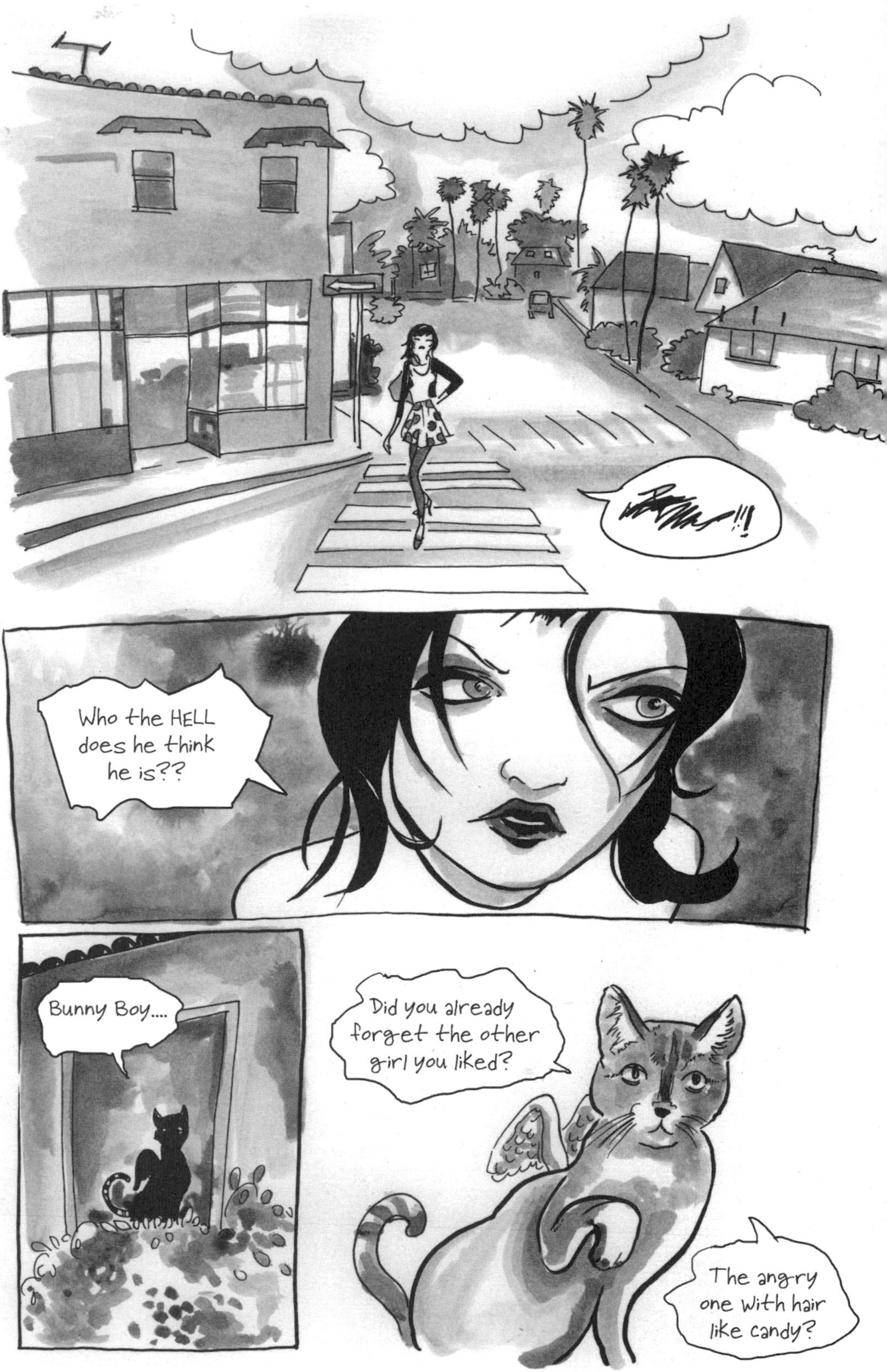

Who the HELL does he think he is??
Bunny Boy....
Did you already forget the other girl you liked?
The angry one with hair like candy?

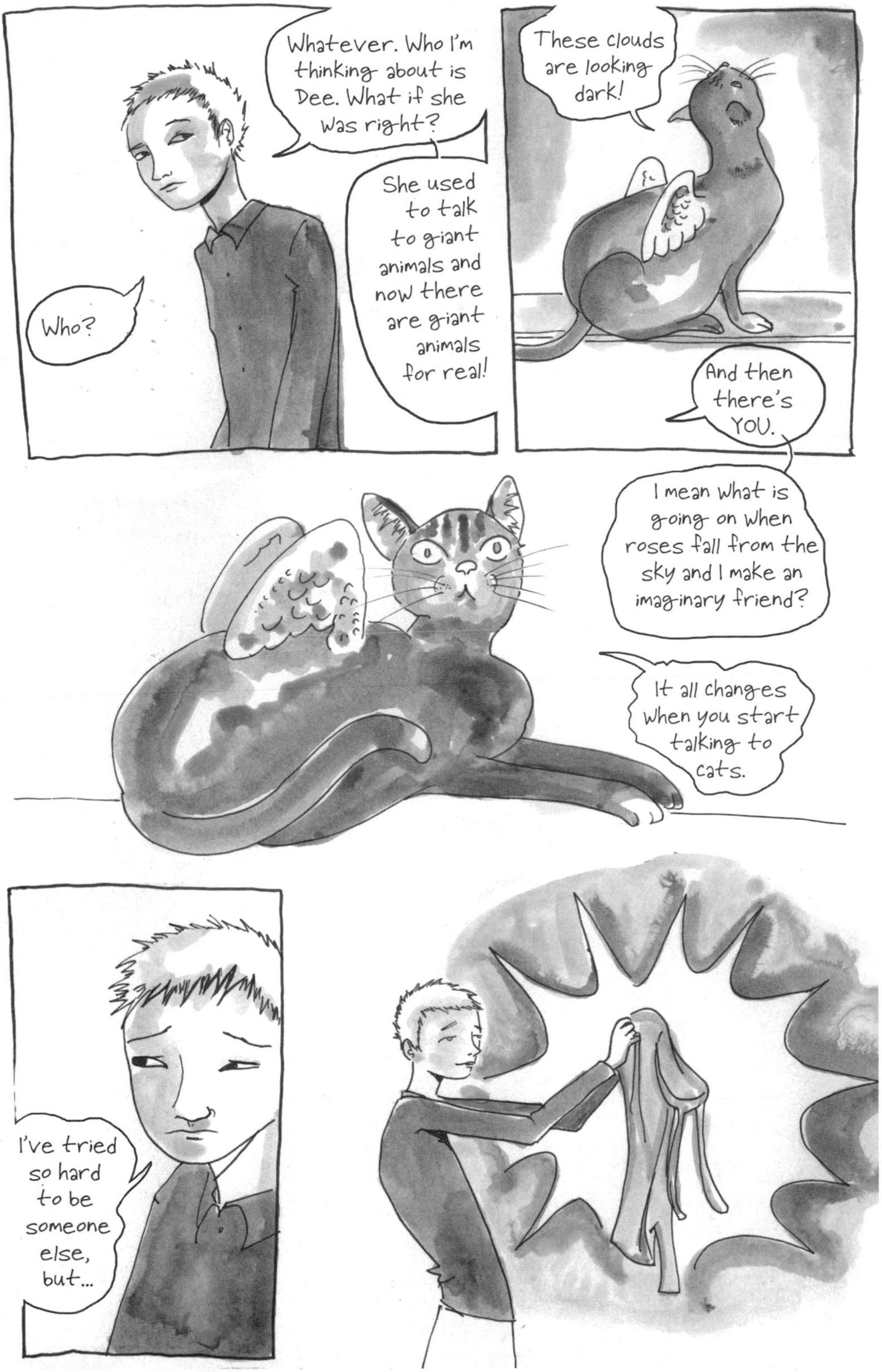
Whatever. Who I'm thinking about is Dee. What if she was right?
Who?
She used to talk to giant animals and now there are giant animals for real!
These clouds are looking dark!
And then there's YOU.
I mean what is going on when roses fall from the sky and I make an imaginary friend?
It all changes when you start talking to cats.
I've tried so hard to be someone else, but...

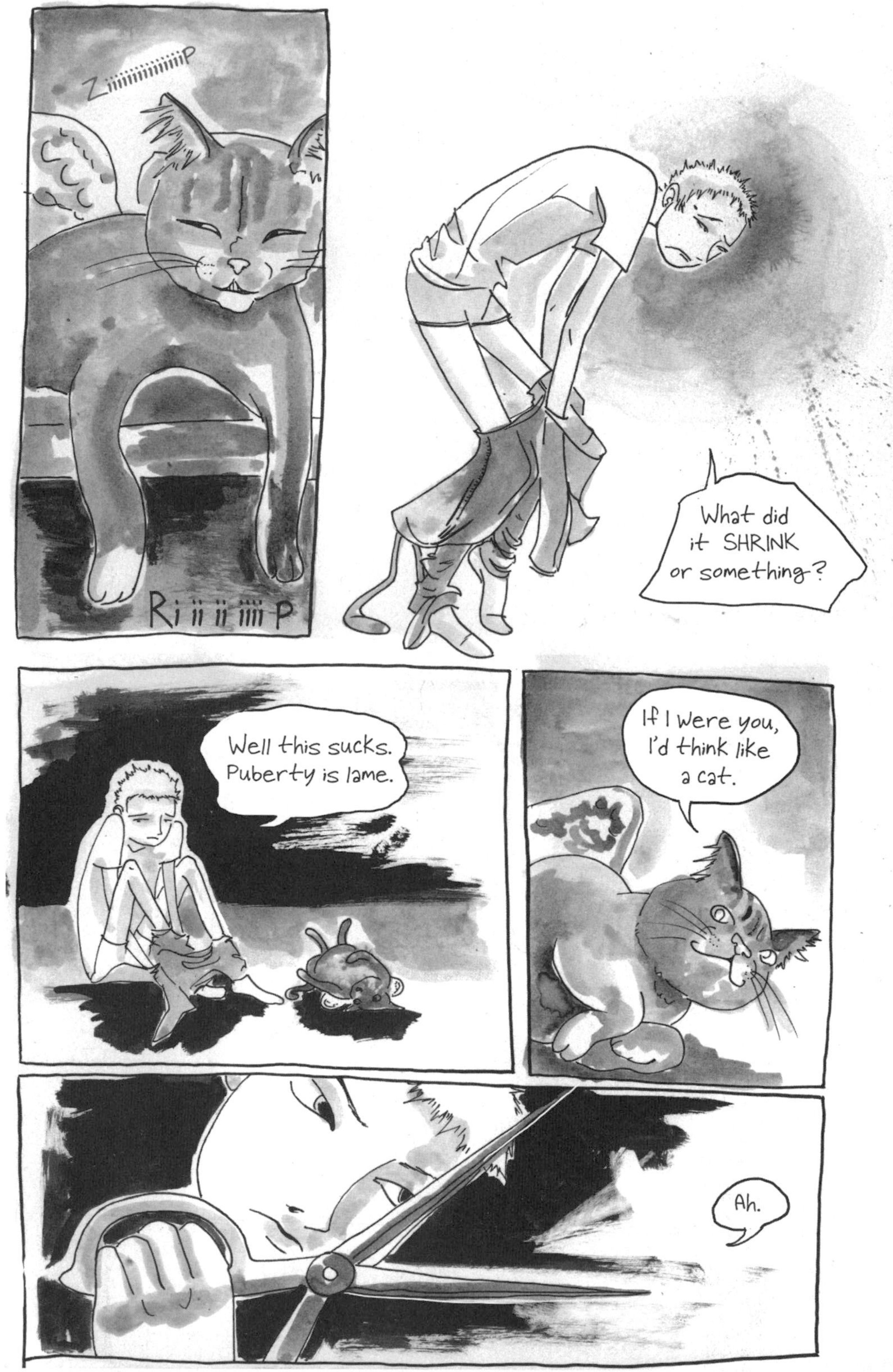
Ziiiiiiiiiiiip
Riiiiiiiiip
What did it SHRINK or something?
Well this sucks. Puberty is lame.
If I were you, I'd think like a cat.
Ah.

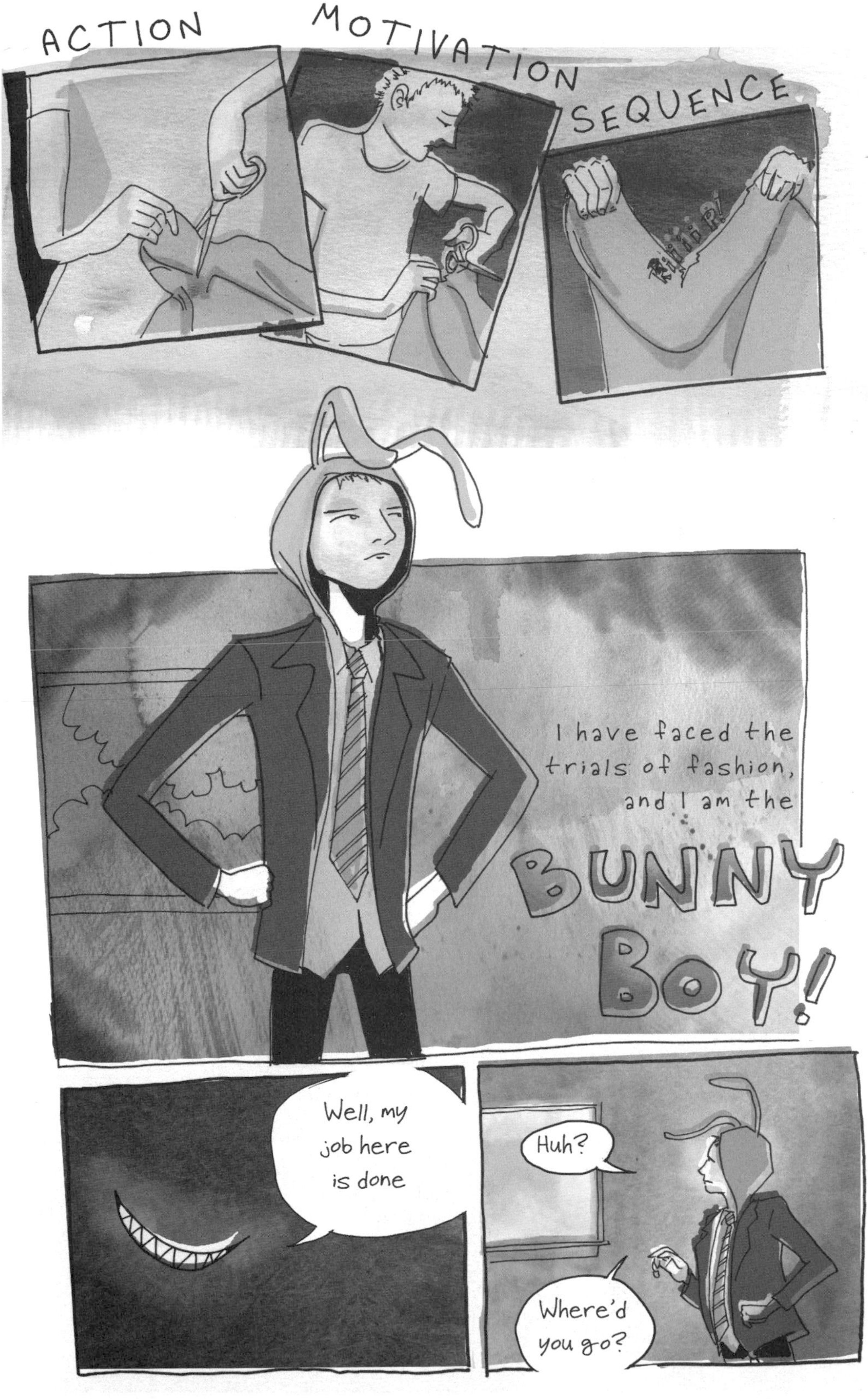
ACTION MOTIVATION SEQUENCE
RIIIIIP!
I have faced the trials of fashion, and I am the
BUNNY BOY!
Well, my job here is done
Huh?
Where'd you go?

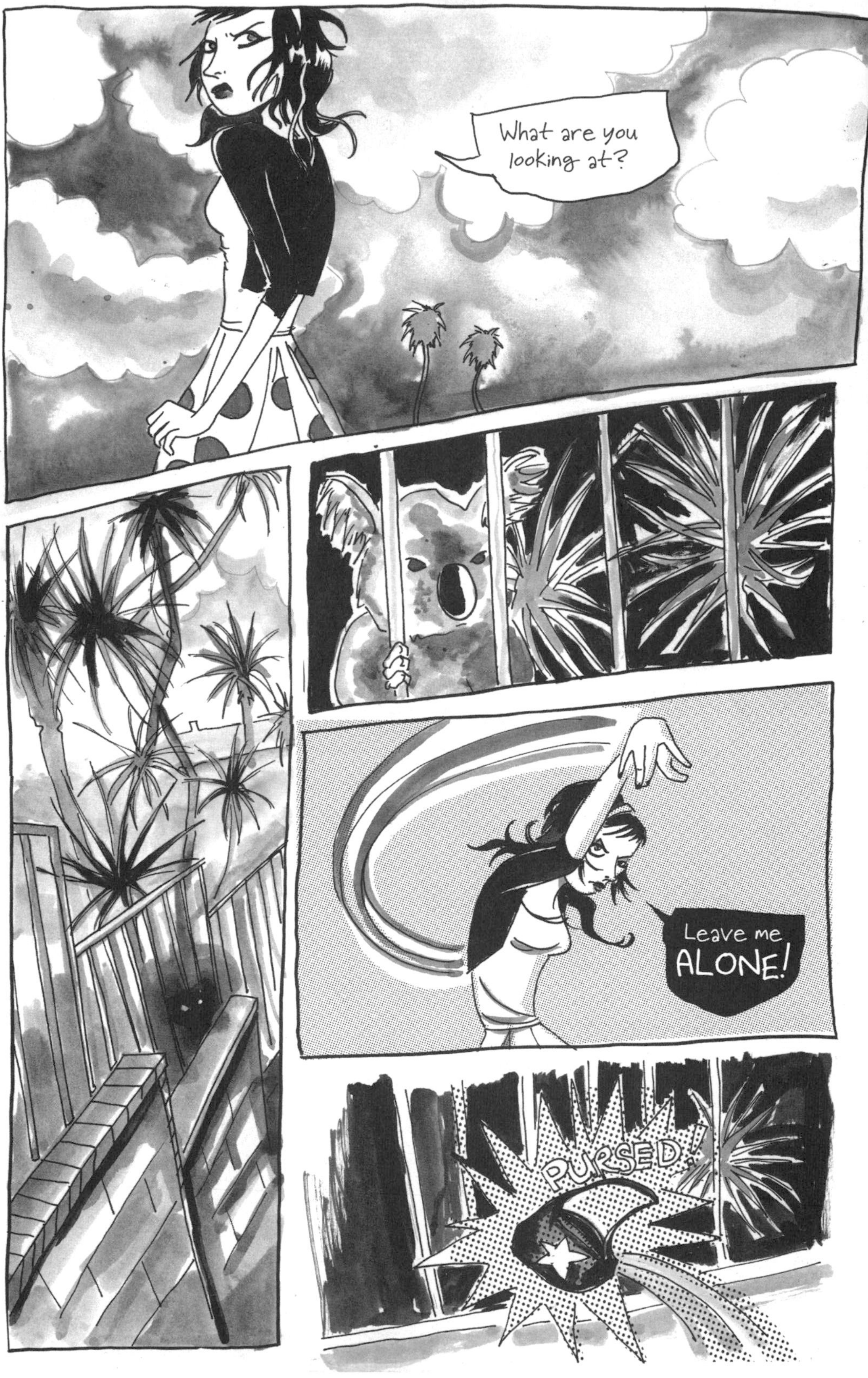
What are you looking at?
Leave me ALONE!
PURSED!

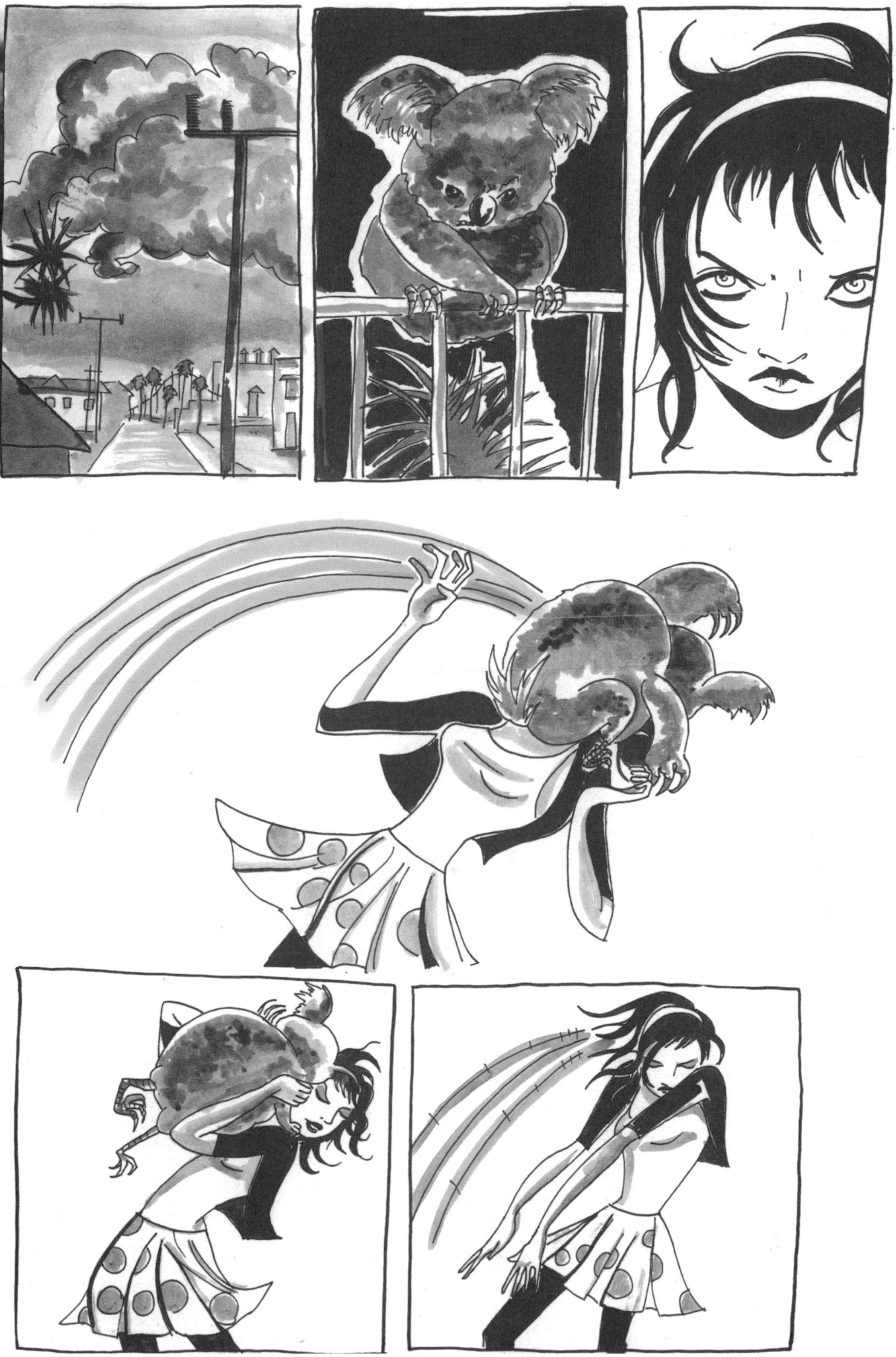

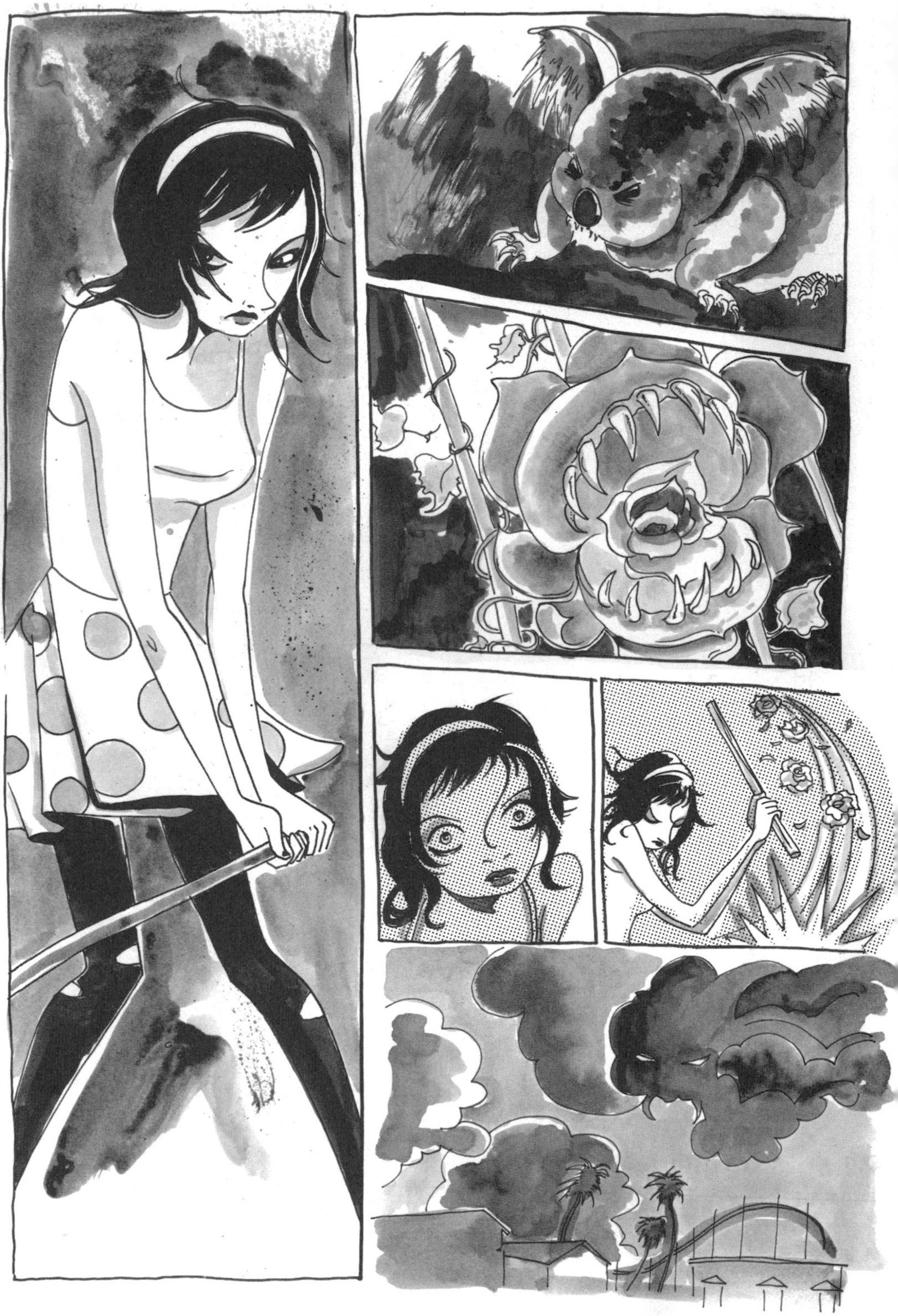

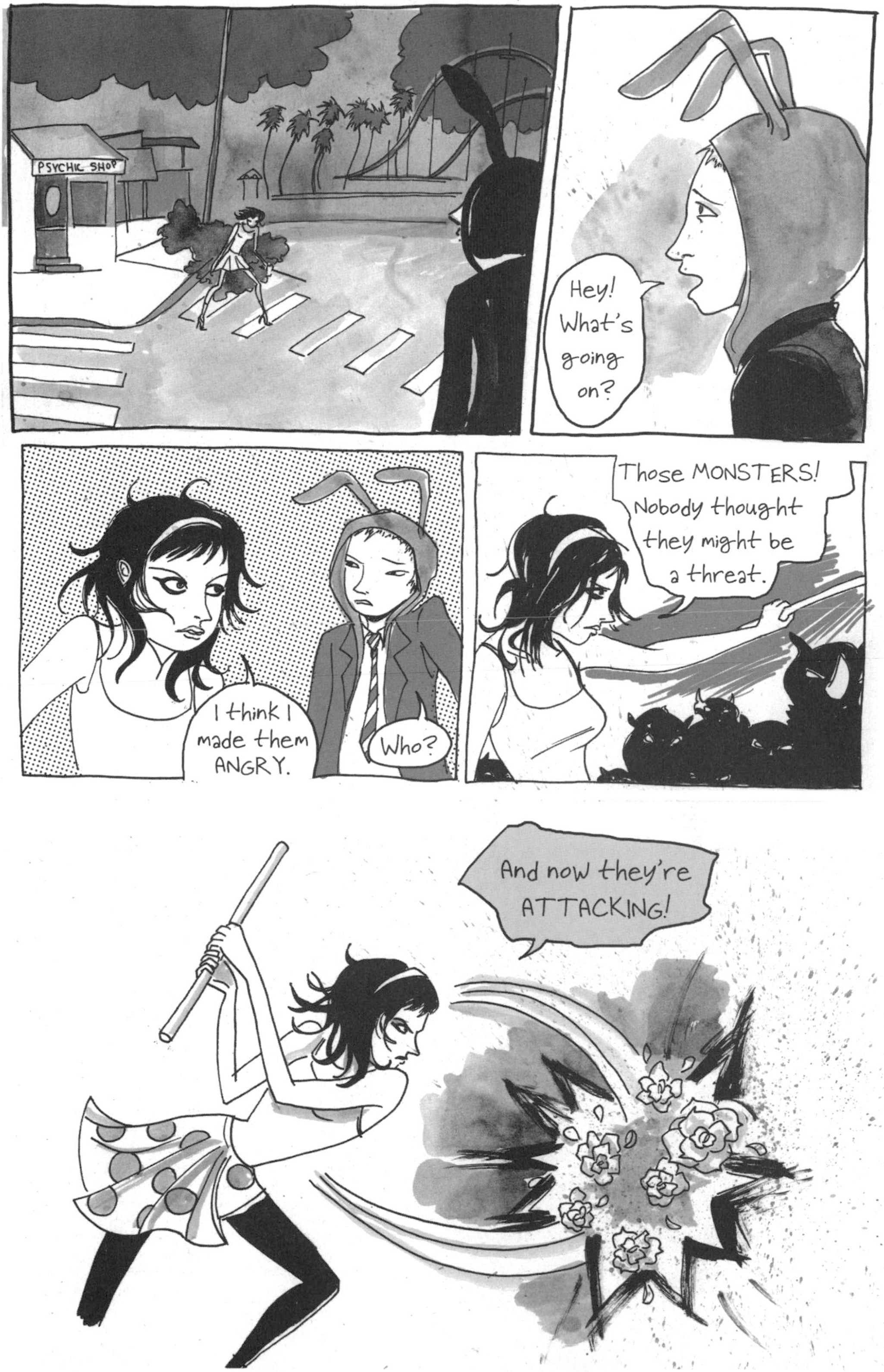
PSYCHIC SHOP
Hey! What's going on?
I think I made them ANGRY.
Who?
Those MONSTERS! Nobody thought they might be a threat.
And now they're ATTACKING!

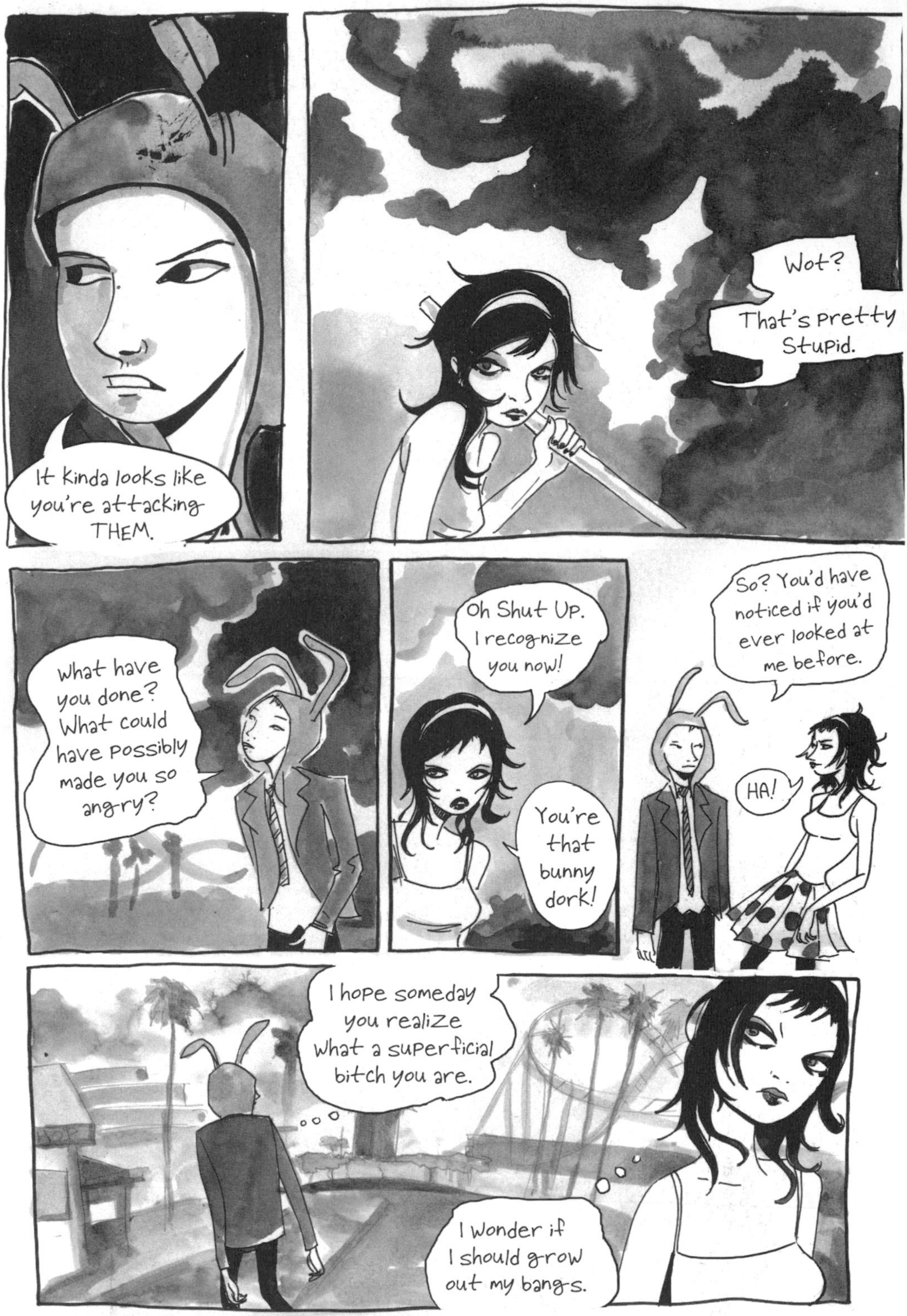
It kinda looks like you're attacking THEM.
Wot?
That's pretty Stupid.
What have you done? What could have possibly made you so angry?
Oh Shut Up. I recognize you now!
You're that bunny dork!
So? You'd have noticed if you'd ever looked at me before.
HA!
I hope someday you realize what a superficial bitch you are.
I wonder if I should grow out my bangs.

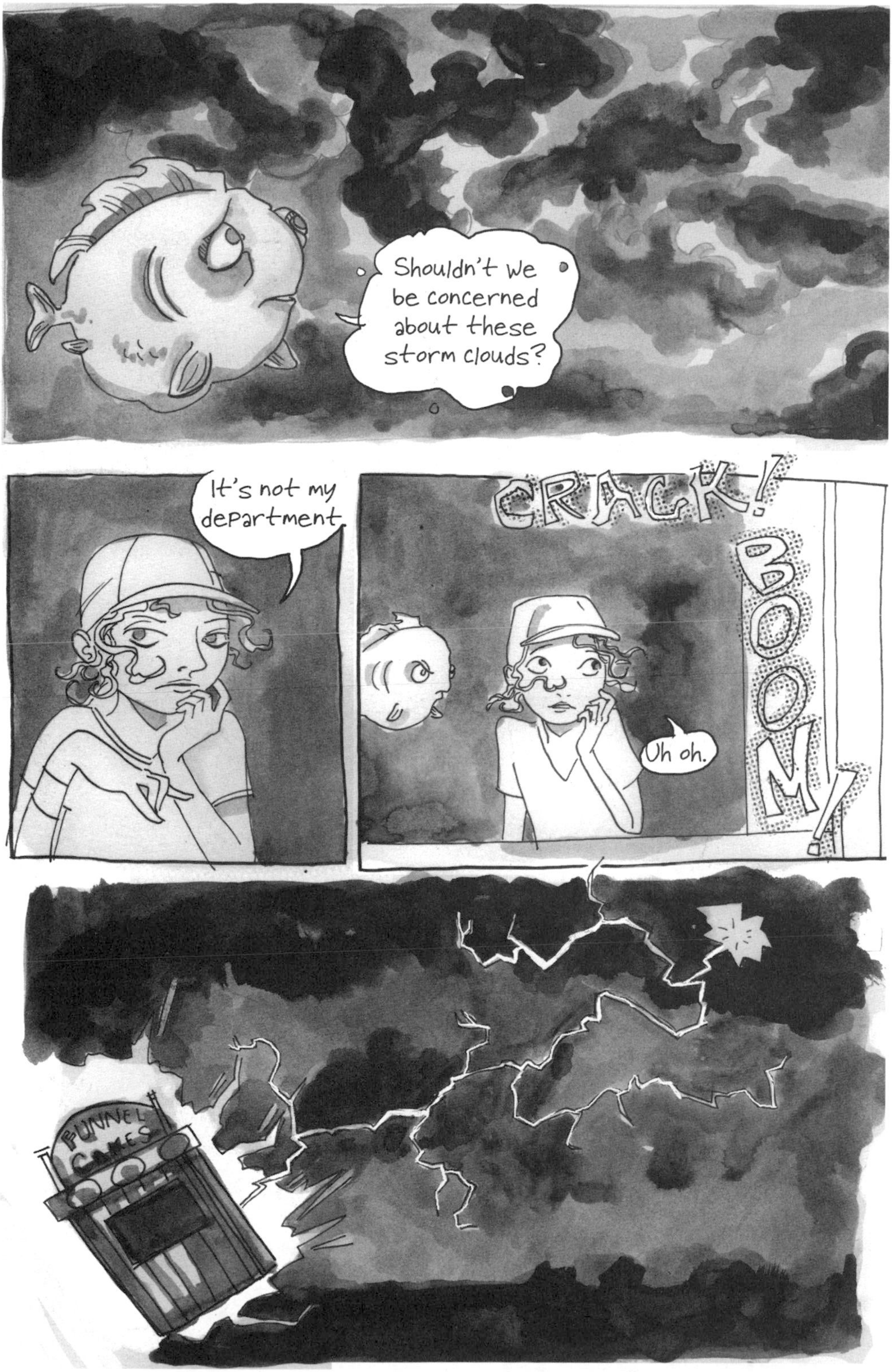
Shouldn't we be concerned about these storm clouds?
It's not my department.
CRACK!
BOOM!
Uh oh.
FUNNEL CAKES

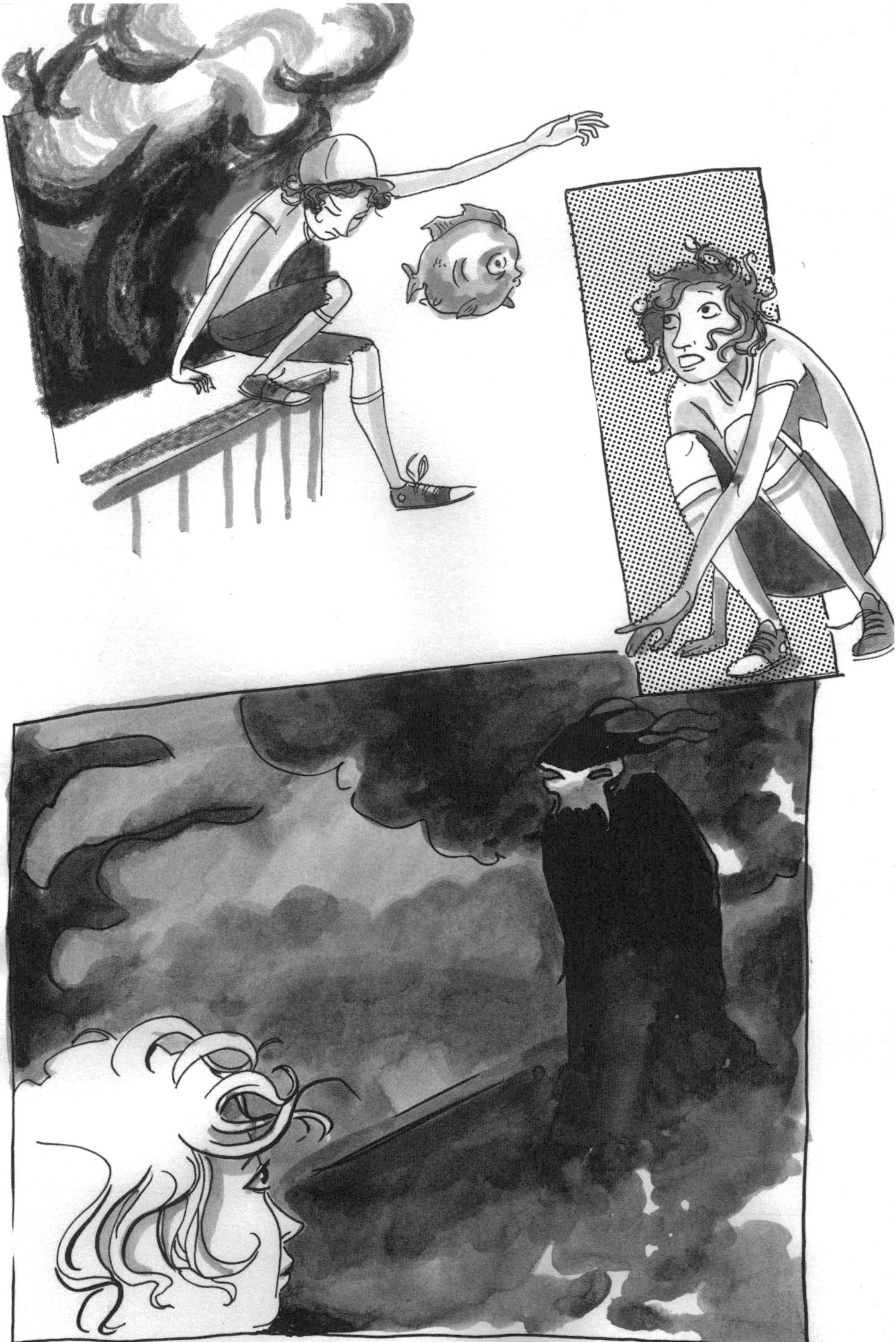

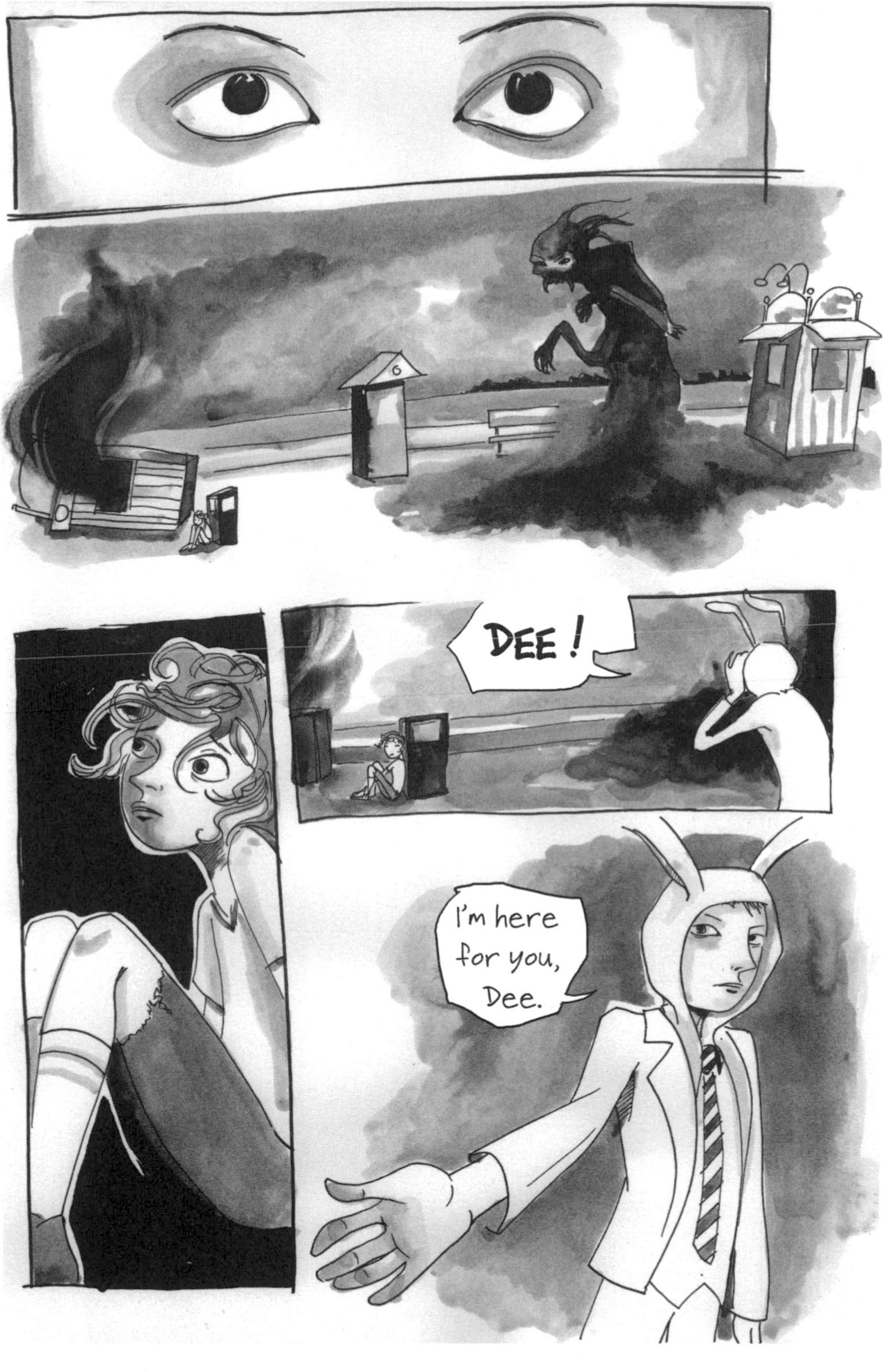
DEE!
I'm here for you, Dee.

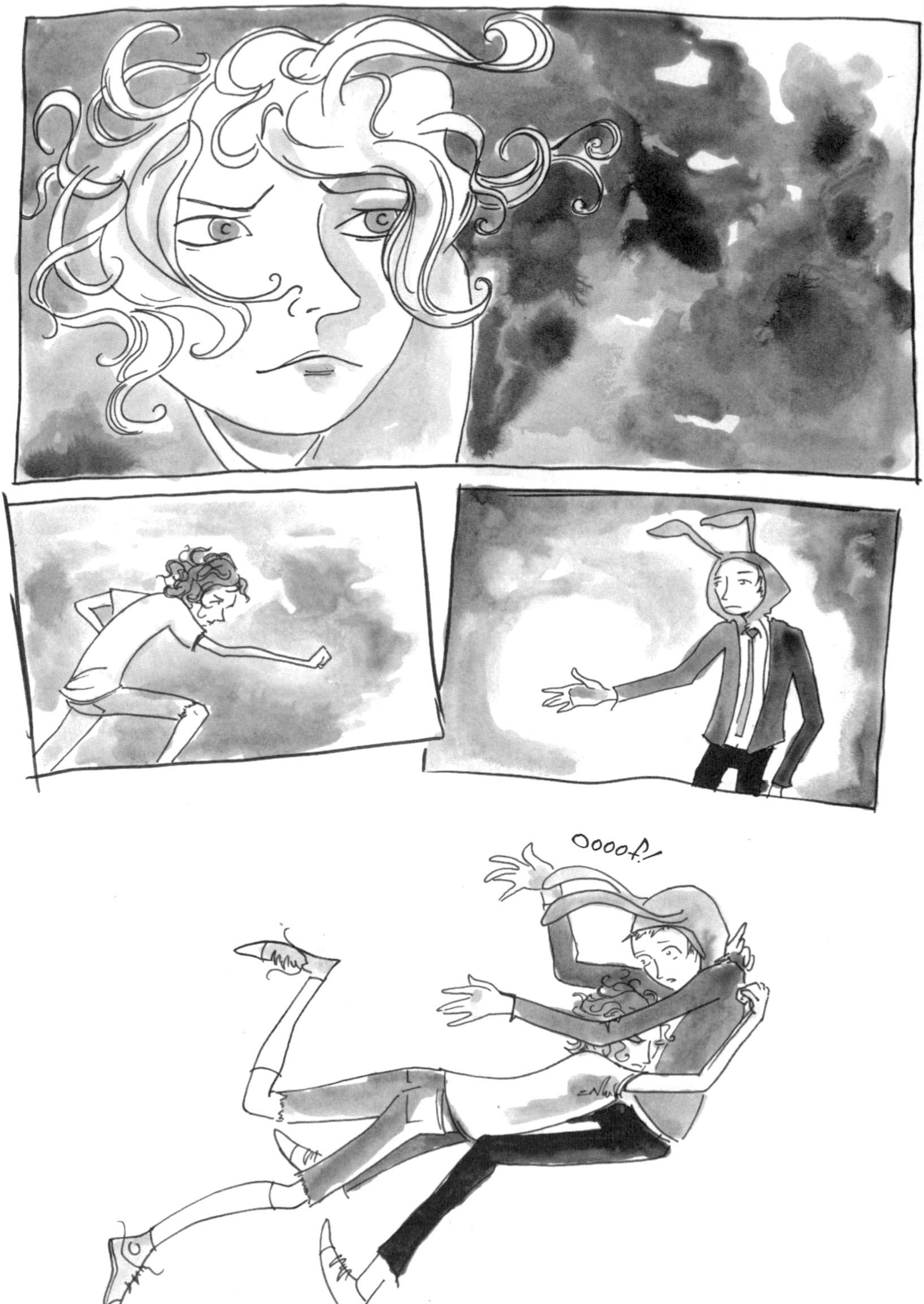
Ooooof!

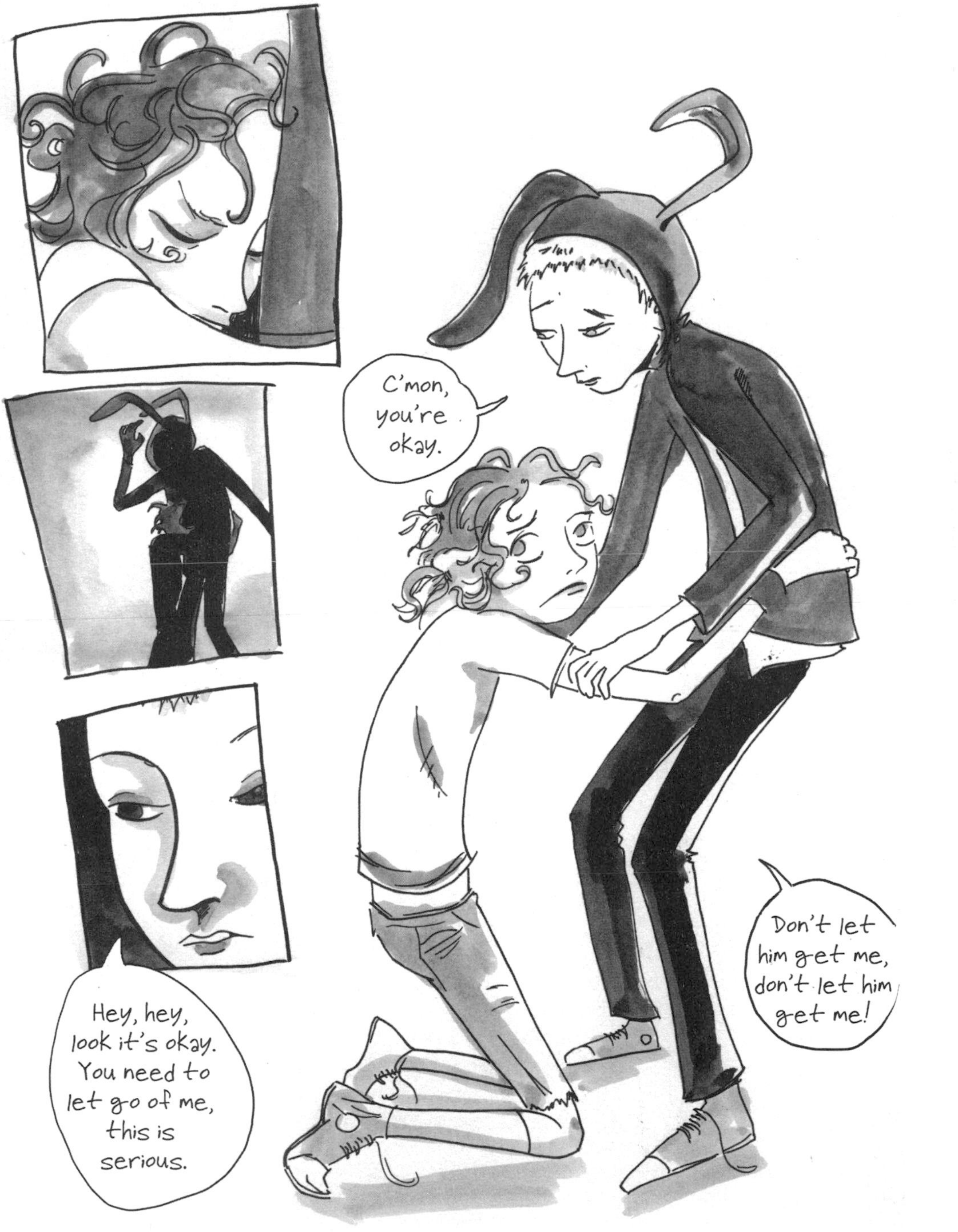
C'mon, you're okay.
Hey, hey, look it's okay. You need to let go of me, this is serious.
Don't let him get me, don't let him get me!

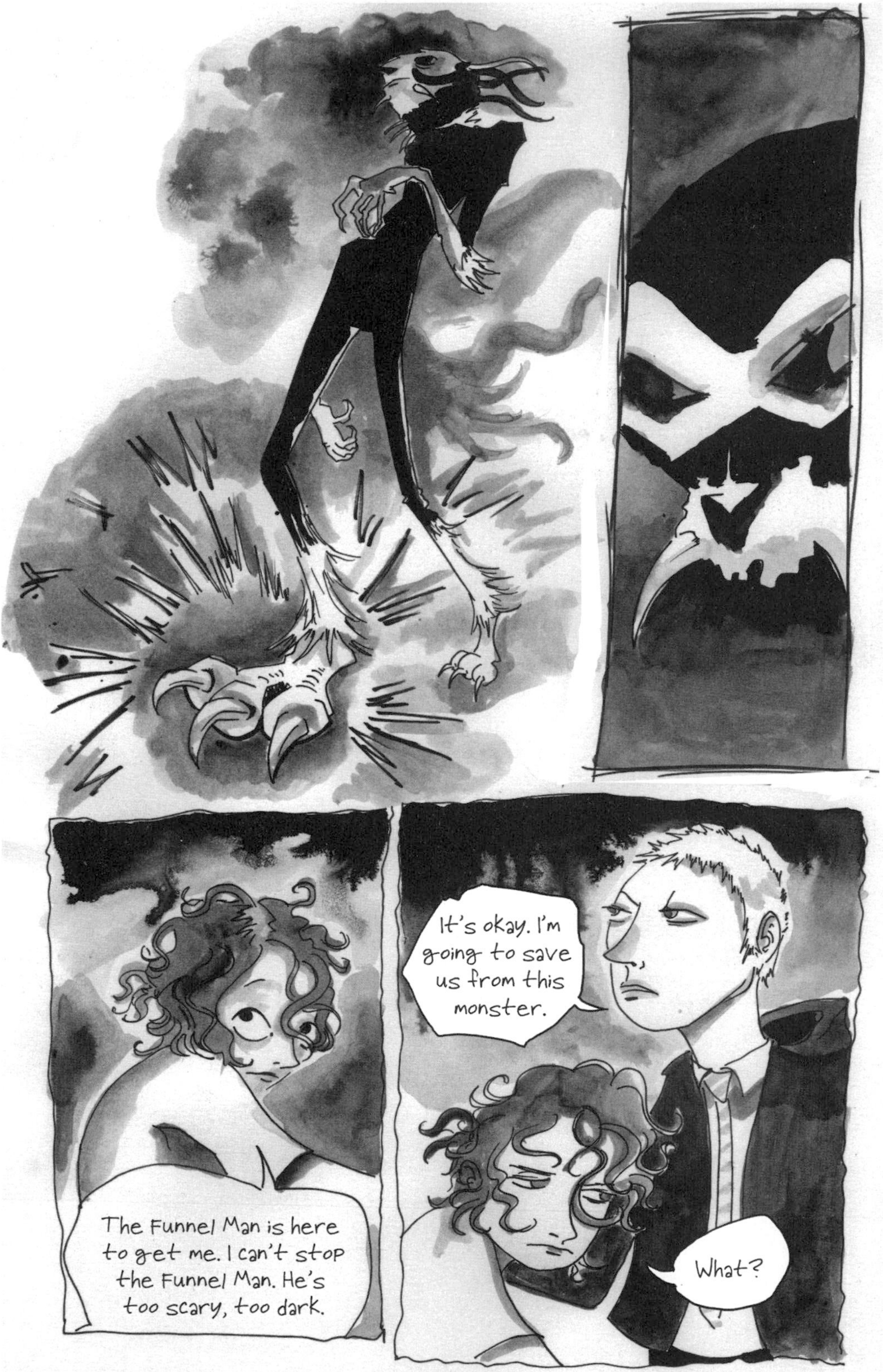
The Funnel Man is here to get me. I can't stop the Funnel Man. He's too scary, too dark.
It's okay. I'm going to save us from this monster.
What?

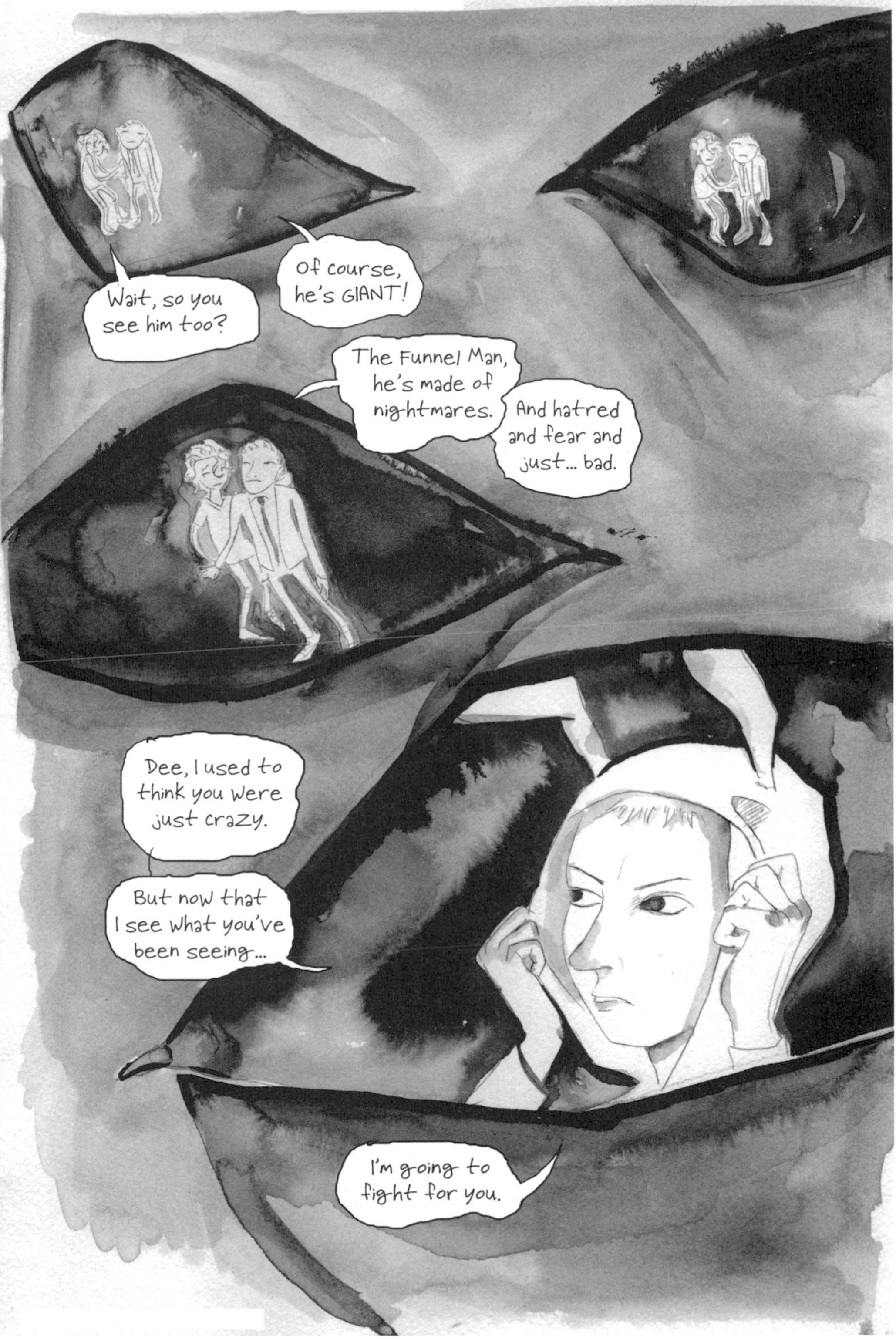
Wait, so you see him too?
Of course, he's GIANT!
The Funnel Man, he's made of nightmares.
And hatred and fear and just... bad.
Dee, I used to think you were just crazy.
But now that I see what you've been seeing...
I'm going to fight for you.

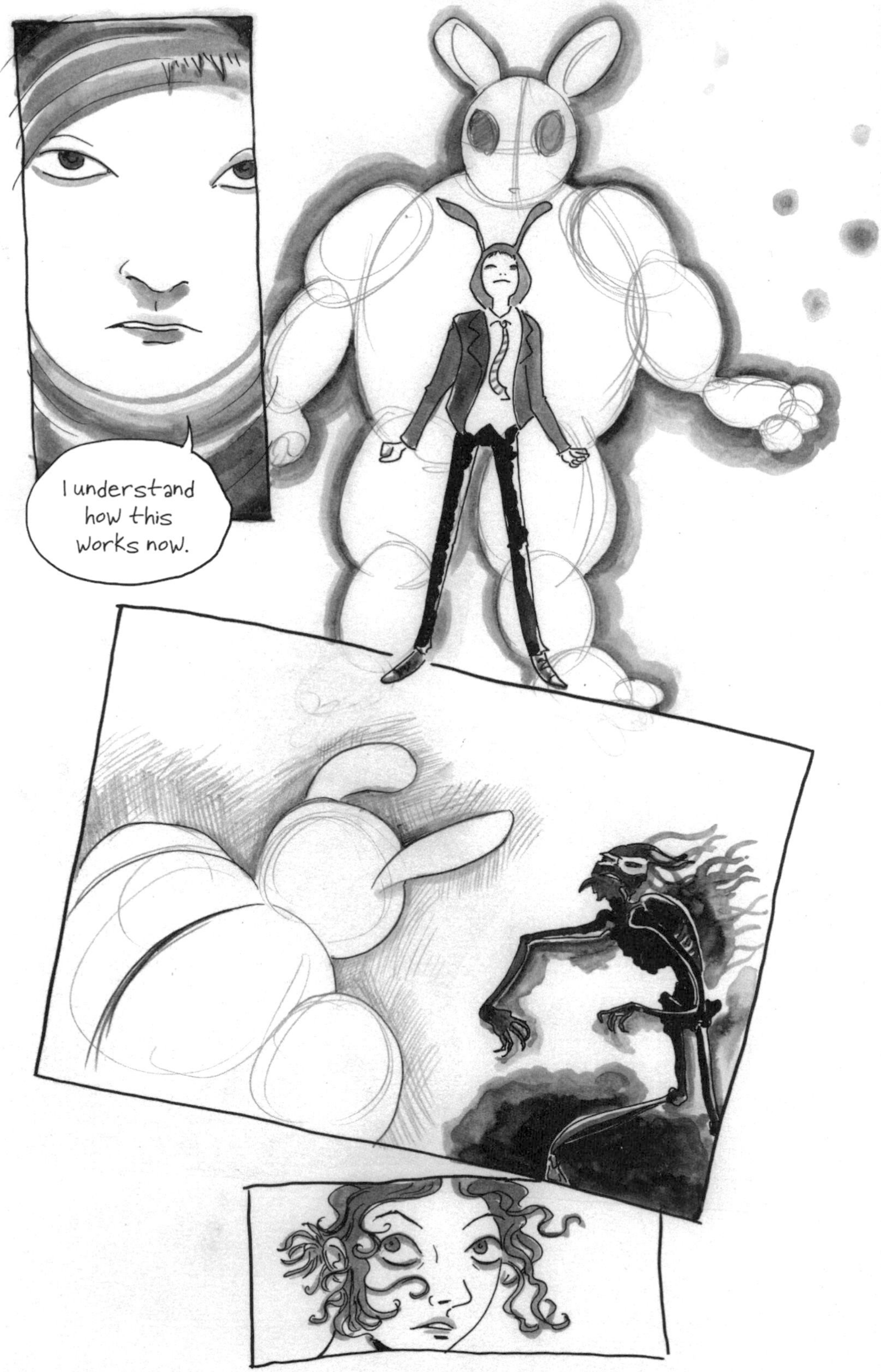
I understand how this works now.

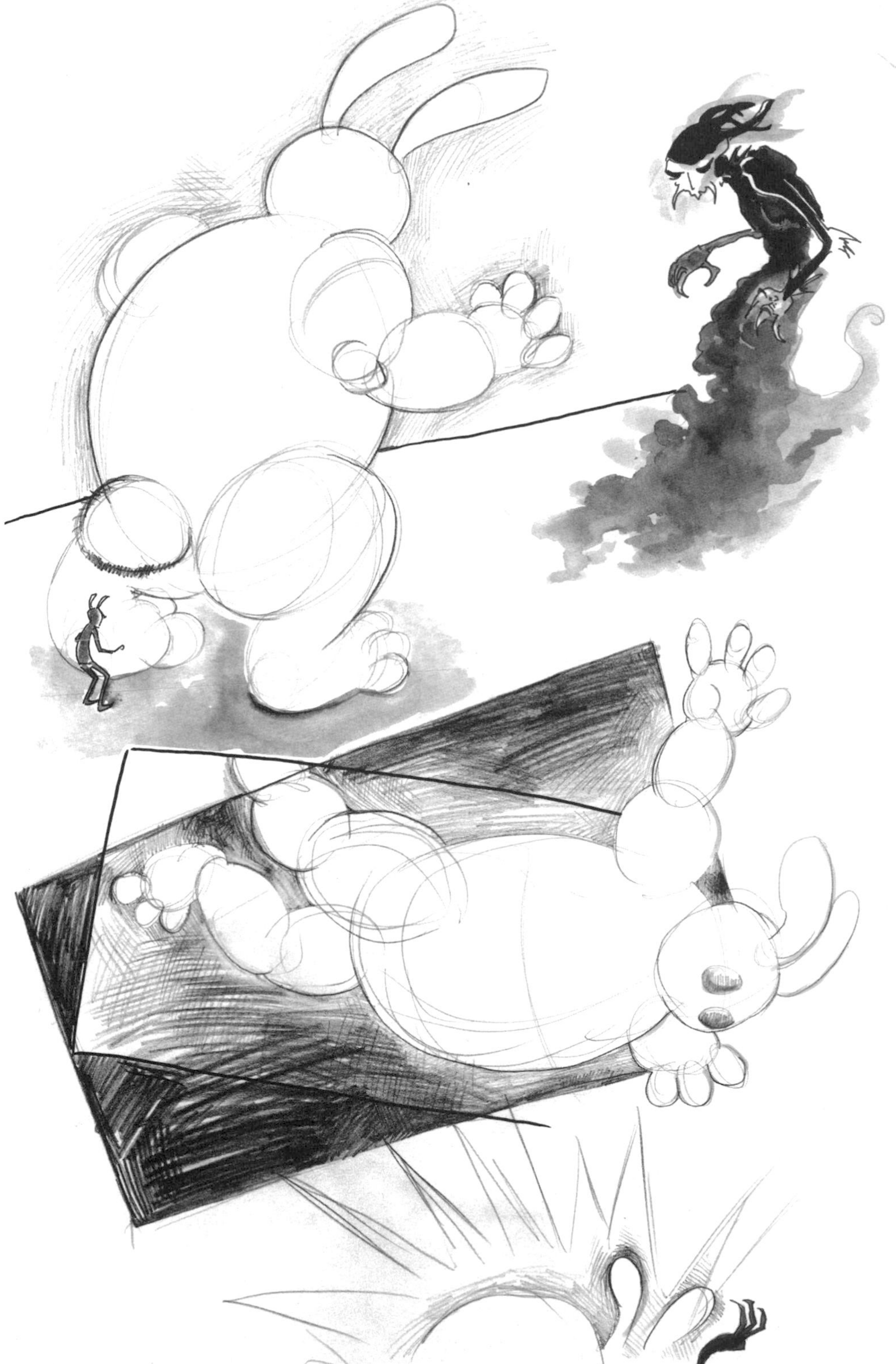

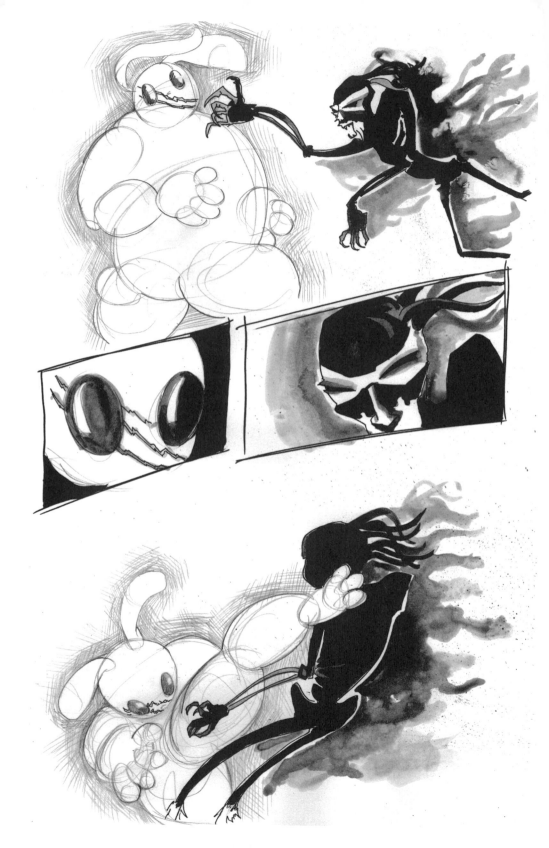

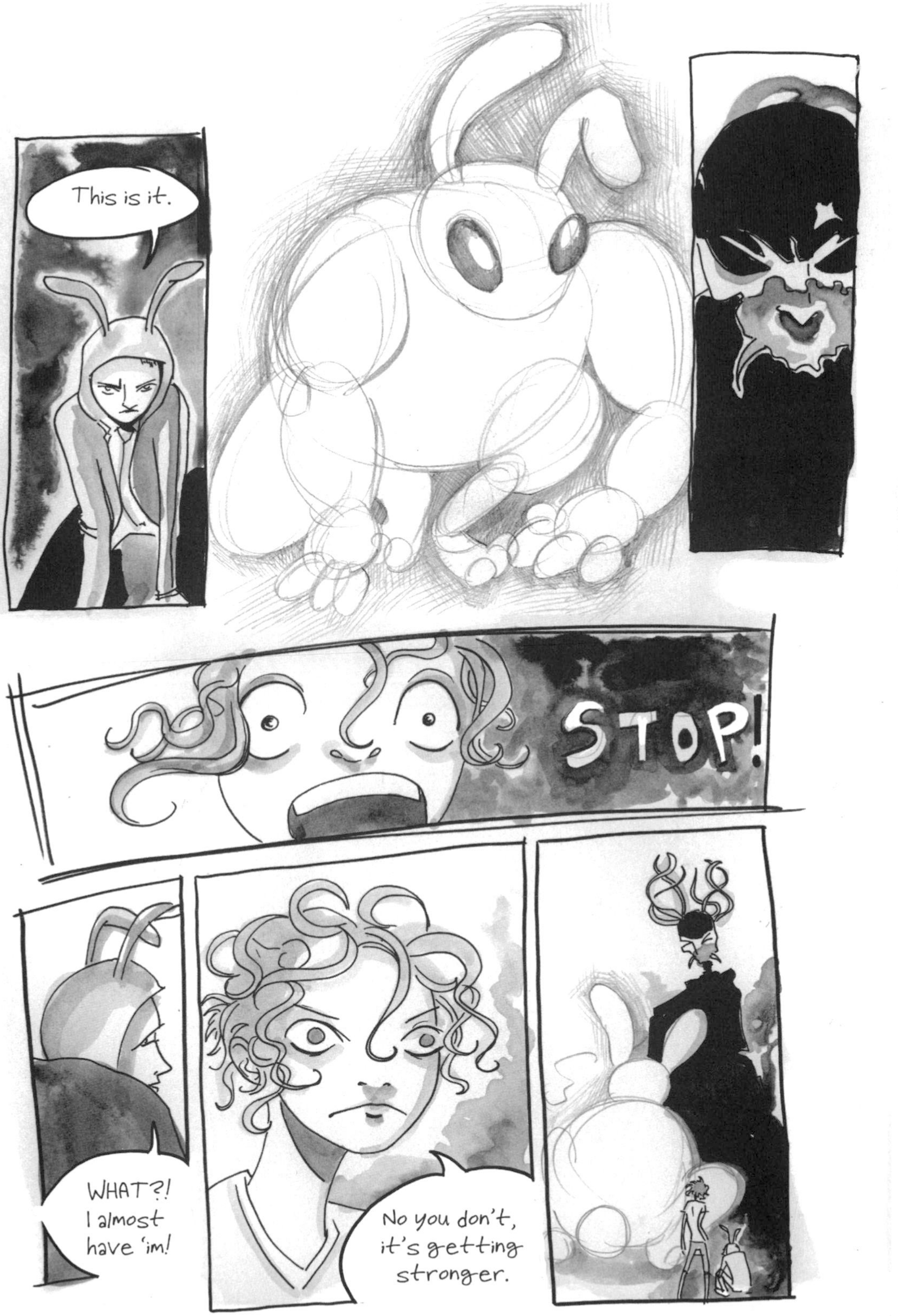
This is it.
STOP!
WHAT?! I almost have 'im!
No you don't, it's getting stronger.

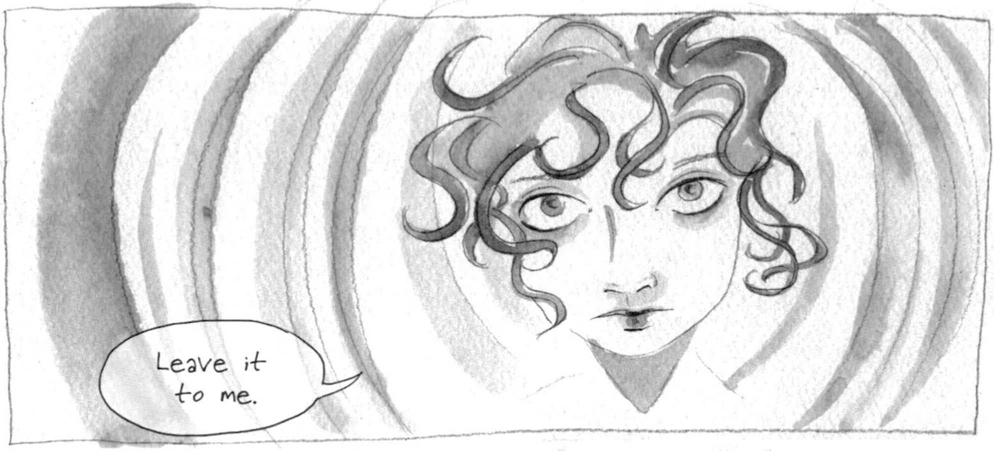
Leave it to me.

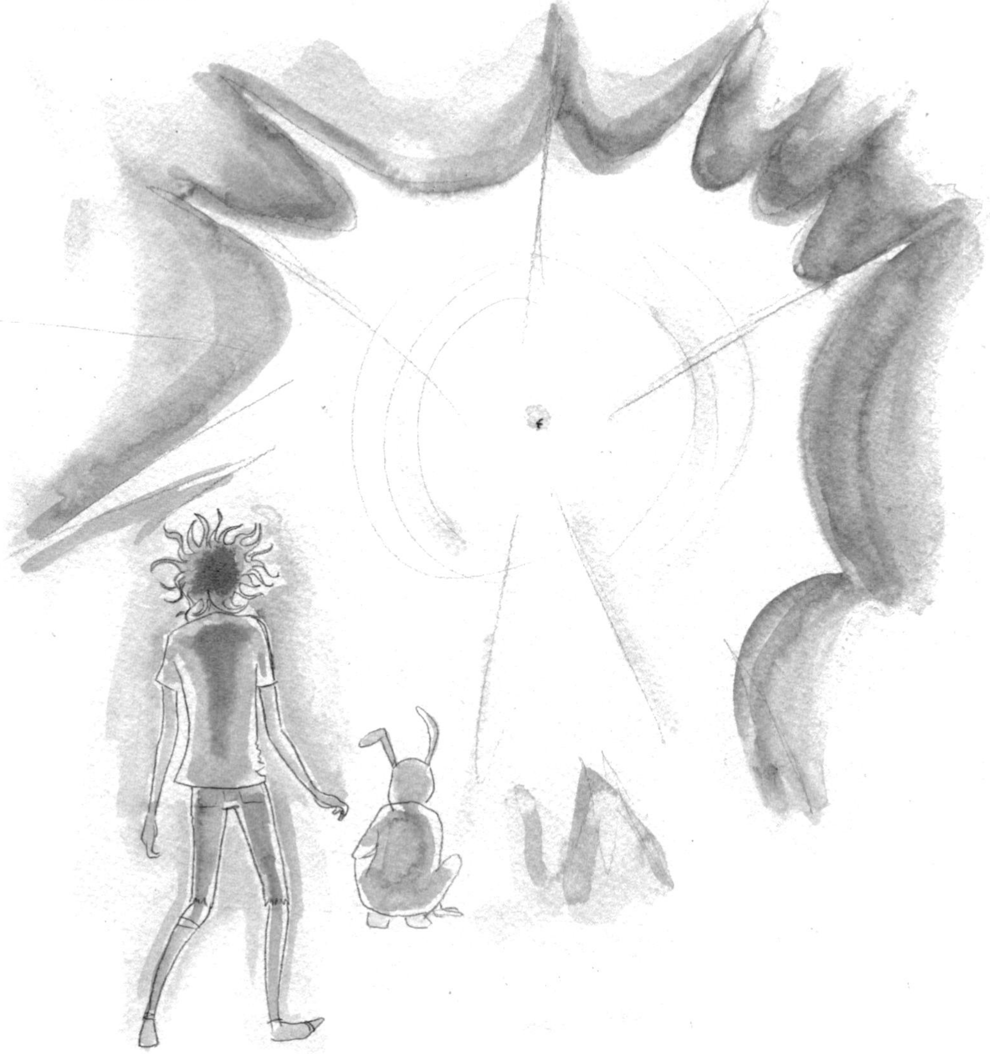

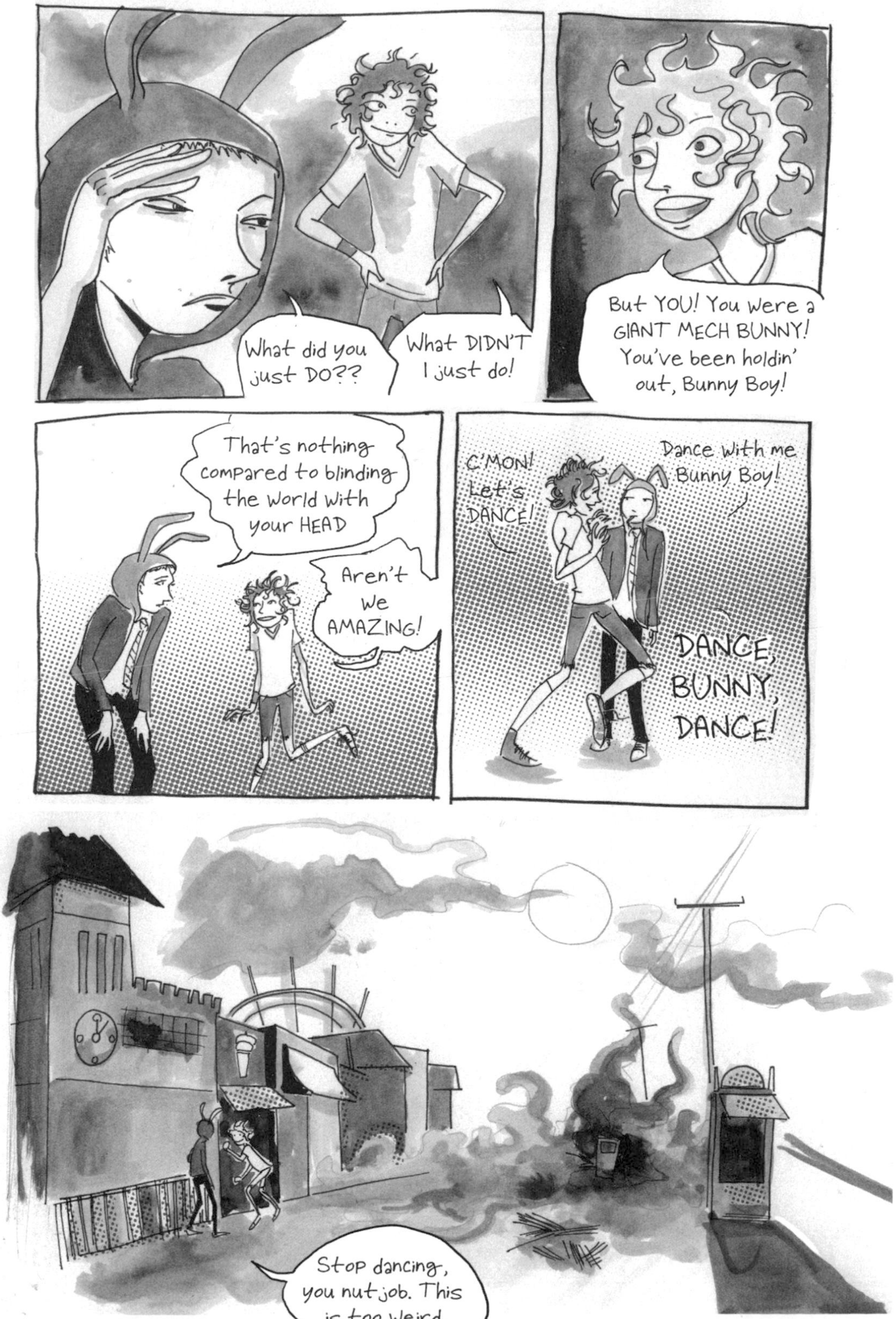
What did you just DO??
What DIDN'T I just do!
But YOU! You were a GIANT MECH BUNNY! You've been holdin' out, Bunny Boy!
That's nothing compared to blinding the world with your HEAD
Aren't we AMAZING!
C'MON! Let's DANCE!
Dance with me Bunny Boy!
DANCE, BUNNY, DANCE!
Stop dancing, you nut job. This is too weird.

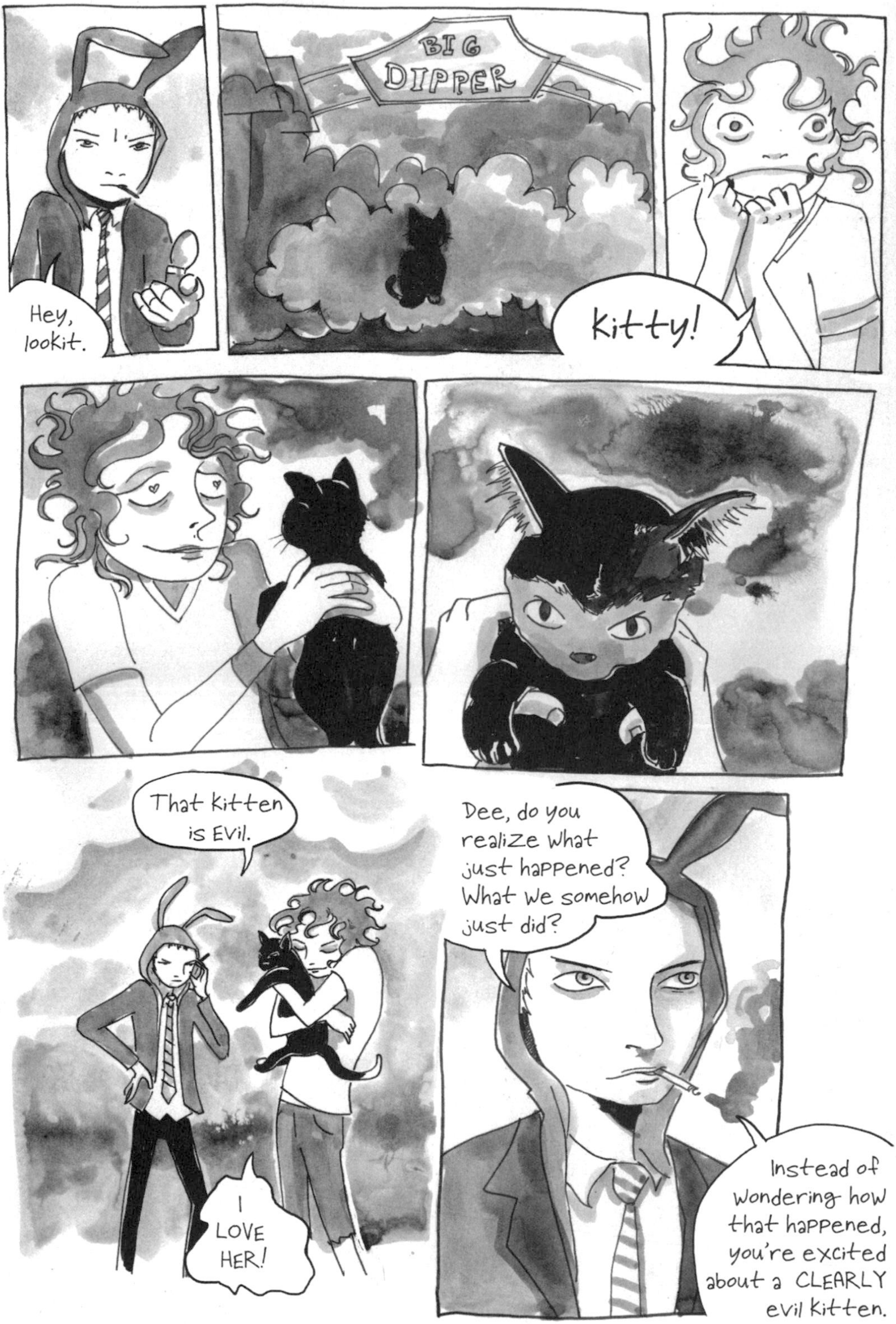
Hey, lookit.
BIG DIPPER
Kitty!
That kitten is EVIL.
I LOVE HER!
Dee, do you realize what just happened? What we somehow just did?
Instead of wondering how that happened, you're excited about a CLEARLY evil kitten.

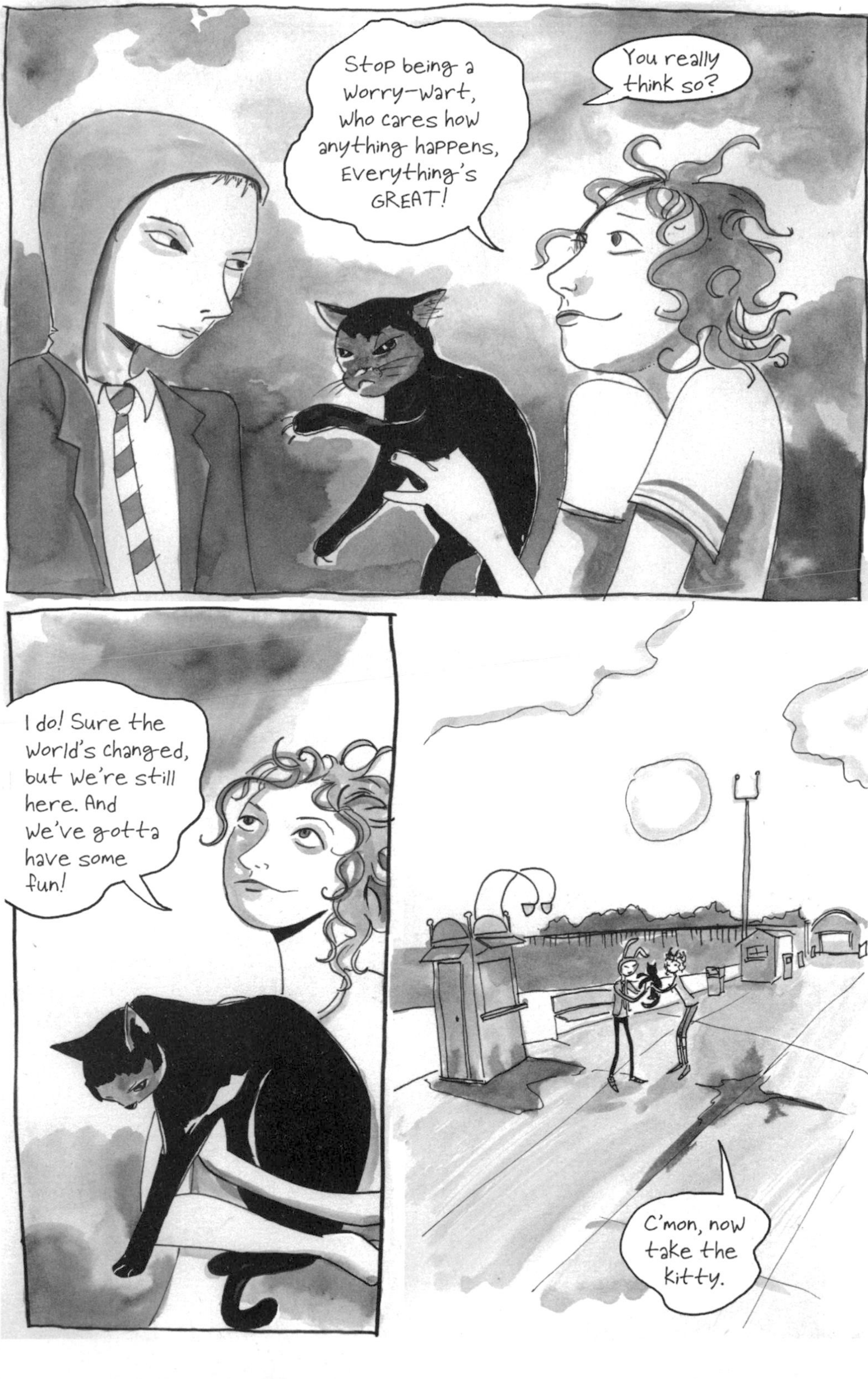
Stop being a worry-wart, who cares how anything happens, Everything's GREAT!
You really think so?
I do! Sure the world's changed, but we're still here. And we've gotta have some fun!
C'mon, now take the kitty.

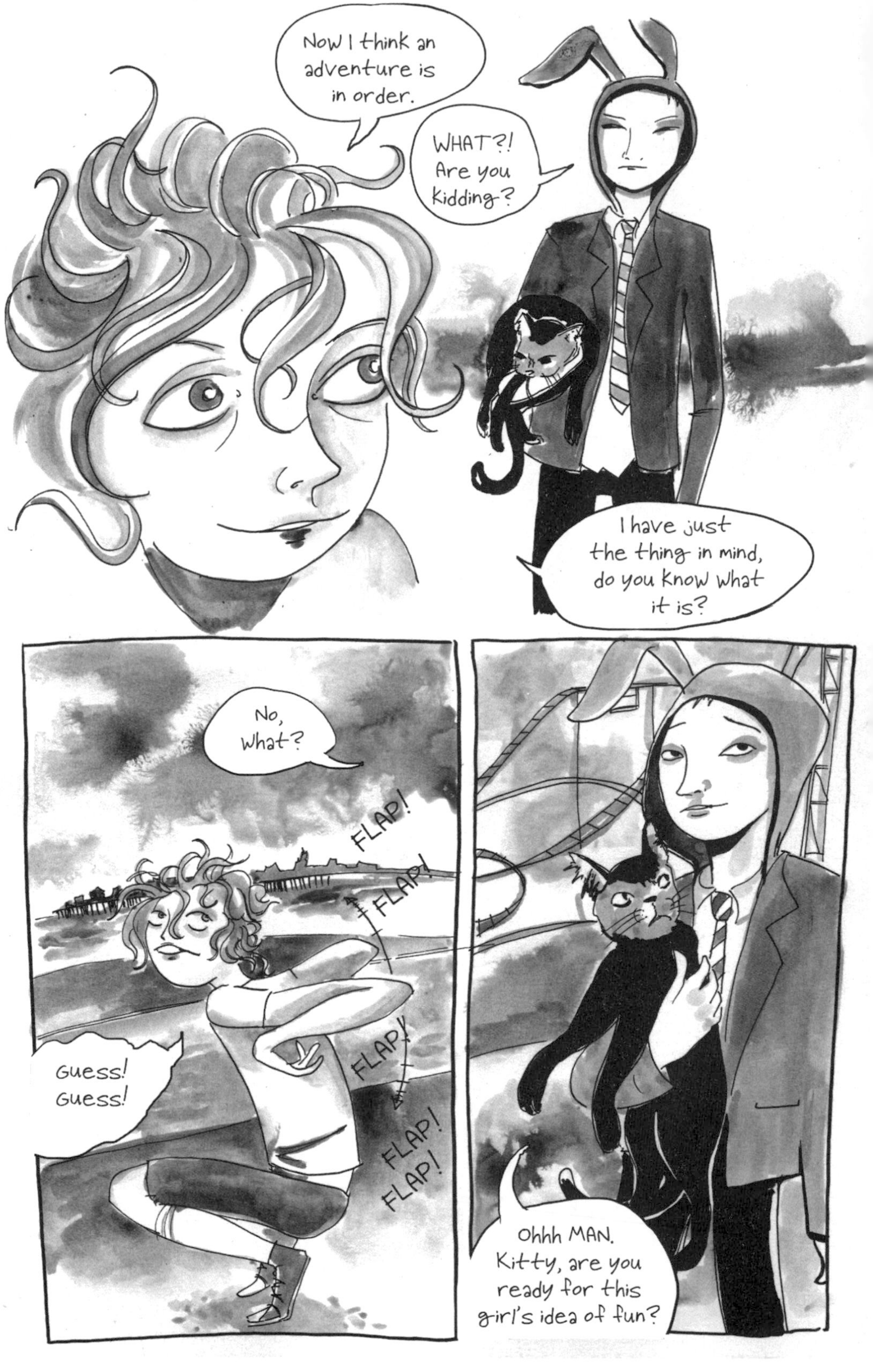

Now I think an adventure is in order.
WHAT?! Are you kidding?
I have just the thing in mind, do you know what it is?
No, what?
Guess! Guess!
FLAP! FLAP! FLAP! FLAP! FLAP!
Ohhh MAN. Kitty, are you ready for this girl's idea of fun?

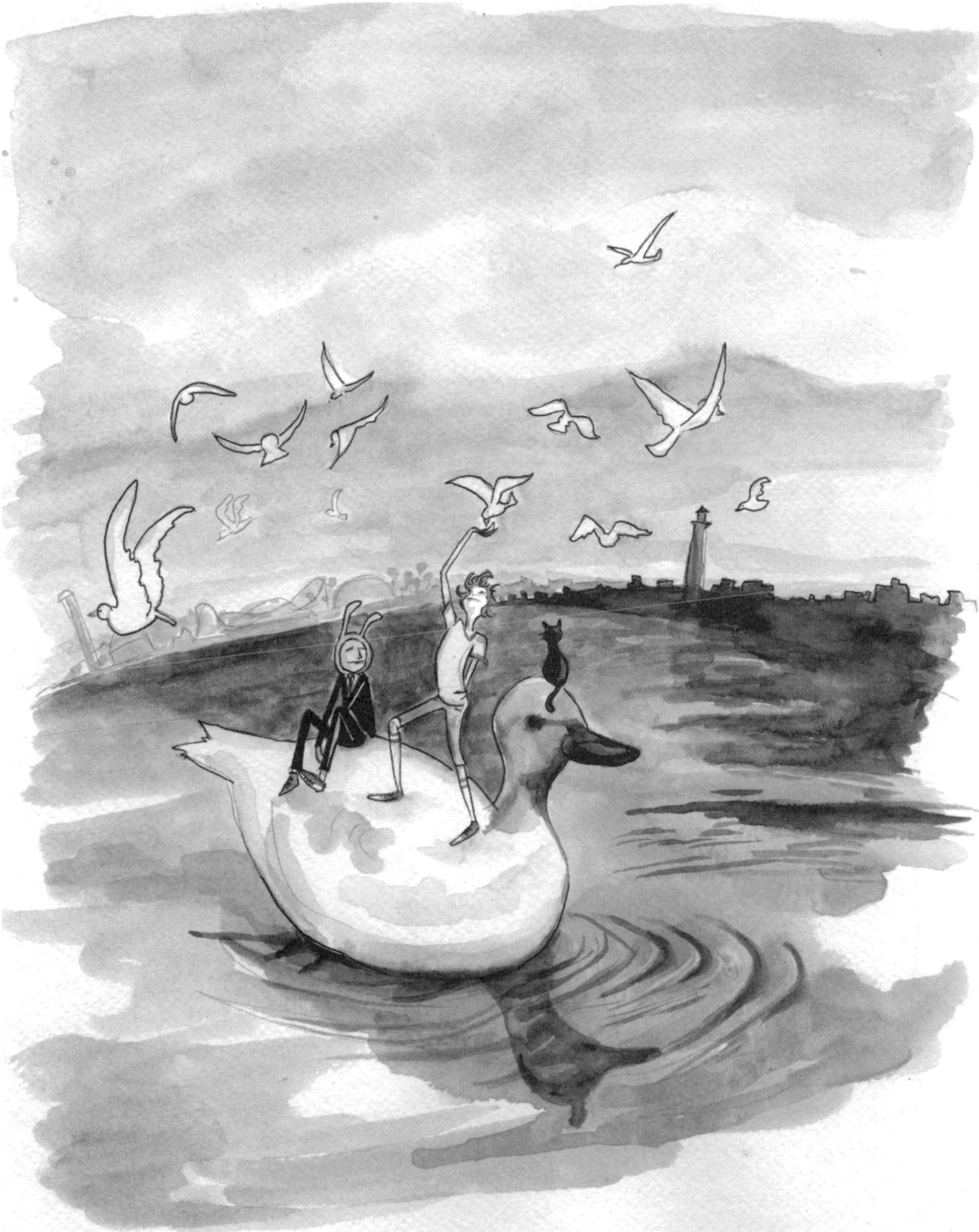

Social Links

What happens next?

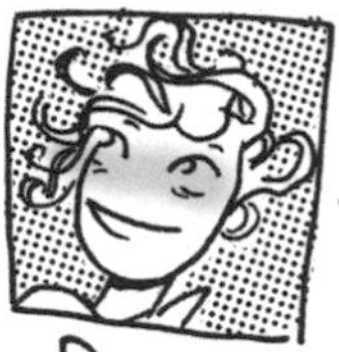

DEE

Has sailed off on a duck, never to be seen again?

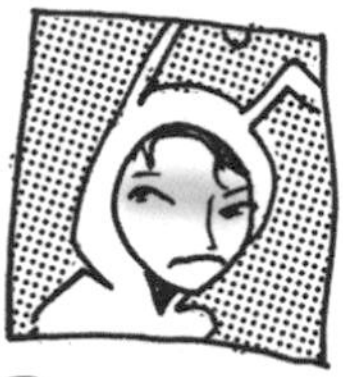

BUNNY BOY

It looks like he's along for the ride. Is he born to be a sailor?

Where is his sister these days?

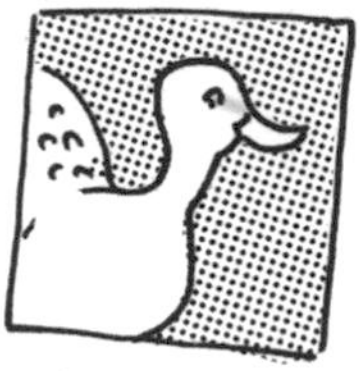

DUCK.

Quack.

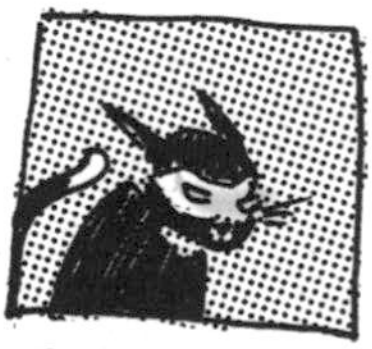

Shadow Cat

Dee used her unusual power to turn the Creature into a Kitten.

It is not pleased.

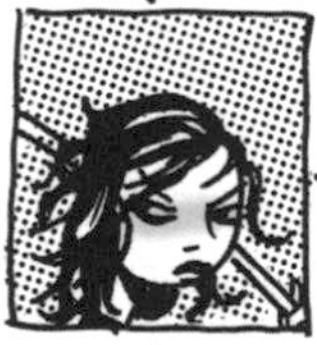

Goth Girl

Bunny Boy's former love interest has become evil. She may be in Jr. High but she's vowed to Kill monsters. VENGEANCE!

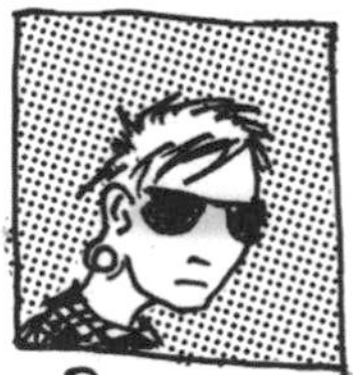

RECORD STORE BOY

Is out of the picture. The only boy to turn down Goth Girl, and the catalyst for her rage streak.

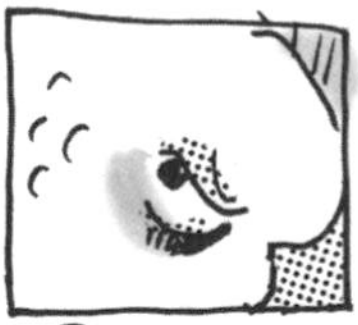

BONES

Has gone AWOL. He does not want to ride a duck

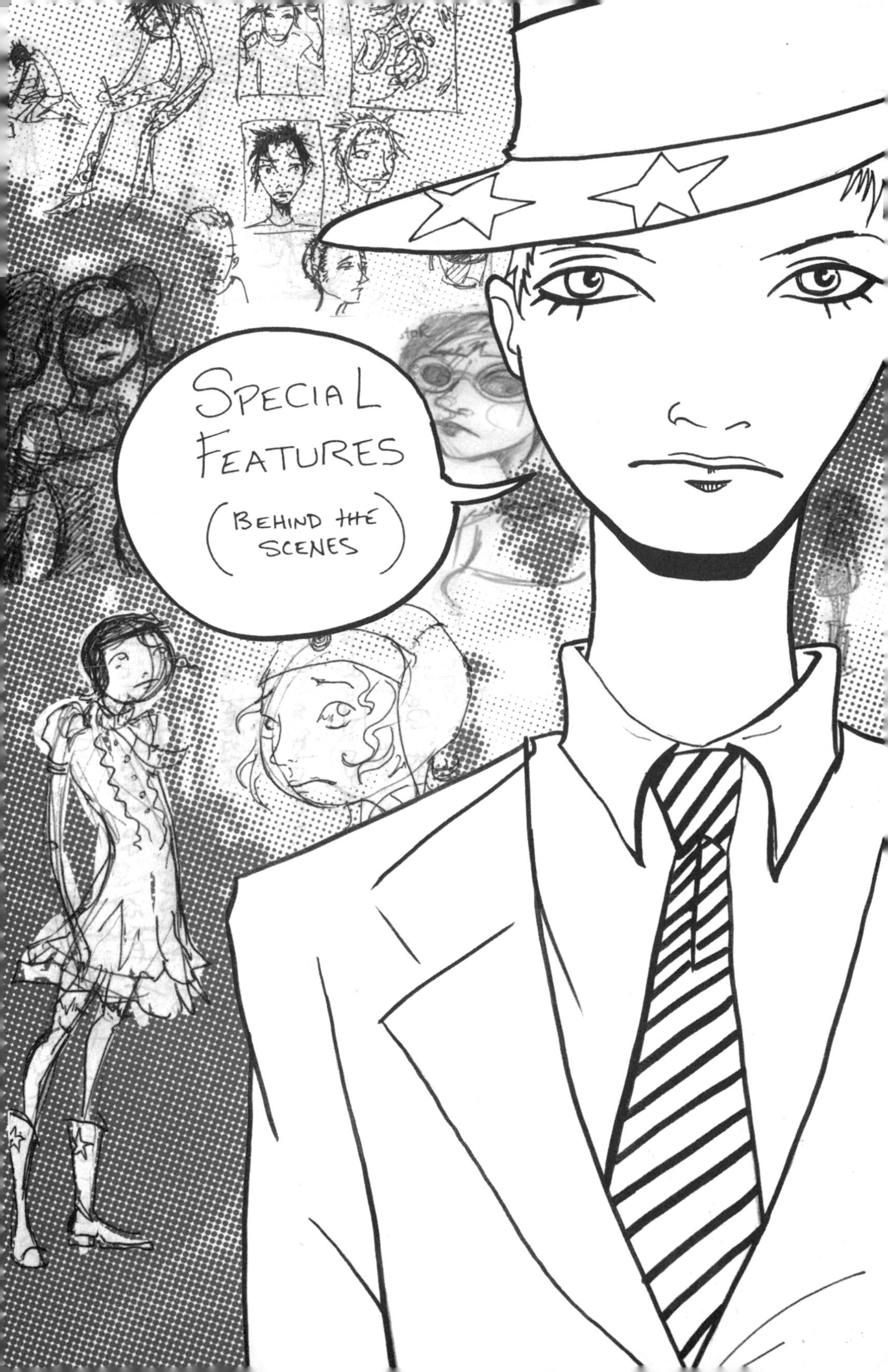
SPECIAL FEATURES
(BEHIND THE SCENES)

Origins

Hi! Are you a new kid? My name's Dee!!

Hi. What's the "D" stand for?

But th' grown ups won't call me that.

Devour!

So we settled on "D".

Mine did the same thing! They won't call me "SUPER FLUFFY BOTTOM"... So they call me "SAM."

DEVOUR © JAMAICA D

A GIRL

Back before Weird Fishes even began, Dee was the star of a strip called "Devour the Child" that was printed in 2005 in my school's paper, the "Spartan Daily." In the strip, morbid little Dee has various adventures with Bones (back when he lived in a bowl) and she eventually meets The Bunny Boy, and he was convinced he was the next Easter Bunny.

My best friend Josh and I were the two cartoonists for the paper that semester, and we submitted strips every week, and every week people came back to us confused about what they'd just read. It was fantastic! By the end of the semester I was waging war with the newspaper itself because of the horrible design, which often put distracting boxes around my comic, and stated "DEVOUR" in some ugly font overtop of my handwritten one.

While my skills grew over the years, these early strips are Dee at her purest, lost in imagination and a distorted view of her surroundings. Plus, they, too, were on a strict schedule much like the "Weird Fishes" webcomic.

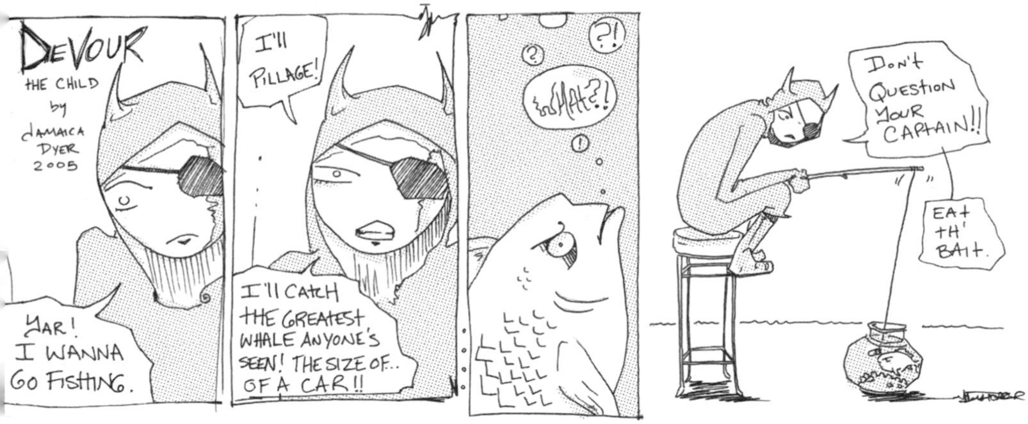
DEVOUR
THE CHILD
by JAMAICA DYER 2005
YAR! I WANNA GO FISHING.
I'll PILLAGE!
I'LL CATCH THE GREATEST WHALE ANYONE'S SEEN! THE SIZE OF.. OF A CAR!!
?!
?
WHAT?!
!
Don't QUESTION YOUR CAPTAIN!!
EAT TH' BAIT.

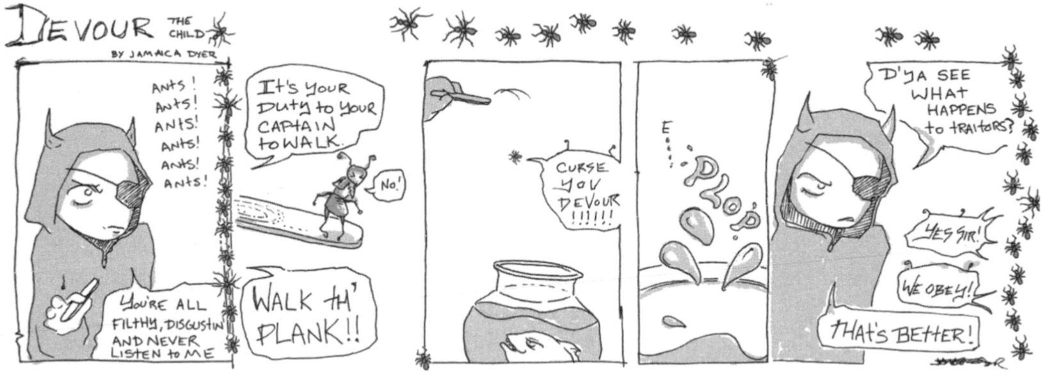
DEVOUR THE CHILD
BY JAMAICA DYER
Ants! Ants! Ants! Ants! Ants! Ants!
You're ALL FILTHY, DISGUSTIN AND NEVER LISTEN to ME
It's your Duty to your CAPTAIN to WALK.
No!
WALK TH' PLANK!!
CURSE YOU DEVOUR !!!!!!
E...
PLOP
D'YA SEE WHAT HAPPENS to traitors?
YES SIR!
WE OBEY!
THAT'S BETTER!

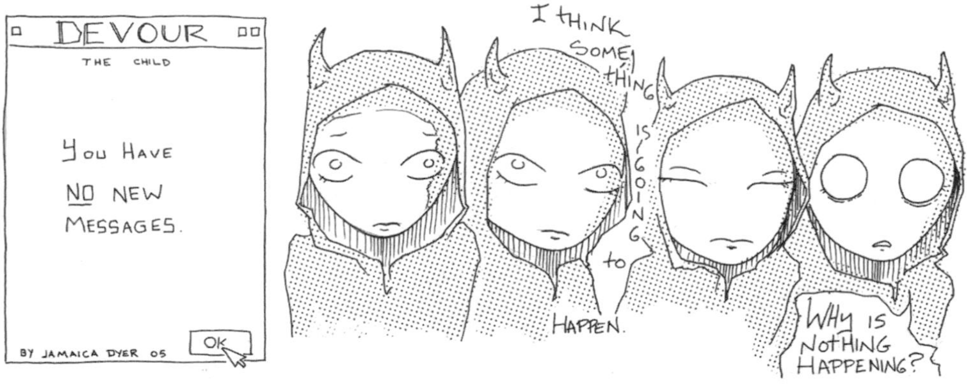
DEVOUR
THE CHILD
You HAVE NO NEW MESSAGES.
BY JAMAICA DYER 05
OK
I THINK SOMETHING IS GOING to HAPPEN.
WHY IS NOTHING HAPPENING?

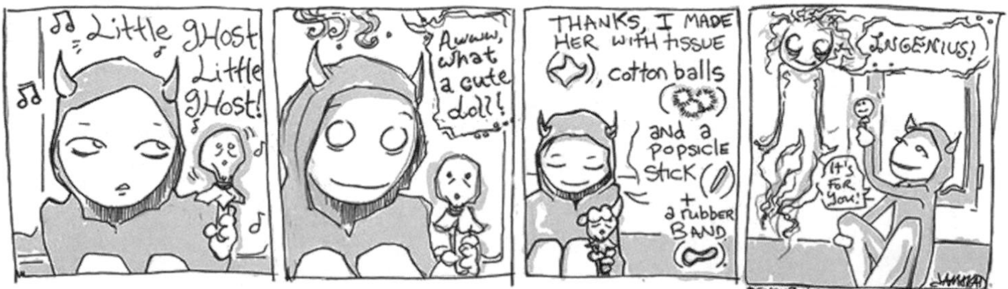
Little gHost Little gHost!
Awww, what a cute doll!
THANKS, I MADE HER WITH tissue ( ), cotton balls ( ) and a popsicle stick ( ) + a rubber BAND ( ).
INGENIUS!
It's FOR You!

DEVOUR THE CHILD © 2005

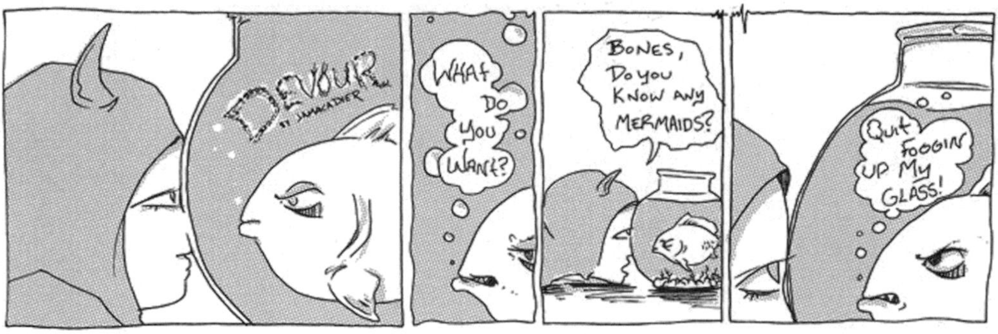
DEVOUR
BY JAMAICA DYER
WHAT DO YOU WANT?
BONES, DO YOU KNOW ANY MERMAIDS?
QUIT FOGGIN UP MY GLASS!

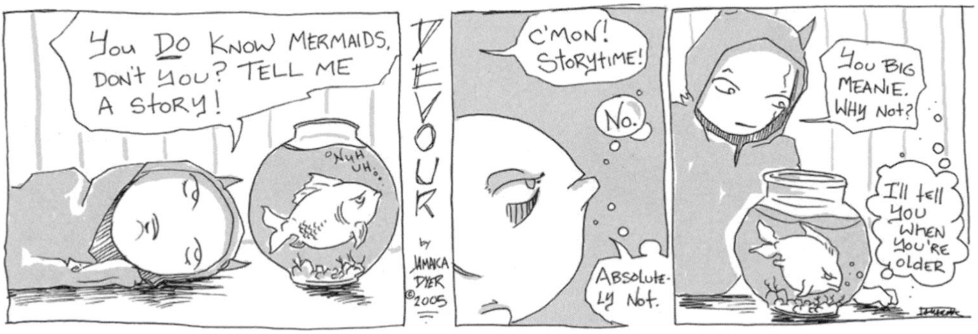
YOU DO KNOW MERMAIDS, DON'T YOU? TELL ME A STORY!
NUH UH...
DEVOUR
by JAMAICA DYER ©2005
C'MON! STORYTIME!
NO.
ABSOLUTELY NOT.
YOU BIG MEANIE. WHY NOT?
I'LL TELL YOU WHEN YOU'RE OLDER

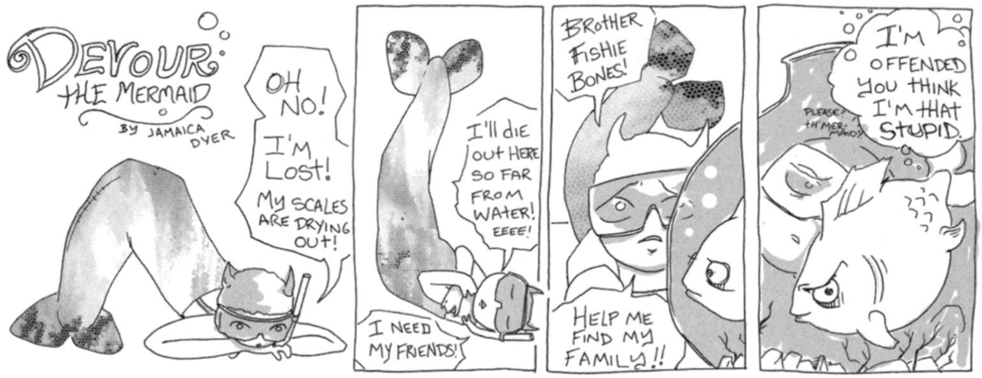
DEVOUR THE MERMAID
BY JAMAICA DYER
OH NO! I'M LOST! MY SCALES ARE DRYING OUT!
I'LL DIE OUT HERE SO FAR FROM WATER! EEEE!
I NEED MY FRIENDS!
BROTHER FISHIE BONES!
HELP ME FIND MY FAMILY!!
PLEASE? TH'MERMAIDS?
I'M OFFENDED YOU THINK I'M THAT STUPID.

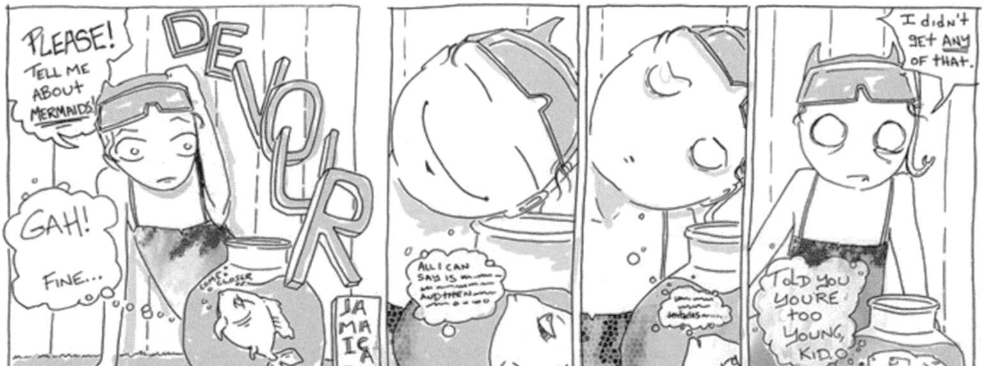
PLEASE! TELL ME ABOUT MERMAIDS!
DEVOUR
GAH! FINE...
COME CLOSER
JAMAICA D.05
ALL I CAN SAY IS
AND THEN
I DIDN'T GET ANY OF THAT.
TOLD YOU YOU'RE TOO YOUNG, KID.

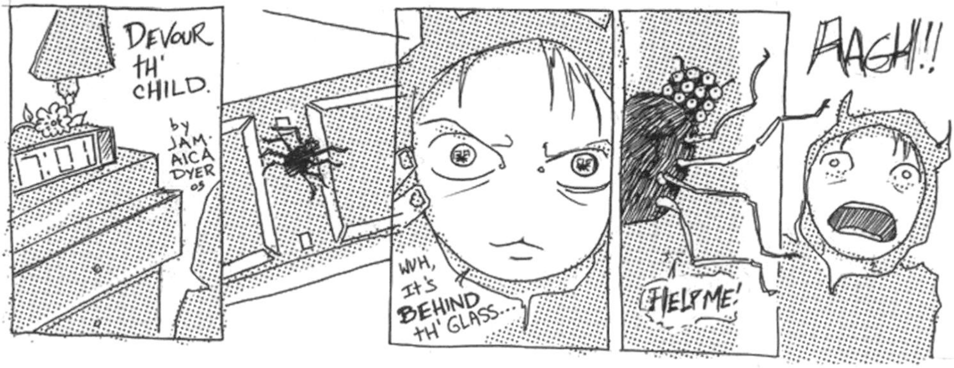
DEVOUR TH' CHILD.
by JAMAICA DYER 05
7:01
WUH, It's BEHIND TH' GLASS...
HELP ME!
AAGH!!

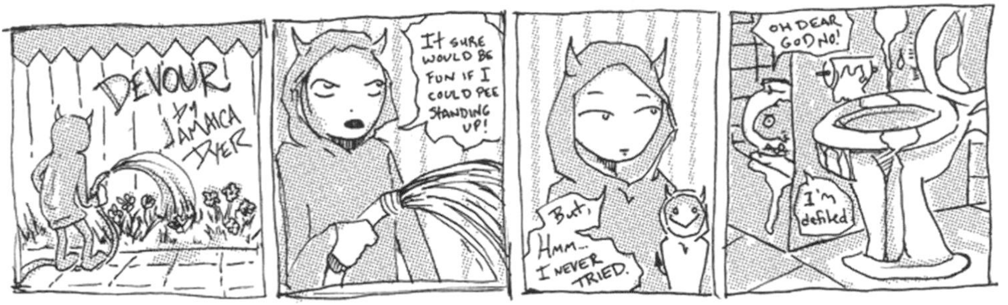
DEVOUR! by JAMACA DYER
It sure would be fun if I could pee standing up!
But, Hmm... I never tried.
OH DEAR GOD NO!
I'm defiled

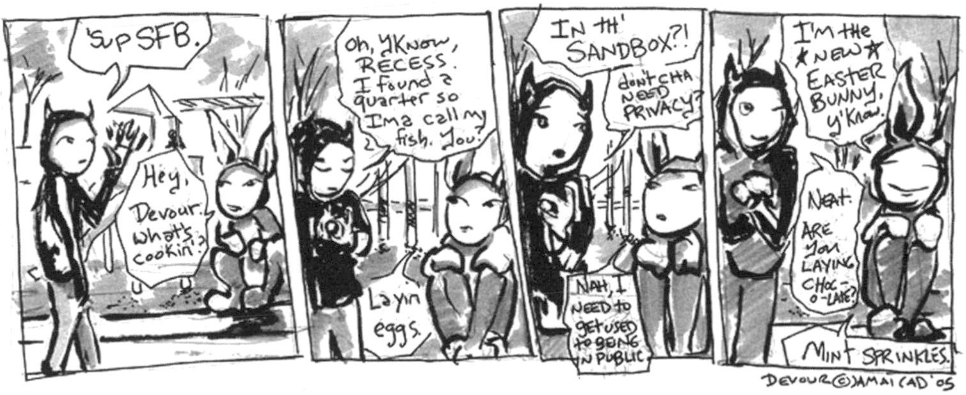
'Sup SFB.
Hey, Devour. What's cookin'?
Oh, y'Know, RECESS. I found a quarter so Ima call my fish. You?
Layin eggs.
IN TH' SANDBOX?!
don'tCHA NEED PRIVACY?
NAH, I NEED to get used to BEING IN PUBLIC.
I'm the NEW EASTER BUNNY, y'Know.
Neat. ARE YOU LAYING CHOC-O-LATE?
MINT SPRINKLES.

DEVOUR © JAMAICAD '05

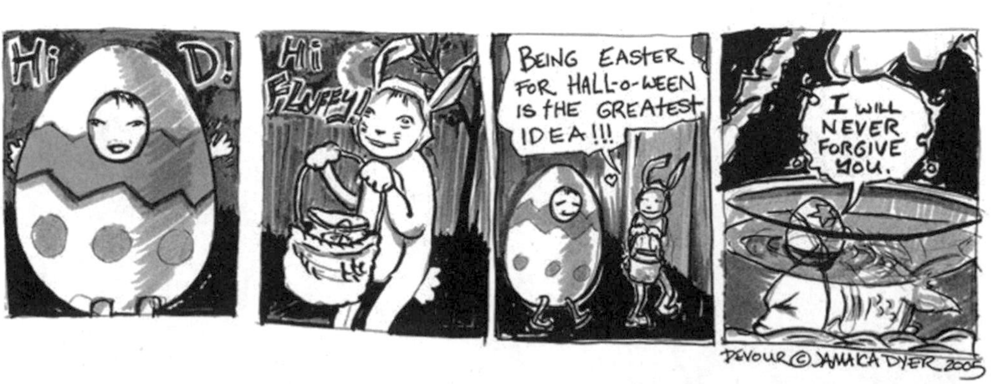
Hi D!
Hi FLUFFY!
BEING EASTER FOR HALL-o-WEEN IS THE GREATEST IDEA!!!
I WILL NEVER FORGIVE YOU.

DEVOUR © JAMAICA DYER 2005

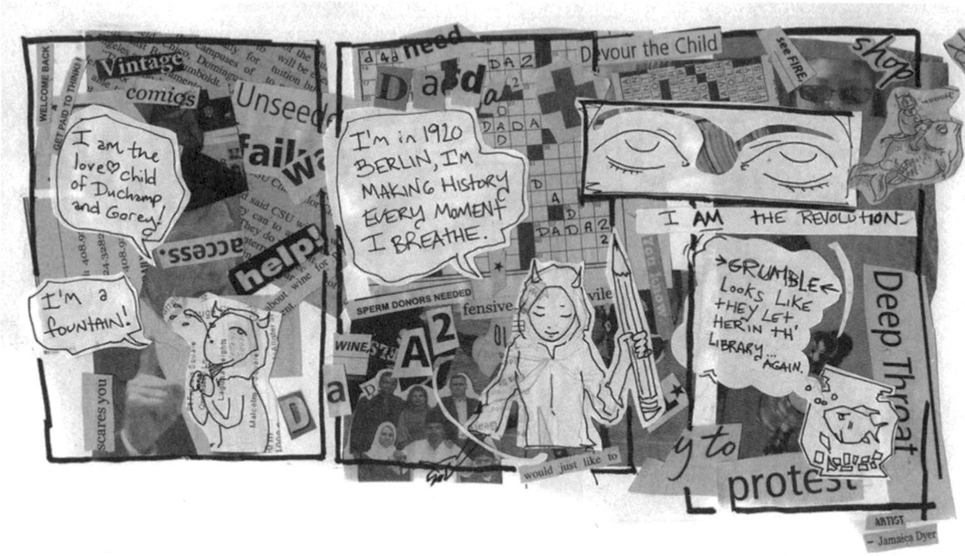
Vintage
comics
Unseed
fail
I am the love♡child of Duchamp and Gorey!
access.
help!
I'm a fountain!
scares you
Dada
Devour the Child
I'm in 1920 BERLIN, I'm MAKING History EVERY MOMENT I BREATHE.
SPERM DONORS NEEDED
fensive
A2
would just like to
shop
I AM THE REVOLUTION
→GRUMBLE← Looks LIKE THEY LET HER IN TH' LIBRARY... AGAIN.
Deep Throat
y to
protest
ARTIST
– Jamaica Dyer

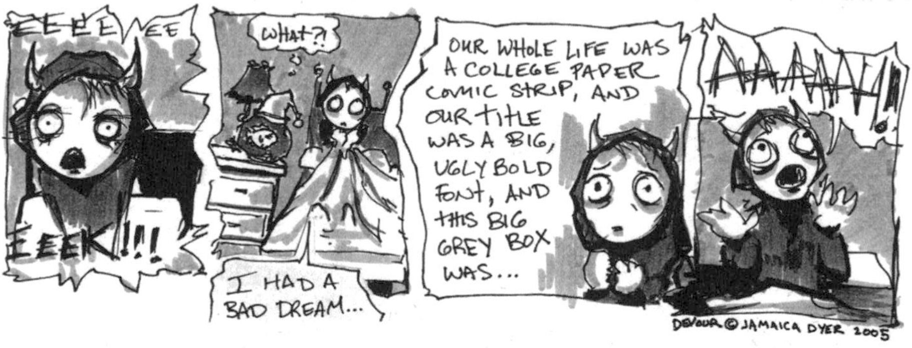
EEEEEE
EEEK!!!
WHAT?!
I HAD A BAD DREAM...
OUR WHOLE LIFE WAS A COLLEGE PAPER COMIC STRIP, AND OUR TITLE WAS A BIG, UGLY BOLD FONT, AND THIS BIG GREY BOX WAS...
AAAAAH!!
DEVOUR © JAMAICA DYER 2005

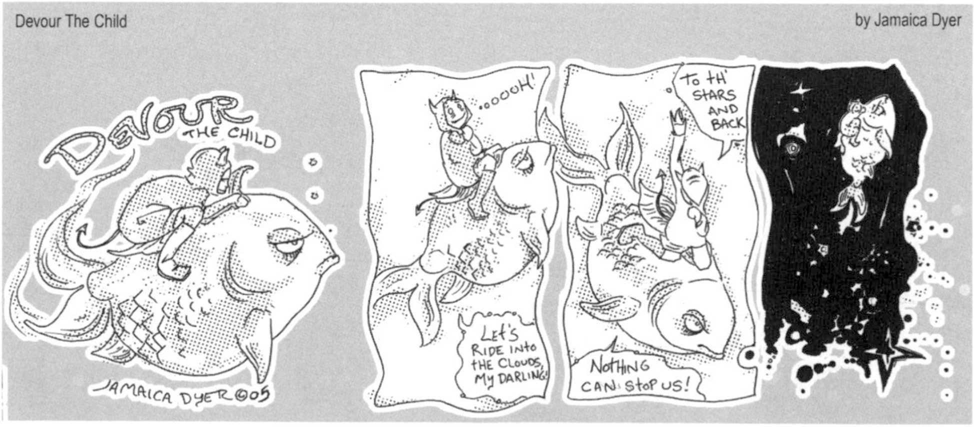
Devour The Child
by Jamaica Dyer
DEVOUR THE CHILD
JAMAICA DYER ©05
...OOOOH!
LET'S RIDE INTO THE CLOUDS, MY DARLING!
TO TH' STARS AND BACK
NOTHING CAN STOP US!

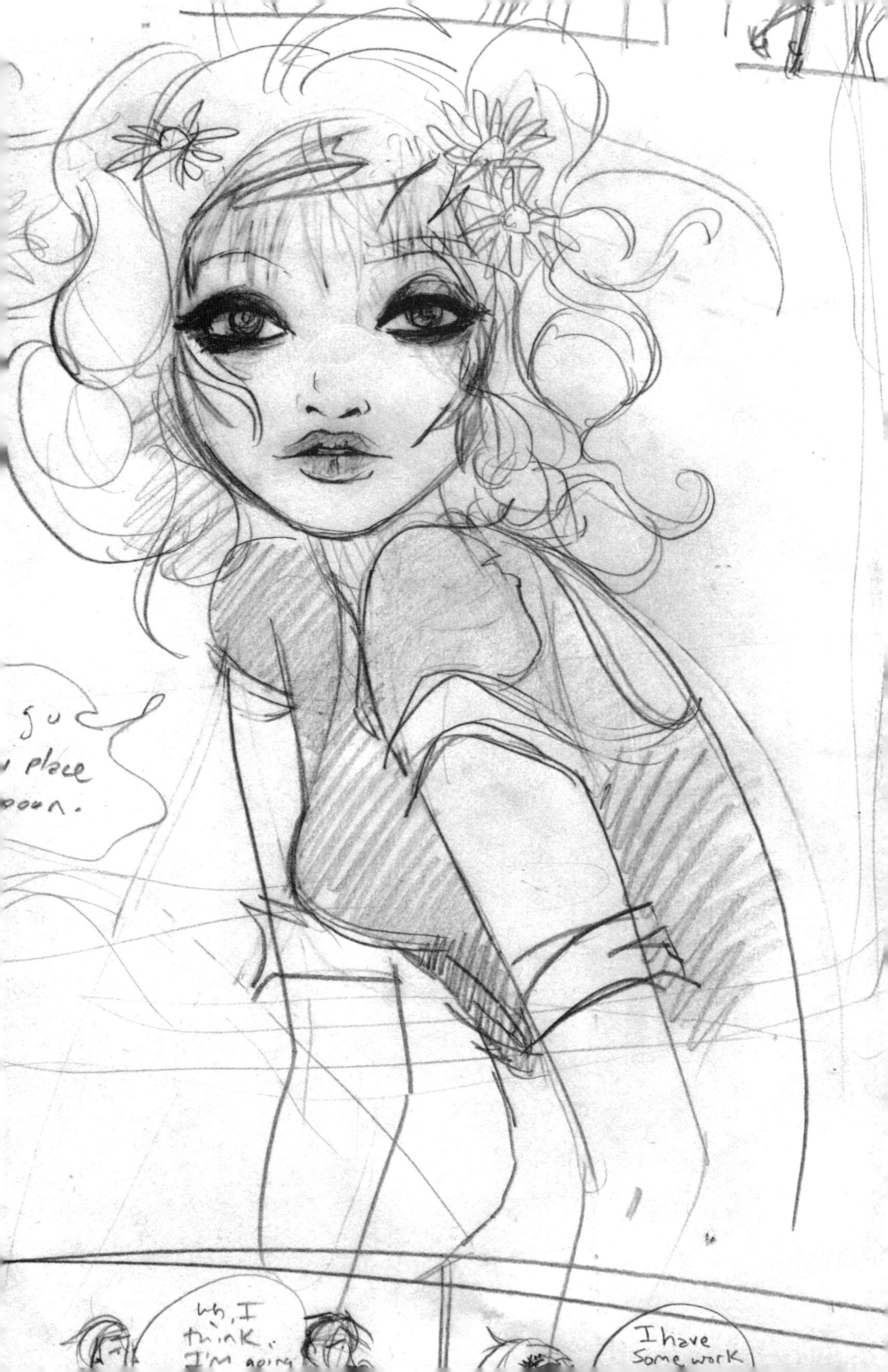
place
uh, I think. I'M
I have Some work

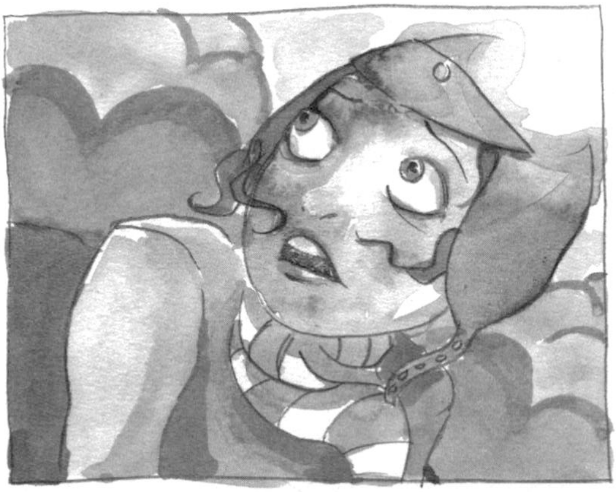

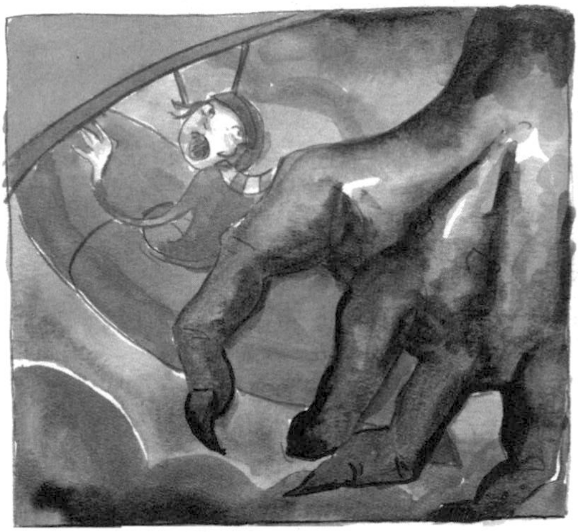

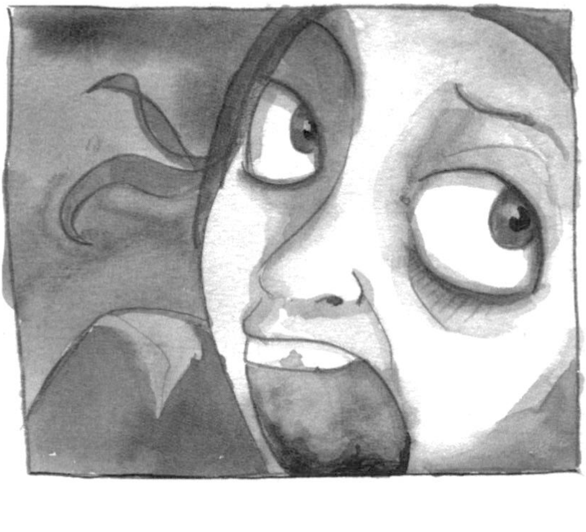

Style is a big part of the storytelling, as well as the process I went through while creating the pages. I was producing about 1 page a week to put online, and didn't want to restrict myself to any one style from the start. I quickly realized that I was imitating watercolors with my computer coloring, and started using watercolors and gouache to paint my pages. Along with this, I varied between wanting nice clean pencil lines and then becoming excited about pens and brushes. The evolution of the characters and craziness of the story seem to go hand-in-hand with my own evolution. When I'm asked "Why watercolor?" I think it's extremely fast and creates great textures and adds a bit of chance to the final page. I scan most of my pages before painting just incase I ruin it, but never had to use that, luckily!

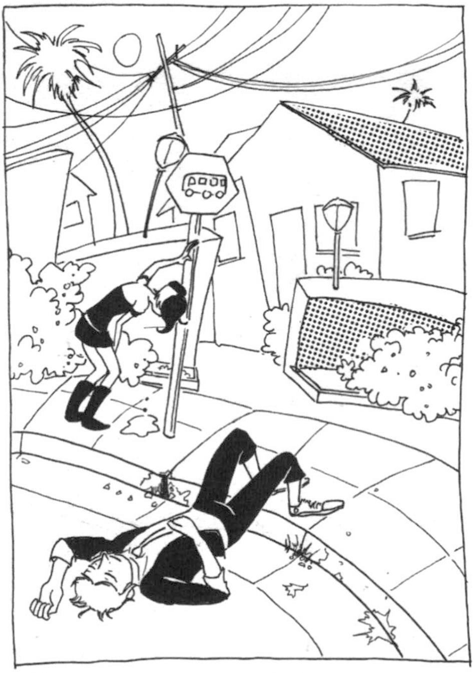

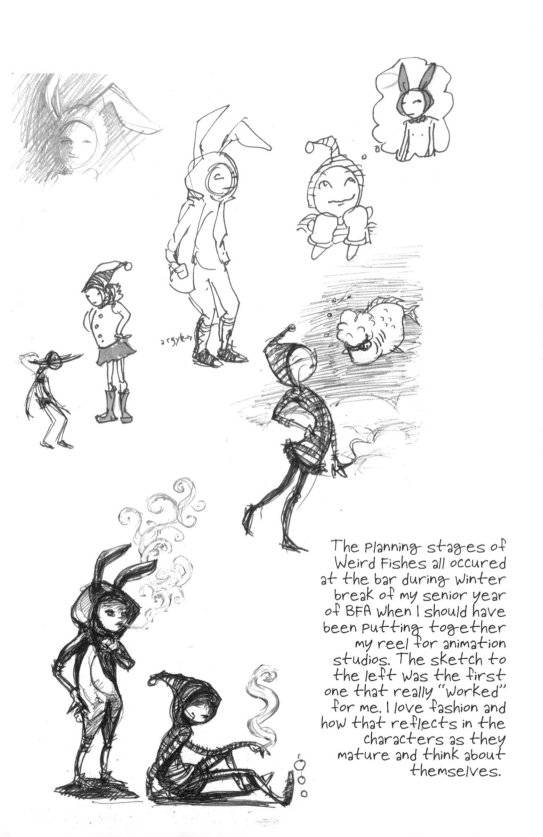

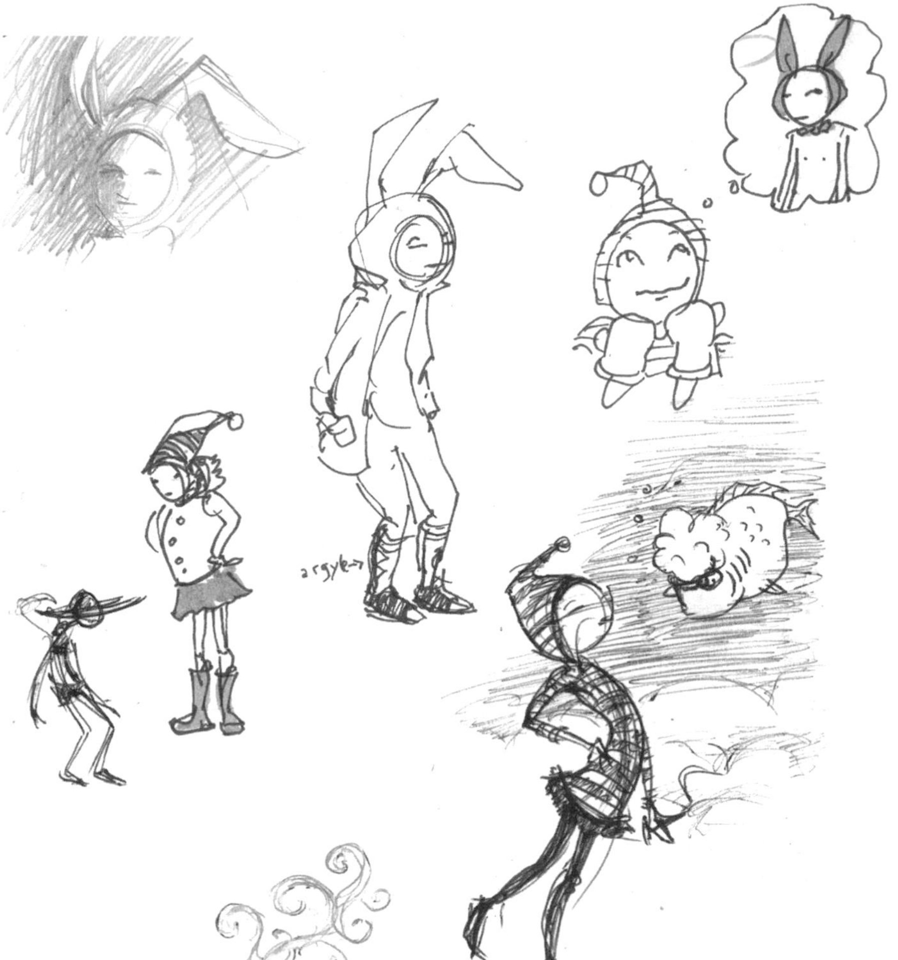
argyle

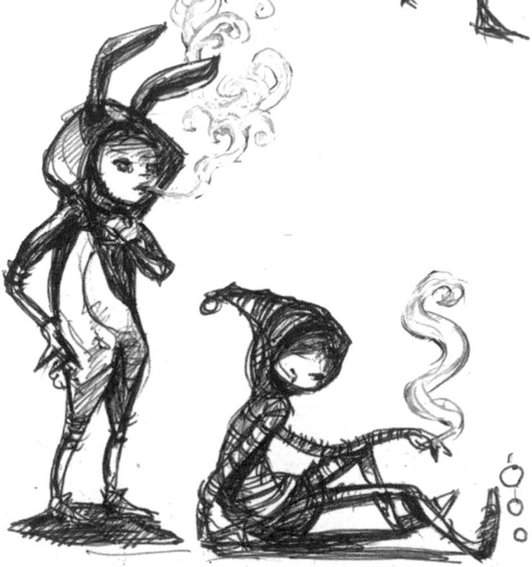

The planning stages of Weird Fishes all occured at the bar during winter break of my senior year of BFA when I should have been putting together my reel for animation studios. The sketch to the left was the first one that really "worked" for me. I love fashion and how that reflects in the characters as they mature and think about themselves.

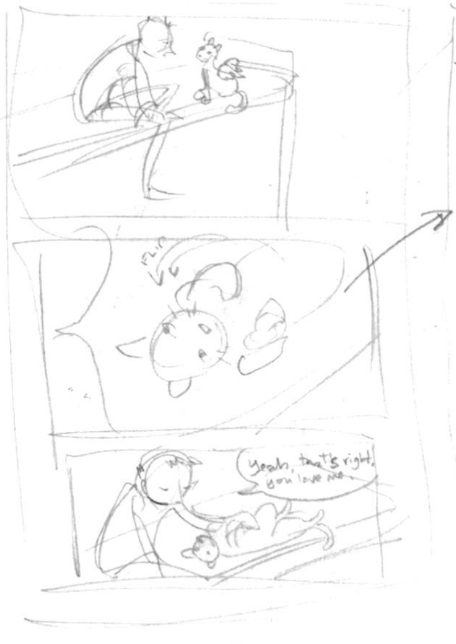
FLIP
Yeah, that's right, you love me.

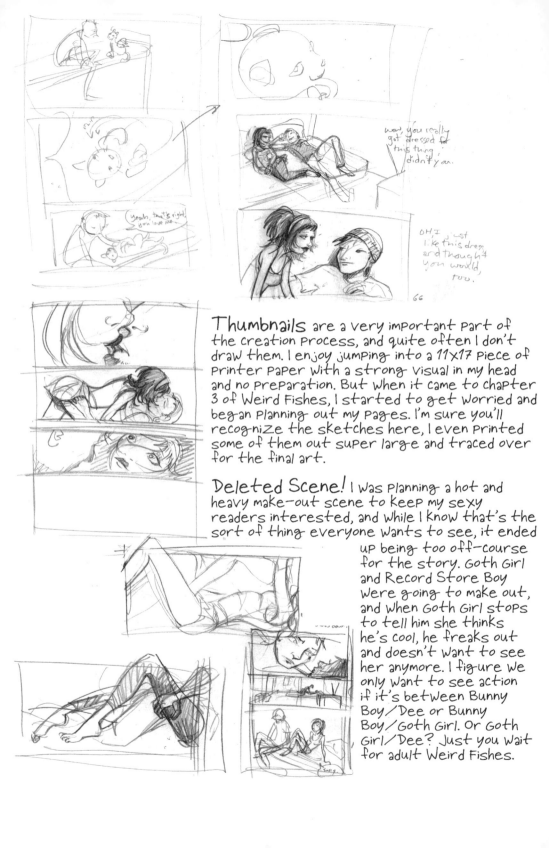

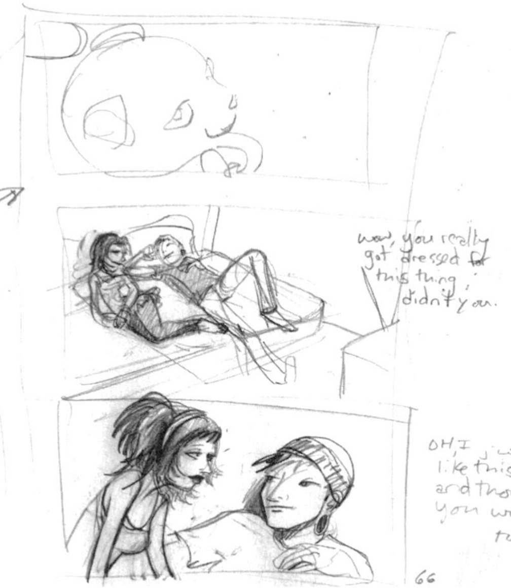
wow, you really got dressed for this thing, didn't you.
OH, I just like this dress and thought you would, too.
66

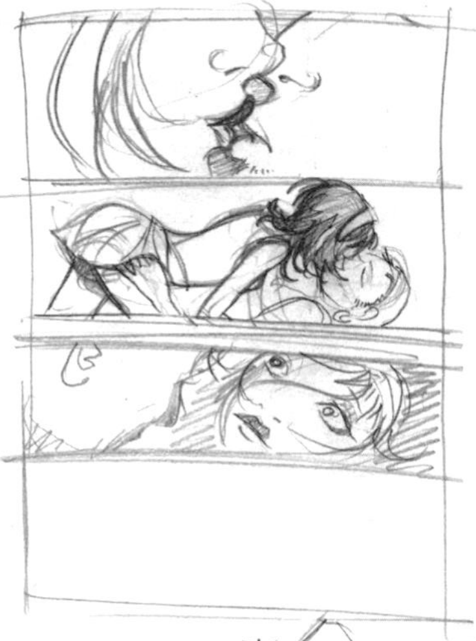

Thumbnails are a very important part of the creation process, and quite often I don't draw them. I enjoy jumping into a 11x17 piece of printer paper with a strong visual in my head and no preparation. But when it came to chapter 3 of Weird Fishes, I started to get worried and began planning out my pages. I'm sure you'll recognize the sketches here, I even printed some of them out super large and traced over for the final art.

Deleted Scene! I was planning a hot and heavy make-out scene to keep my sexy readers interested, and while I know that's the sort of thing everyone wants to see, it ended up being too off-course for the story. Goth Girl and Record Store Boy were going to make out, and when Goth Girl stops to tell him she thinks he's cool, he freaks out and doesn't want to see her anymore. I figure we only want to see action if it's between Bunny Boy/Dee or Bunny Boy/Goth Girl. Or Goth Girl/Dee? Just you wait for adult Weird Fishes.

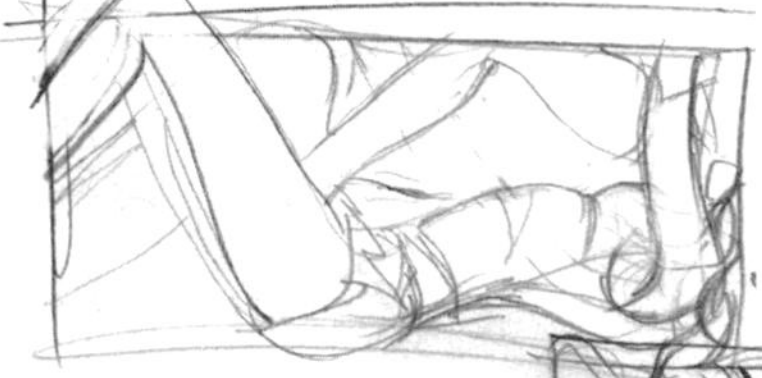

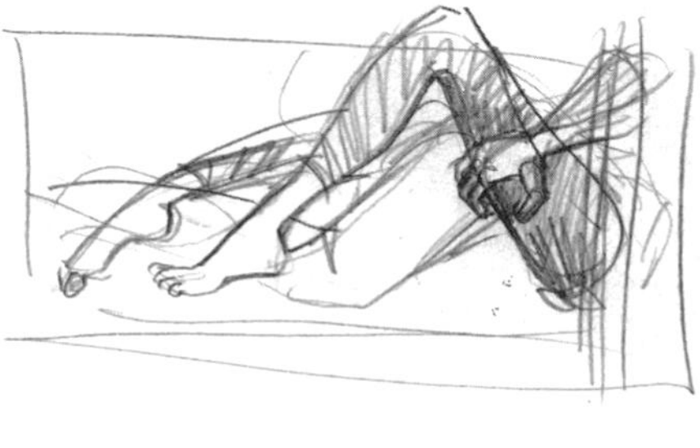

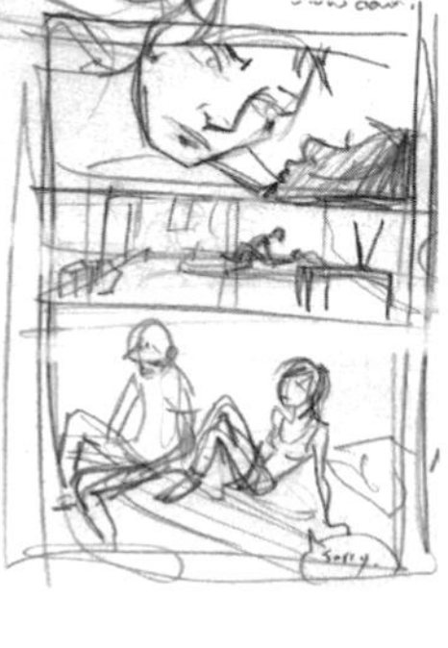
sorry.

I have a special skill for weird names. I used to make up words or just give characters object names like Pixel, Nettle or Dune. Goth Girl was originally named "Kitty" but that was a little too cute, and the other ones didn't stick. So she got a label instead of a name.

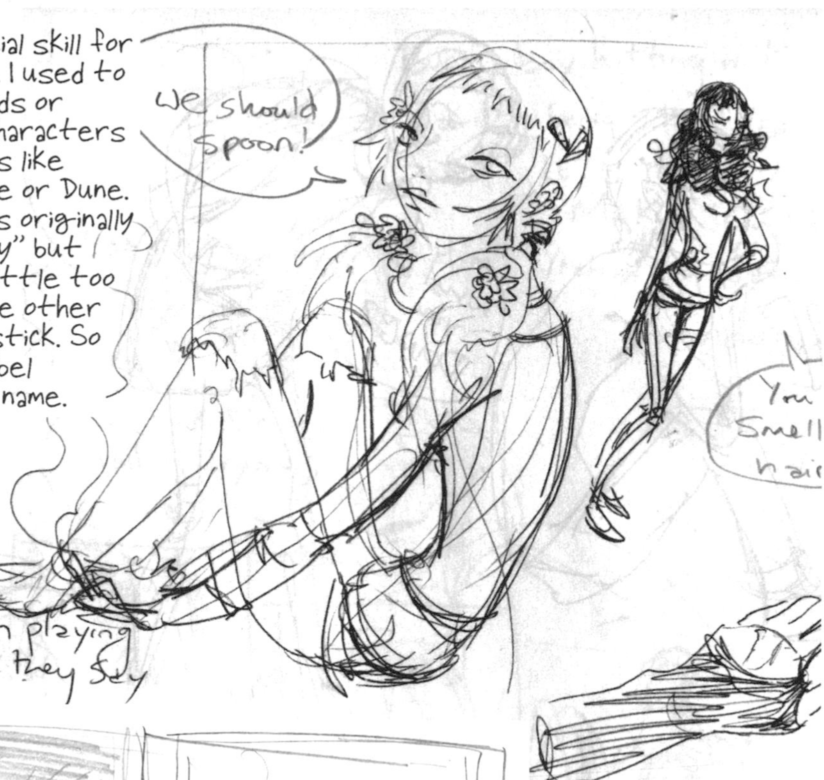
We should spoon!

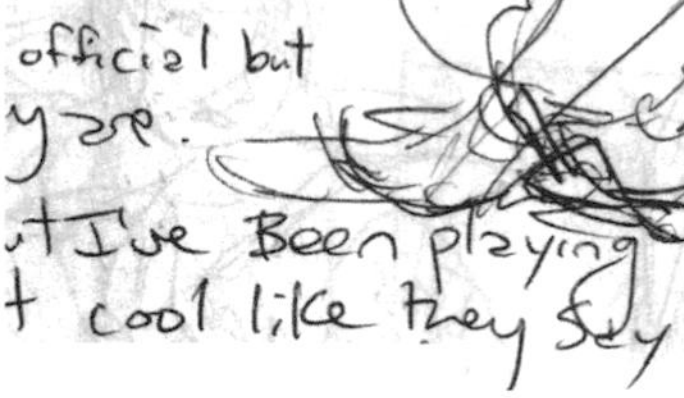
official but
yare.
t I've Been playing
t cool like they say

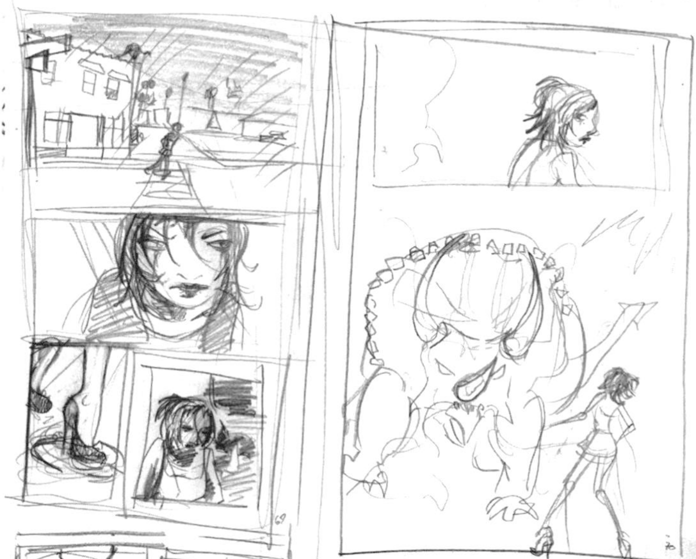

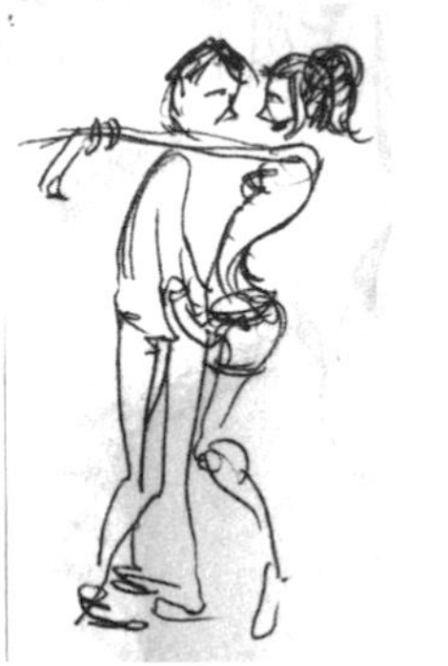

Deleted Scene #2

Goth Girl Was totally going to fight a dinosaur! Somehow that didn't pan out, either. I like the absolute brutality that goes along with throwing a purse at a koala.

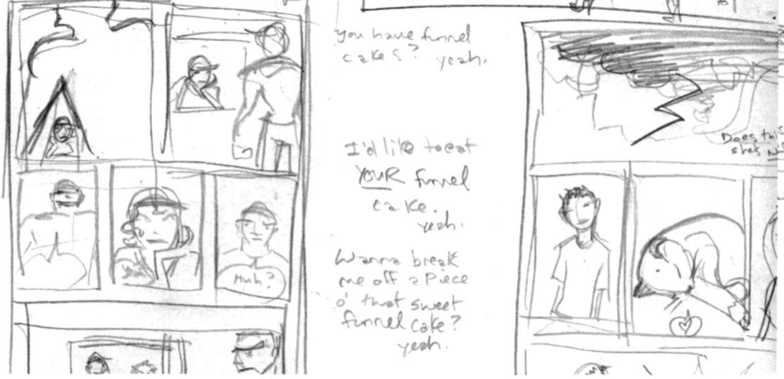
you have funnel cakes? yeah.
I'd like to eat YOUR funnel cake. yeah.
Wanna break me off a piece o' that sweet funnel cake? yeah.
Huh?

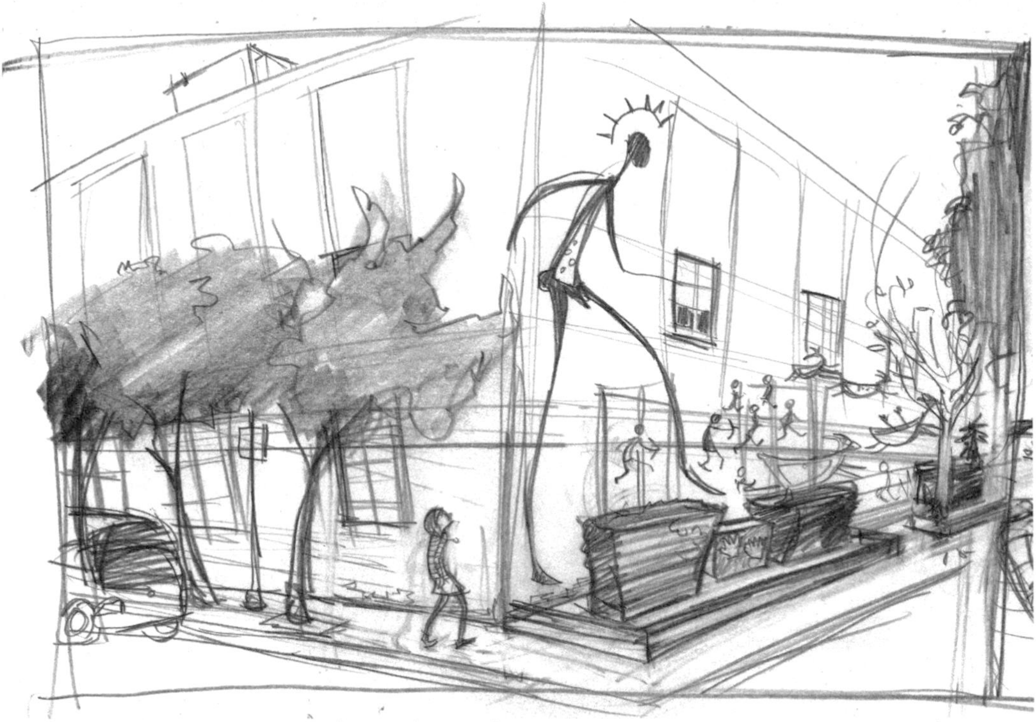

I love sketching, and for a few of the scenes I went out and took a bunch of photos to draw from. A lot of the outdoor scenes in the book come from locations around Santa Cruz, like this big building I've always imagined cave paintings dancing across, or a bus stop curb.

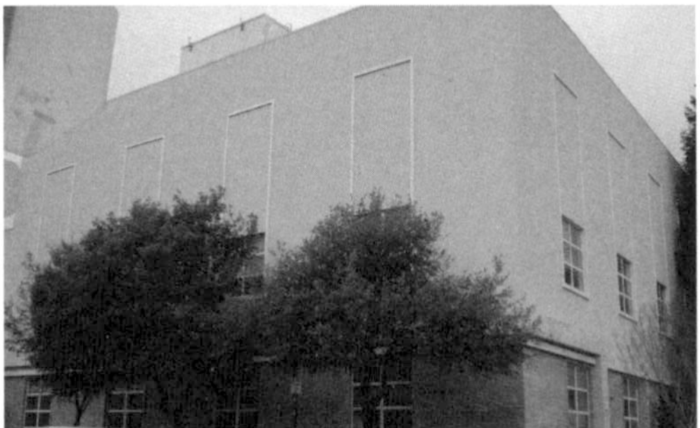

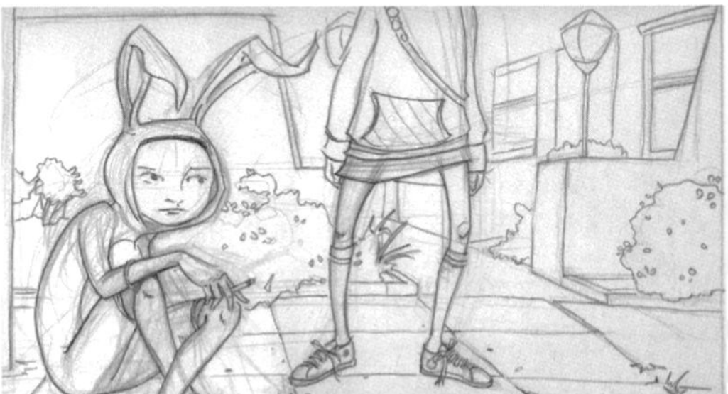

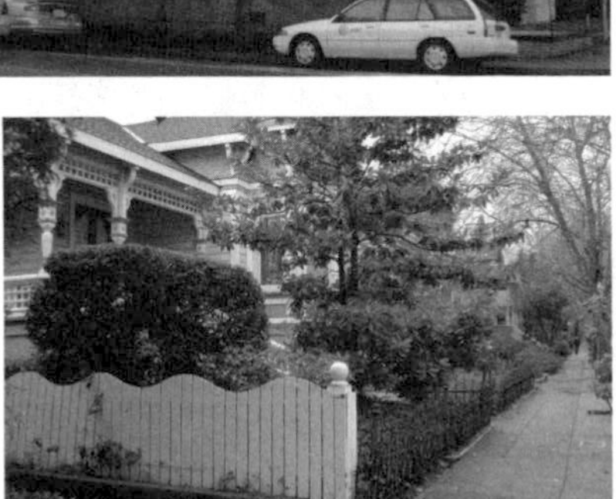

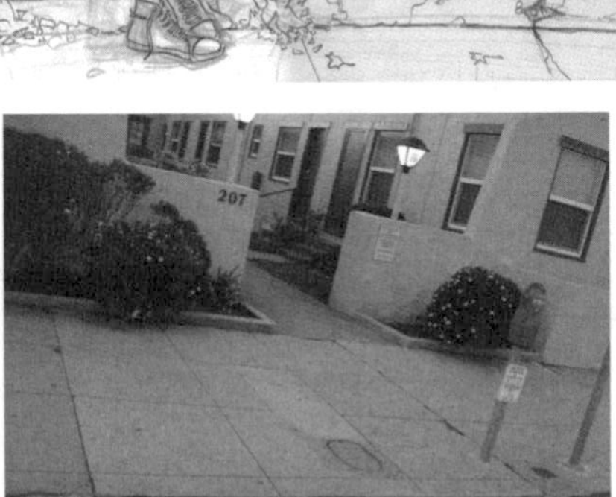

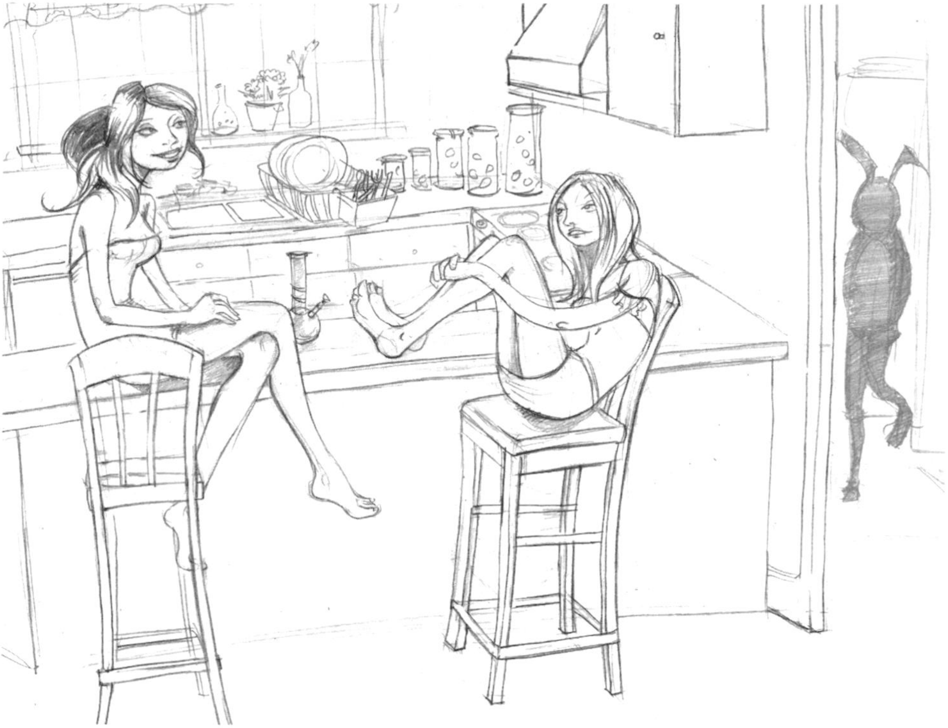

The kitchen scene is one of the few times I used the sketch as the final image for the comic. I love the look of quick pen drawings, but I usually redraw them on nice watercolor or bristol paper for the final piece. I have sketches drawn on reams of cheap printer paper all around my apartment, getting stomped on and eaten by the kittens.

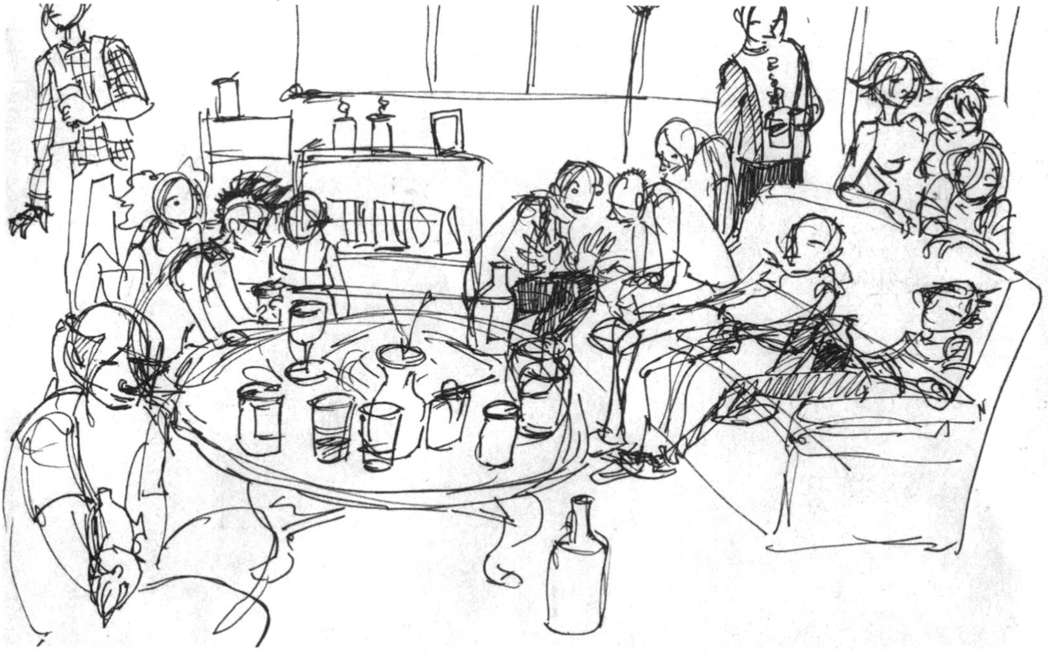

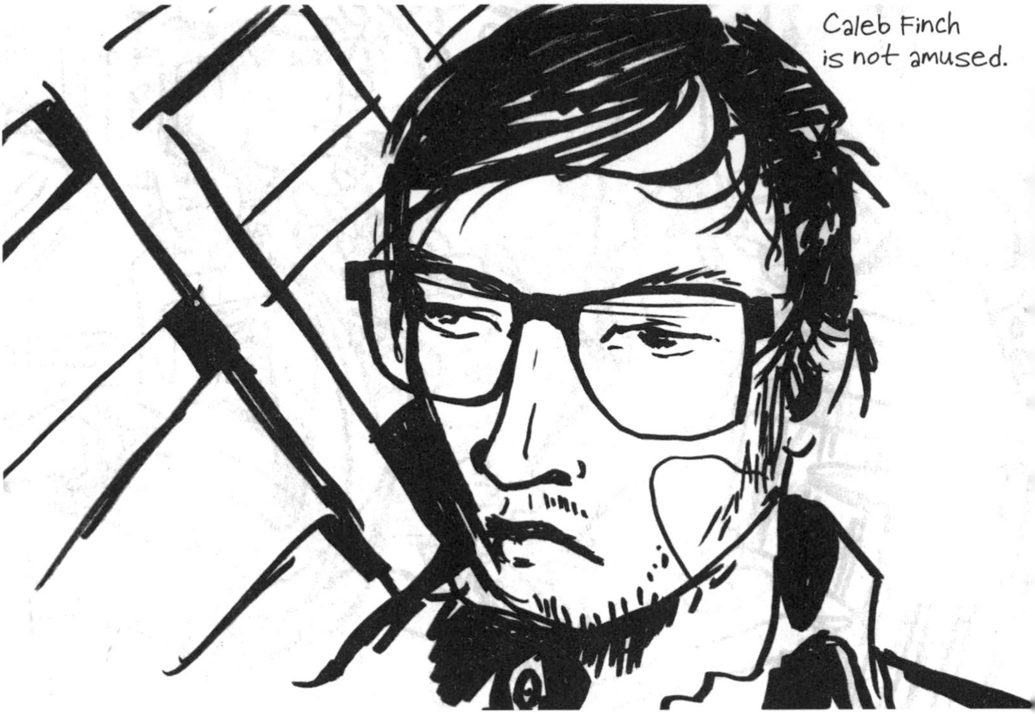
Caleb Finch
is not amused.

My comic tends to be a tiny bit unusual, even for me sometimes. Luckily I have Caleb Finch to help take my blurry dreams and ideas and bring them into reality. We might be walking downtown and I blab on about what I want to happen in the story and five minutes later he responds with a perfectly logical outline to make that happen beautifully. And then I go and draw the page back in crazyland, and thing shift around, but some of my favorite scenes and dialogue happened in these conversations.

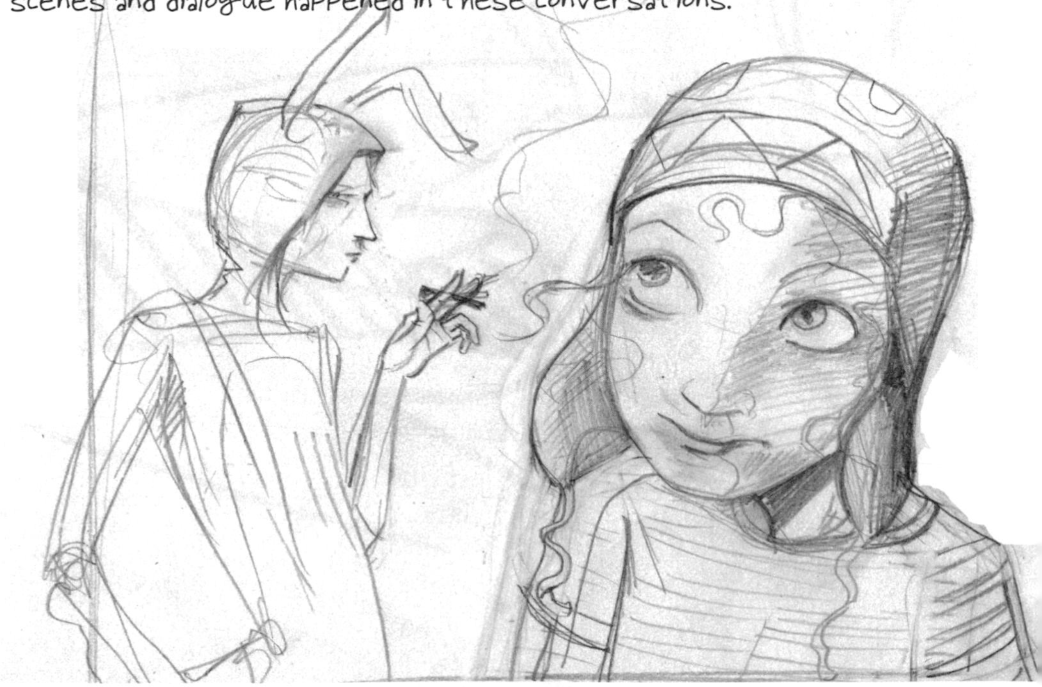

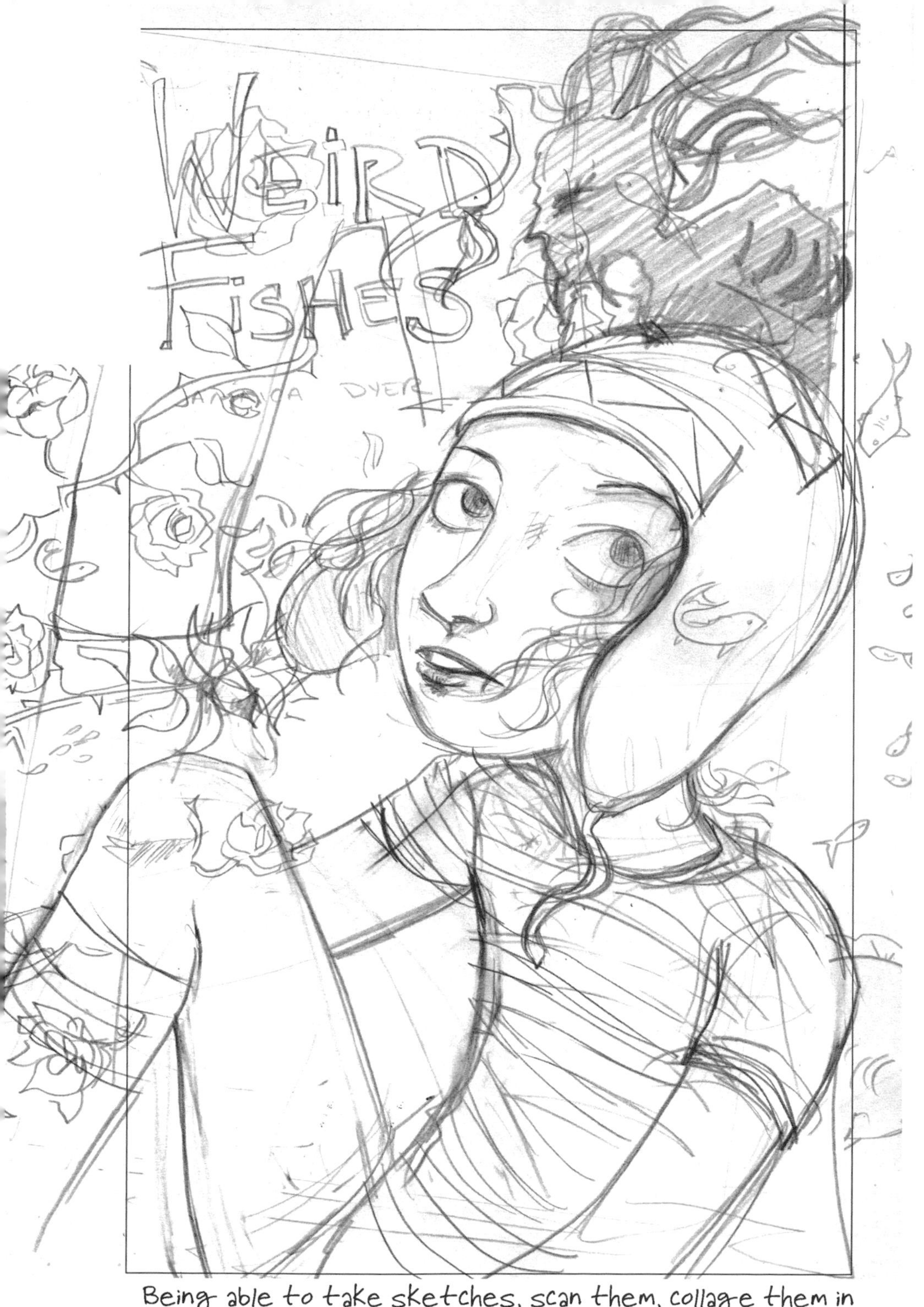
WEIRD
FISHES
JAMAICA DYER

Being able to take sketches, scan them, collage them in Photoshop, and then print them out on giant paper to trace on a lightbox onto watercolor paper and then paint it... Priceless. Even for images that never ended up being used for the book, like this potential cover.

Jamaica Dyer has been drawing to entertain herself since she was very little, became obsessed with Catwoman at a young age, began working in a comic store as a teen and started making her own books. Her photocopied comics graced Bay Area convention floors, and she collaborated in anthologies like "Dark Horse Myspace Presents 3", "Spark Generators 2", and "Juicy Mother 2". One day she hopes to get into a first edition of an anthology. "Weird Fishes" marks her first graphic novel published by SLG.

When not dreaming about comics, she's animating Flash cartoons.

jamaicad.com